Larry Writer was born in Sydney in 1950, spending part of his growing-up years in Kings Cross and attending Darlinghurst Public School. Today he lives in Woollahra with his wife, two sons, Labrador and ginger cat. For twelve years, Writer worked for Australian Consolidated Press as an editor and writer, and from 1981 to 1984, as European editor and London bureau chief. In 1989, he co-founded Ironbark Press. From 1992 to 2003, he was a writer, editor and London bureau chief with Time Inc. In recent years he has been a freelance writer for *The Weekend Australian Magazine*, *The Australian Financial Review*, *The Sydney Morning Herald*'s *Sydney* magazine, *The Bulletin*, *Madison* and *The Australian Women's Weekly*. As well as *Razor*, his books include the critically acclaimed *Never Before, Never Again*, the story of the record-breaking St George Rugby League team of the 1950s and '60s; *Newk*, the biography of John Newcombe; *Pleasure and Pain*, the biography of Chrissy Amphlett; *The Australian Book of True Crime*; and *First Blood*, the story of the sea battle between HMAS *Sydney* and SMS *Emden* in 1914.

# RAZOR

# RAZOR

Tilly Devine, Kate Leigh and the razor gangs

## LARRY WRITER

**MACMILLAN**
Pan Macmillan Australia

First published 2001 in Macmillan by Pan Macmillan Australia Pty Limited
This Macmillan edition published 2009 by Pan Macmillan Australia Pty Limited
1 Market Street, Sydney

National Library of Australia
Cataloguing-in-Publication data:

Writer, Larry.
Razor

ISBN 978 1 4050 3951 2.

1. Criminals – New South Wales – Sydney. I. Title.

364.3099441

Cover photograph: Main image is Tilly Devine, courtesy of the State Library of
New South Wales. Images of Kate Leigh, Phil Jeffs and Nellie Cameron courtesy of State
Records New South Wales. Image of Guido Calletti courtesy of the Fairfax Photo Library.
Image of Norman Bruhn courtesy of the London Metropolitan Archives.

Typeset in 11pt Garth Graphic by Post Pre-Press Group
Printed in Australia by McPherson's Printing Group

Every endeavour has been made to source the photographs and to contact
copyright holders to obtain the necessary permission for use of photographic
and other material in this book. Any person who may have been
inadvertently overlooked should contact the publisher.

To Carol, Tom and Casey, with love

*The greatest happiness is to scatter your enemy, to drive him before you, to see his cities reduced to ashes, to see those who love him shrouded in tears.*
Genghis Khan, 1226

# Contents

## Part 3 – Colourful Identities

## Part 4 – The End of an Era

# Acknowledgments

One of the very best things about researching and writing *Razor* was interviewing a number of former police officers who knew the people and experienced first-hand many of the events chronicled in this book. The memories they shared brought the long-ago period to life for me. So my appreciation to Ray Blissett, Lua Niall, Lance Hoban, Bill Harris, Greg Brown, and the former policewoman who gave freely of her time on the proviso that I preserve her anonymity. Respecting her wishes, I have called her 'Maggie Baker'.

Sadly, in some ways, especially when one considers the wonderful information they might have divulged, none of the major villains from the razor-gang years survives, but I am grateful for the recollections of many who knew them.

Nor could this book exist without the insights and knowledge, and many courtesies and encouragements, of Professor Frank Clarke of Macquarie University; East Sydney historian Brian Kelleher; Bernie Purcell; Leicester Warburton; Len Smith; the late Ennis Firth; Elva Blissett; Kate McClymont; Pete 'Super Sleuth' Norman; Jane and Chris Mathews; Justin and Helen Bairamian; Paul Isgro; Ian Heads; Helen Martin; Terence McCann; Ross and Lenore Adamson (for all the love and wisdom); Marie Sampson (for listening); my mother, June Samuels; my father, the late Ray Writer; the talented professionals at

*Who Weekly* and John Partridge, corporate records manager and archivist of the New South Wales Department of Corrective Services.

For his invaluable childhood memories and insight into the character of his aunt, Tilly Devine, and uncle, Eric Parsons, I thank Dr George Parsons, senior lecturer in Australian History at Macquarie University.

My gratitude, as well, to the many current and former police officers who responded generously to my notices in police journals seeking information about the era, for their memories and anecdotes, and for giving me the chance to verify names, dates and places. Thanks to the editors of those journals, Mrs Silva of *The Police News*, and Mrs Armstrong of the *Retired Police Association Journal*, who published my calls for information. Thanks to Professor Edward Jaggard, historian of Surf Life Saving Australia.

A special salute to Michaela Perske, who wrote and produced the fine ABC Radio National *Hindsight* documentary on the female criminals of East Sydney.

Stuart Pendlebury, Caleb Williams and their colleagues at Sydney's Justice and Police Museum encouraged my efforts from the outset. They gave me a desk, taught me how to work the photocopier, and swamped me with the museum's trove of files, exhibits and photographs. These documents shed light on police work of the period, the uniformed and plain-clothes officers, and their quarries. The material from the museum was indispensable in checking the facts about events that took place sixty, seventy and eighty years ago. (That said, when in a few instances I have been unable to locate irrefutable, definitive proof of an event or conversation, I have taken the liberty of arriving at a version that seems most likely, using as a touchstone the wealth of information at my disposal.)

Of inestimable assistance to me in this project was the research of Michelle Linder, who toiled with diligence and skill for many months in the newspaper archives of the State Library of New South Wales; and Scotland Yard researcher and writer Keith Skinner, who opened doors for me in London, where I went in search of details on the young Tilly Devine. The brilliant and resourceful photo editor Amy Reedy tracked down the photographs that enrich this book. I also thank the staff of the State Library of New South Wales, Ross Connell and the staff of the City of Sydney Library and Photo Archive, Paddington Library and the New South Wales Premier's Department. I thank in London, the Public Record Office; the General Register Office; the Borough of Southwark Library and Photographic Archive at Camberwell; the British Library's Newspaper Library; London Metropolitan Archives; Time Inc; Roy Felton and the staff at Bow Street Magistrates' Court and Police Station; and the Department of Births, Deaths and Marriages.

For helping me to understand the lives, times and crimes of the central figures of Razorhurst, I thank the courtroom and police stenographers of the era who recorded the trials and hearings recounted in this book. I also owe a debt to the (mainly un-bylined) reporters of *Truth*, the *Sydney Morning Herald*, *Smith's Weekly*, *People*, the *Daily Mirror*, the *Daily Telegraph* and the *Bulletin*, who covered Sydney and the lives of its more colourful denizens over the ninety-year span of my story. Reading their articles and features, which still leap from the yellowing newsprint today, was — along with interviewing the aforementioned survivors of the era — the next best thing to being there.

Books and other publications I consulted in my background research include: the landmark and estimable *Drug Traffic: Narcotics and Organised Crime in Australia* by Dr Alfred McCoy; Dr McCoy's chapter in *The Sydney–Melbourne Book* edited by Jim Davidson, 'Two Cities and their Syndicates — A Comparative Urban History of Organised Crime'; the poems of Kenneth Slessor; *Surry Hills: The City's Backyard* by Christopher Keating; *Wild Women of Sydney* by George Blaikie; *The Story of Camberwell* by Mary Boast; *Life and Labour of the People of London* by Charles Booth; *Faces of the Street: William Street, Sydney, 1916* by Max Kelly; *Larrikin Crook: The Rise and Fall of Squizzy Taylor* by Hugh Anderson; *The Oldest Profession* by Hilary Evans; the splendid *Chow Hayes — Gunman* by David Hickie; *The History of Female Prostitution in Australia* by Raelene Francis; *As Crime Goes By: The Life and Times of 'Bondi' Bill Jenkings* with Norm Lipson (who would have loved to have reported the razor-gang wars) and Tony Barnao; *Australian Photographs* by Helen Ennis and Isobel Crombie; *Gullible's Travails* by Geoff Allen; *A Hack's Progress* by Phillip Knightley; the article 'Pretty Dulcie Markham and the St Kilda Realists: Some Literary Byways and Digressions', reprinted from a speech by Brian Matthews in *Overland* magazine (issue 118, 1990); and Matthews's rich and evocative memoir, *A Fine and Private Place*. Also shedding light on my subject were: Britain's *People* weekly; Part V of Dennis Whitburn's *Penthouse History of Crime in Australia*, 'The Law of the Razor'; *Larrikins: 19th Century Outrage* by James Murray; Ruth Park's poignant classics of Surry Hills life between the wars, *The Harp in the South* and *Poor Man's Orange*; *With Just But Relentless Discipline: A Social History of Corrective Services in New South Wales* by John Ramsland; *Long Bay Correctional Complex: Conservation Plan*, published by the Department of Corrective Services; *Australian Children Through 200 Years* by Suzane Fabian and Morag Loh; *Backpage: Australia's Greatest Sporting Moments* by Ian Heads; *Growing Up in the '30s* by Brian Carroll; *Inside Kings Cross* by James Holledge; *The Racket Buster* by Vince Kelly; *Rugged Angel: the Amazing Career of Policewoman Lillian Armfield*, by Vince Kelly; *Weevils in the Flour: an Oral Record of the 1930s Depression* by Wendy Lowenstein; *Gangland International: The Mafia and Other Mobs* by James Morton; and *Out of the Bakelite Box: the Heyday of Australian Radio* by Jacqueline Kent.

Tom Gilliatt, my publisher at Macmillan, has been a tower of strength and encouragement through the two years of researching and writing. Editor Sarina Rowell's wise cutting and restructuring and Jon Gibbs's meticulous and learned line editing improved this book immeasurably.

Jeremy Nicholson's design evokes the era beautifully. Thanks, too, to James Fraser, Jeannine Fowler, Tracey Cheetham, Amanda Hemmings and everyone at Macmillan for their belief and support.

To my wife Carol and my sons Tom and Casey, I love you, love you to bits. Thanks for putting up with all my angsting and endless droning on about long-dead gangsters. Thanks, always and forever, for the love and the fun.

# Introduction

Today, East Sydney is a fine place to live. People can pay from $500 000 to more than $1 million to dwell in its iron-laced, lovingly restored Victorian terrace homes and apartments in stately older buildings and soaring new tower blocks. Although seedy pockets remain, the gentrified and cosmopolitan suburbs of Darlinghurst, Kings Cross, Surry Hills, Woolloomooloo and Paddington are addresses prized for their proximity to nightlife, art galleries, shops, restaurants and coffee bars, pubs, parks, Sydney's central business district and the harbour.

East Sydney has not always been so salubrious. Unimaginably perhaps, to those who know it only as it is now, for a time in the century just past it was one of the most dangerous areas in Australia. For it was here, among the desperately poor and dispossessed, that some of the worst criminals the nation has seen waged war with razor, gun and blunt object over the spoils of illegal drugs and alcohol, prostitution, gambling and extortion. As the body count rose, law-abiding citizens, angered and terrified by the activities of these gangsters, christened East Sydney 'Razorhurst'.

My interest in Razorhurst began way back with the many colourful stories my late father, who worked at harbourside Sydney's Cockatoo Docks and Garden Island in the 1930s and '40s and knew the milieu well, told me. For a time, too, in the late 1950s, when I was an impressionable child attending Darlinghurst Public School, I lived at Hensley Hall, a block of flats in Bayswater Road, Kings Cross. In the bad old days of the '20s, this was a mob haunt — and it still had an uneasy atmosphere thirty years later. Then, at a family dinner a few years ago, my parents-in-law recalled how when they bought the block of land on which their present home now stands in Sydney's Rose Bay, there had stood a bungalow previously used as a brothel and shelter by the infamous gang leader and madam Tilly Devine in the 1940s. Tilly, they explained, had divided up the old house into small rooms and it was in these compartments that her 'girls' entertained their clients. When it came time to knock down Tilly's house to build their new one, my in-laws had come upon a cache of women's shoes. Tilly's? The prostitutes'? No one knew, and it didn't really matter, because by then I was beguiled by the thought of what dark and racy deeds had been perpetrated perhaps on the very spot where I sat eating dinner.

Later, I asked the woman next door, who had grown up and lived there for half a century, if she could remember her notorious neighbour, Tilly Devine. She said that she knew Tilly owned the house and visited it from time to time, but she never saw Tilly because her parents would sternly discourage questions about the source of the raucous laughter, squeaking bedsprings and loud music emanating from over the back fence.

My curiosity about Tilly Devine and her world was intensified when, a decade ago, I became a resident of Paddington, one of the suburbs that comprised Razorhurst. A benefit of having an active preservation society is that my suburb of terrace houses and winding streets and lanes looks much as it did eighty or so years ago, and it is easy to imagine the desperado days. I began reading everything I could find about the era and talking at length to the people who lived through it. Entranced by the stories I gleaned, I wanted to write about this wild, romantic, dreadful period in Sydney's history.

So I learned about Tilly, and her great rival, the sly-grog queen Kate Leigh, both, I feel, so memorably portrayed by Ruth Park in the composite character Delie Stock from *The Harp in the South* and *Poor Man's Orange*, Park's evocative novels of 1930s Surry Hills life. I learned about the hair-trigger gangsters Guido Calletti, Frank Green, Norman Bruhn and Tilly's husband, Jim Devine. I was entranced by the tragic, seamy lives of the beautiful prostitutes Nellie Cameron and Dulcie Markham, and awed by the exploits of some of the police officers who opposed them — William Mackay, Lillian Armfield, Frank Farrell and Ray Blissett. I interviewed Ray Blissett, the only survivor of that formidable quartet, looking, at ninety-two, as if he was still capable of hurling any hoodlum into the back of a black maria. I talked to many other police officers of the time, notably Blissett's friend Greg Brown, Lua Niall and Lance Hoban, the latter of whom led me to a stash of razors owned by Guido Calletti, who armed himself with the fearsome weapons after laws outlawing the carrying of handguns were enacted in early 1927. I recorded the theories and observations of those who had studied and written about the period. Descendants of the gangsters happily shared their memories.

I spent weeks going through the criminal registers and records in Sydney's Justice and Police Museum and photostatting the newspapers on microfilm at the City of Sydney Library. Ace police researcher Michelle Linder combed the archives of the New South Wales State Library for me. After I was interviewed by broadcaster Michaela Perske for her 1999 ABC Radio National *Hindsight* documentary on Tilly Devine, Kate Leigh, Dulcie Markham and Nellie Cameron, Michaela graciously made her research and contact details available to me. I travelled to London to find out about Tilly's life and criminal career before she emigrated to Australia in 1920. My home study became a repository of books and notebooks, tapes, transcripts, photographs and documents, the fruits of two years' research.

I walked the streets of East Sydney, alone and with historian Brian Kelleher, an authority on crime in the area. The wondrous thing about the hive of suburbs once known as Razorhurst is that today, seventy-odd years later, it requires only a little imagination to mind-travel back to those long-gone wild years.

Charlotte Lane, near the Australian Museum, Police Headquarters and Sydney Grammar School, is a nondescript clutch of tiny terraces, offices and small factories. But in the dead of night when the office workers and factory hands have departed, it bristles with a claustro-phobic chill that recalls its years as an epicentre of vice. One can almost picture the laneway's cobblestones sticky-wet with the blood of Norman Bruhn, leader of the original razor gang, who was ambushed and gunned down in 1927, and hear his cries, 'Help, I'm shot! Oh, I'm shot!'

Stroll along Kellett Street, Kings Cross, and you'll see a strip of restaurants and coffee houses, pastel-painted terrace homes and a few discreet and legal brothels frequented by respectable, if furtive, busi-nessmen. On 8 August 1929, Kellett Street was the site of a vicious and prolonged brawl between the warring gangs of Kate Leigh and Tilly Devine that ended with shopfronts and cars destroyed, windows smashed, and a dozen combatants hospitalised with serious razor slashes and gunshot wounds. Stand there, perhaps touching the bricks of the same buildings showered by bullets in that skirmish, and it is possible to conjure up the din of breaking glass and thwacking fists.

Drive south along Malabar Road to the corner of Torrington Road at Maroubra, where Tilly Devine and her husband Jim lived. This was where 'Big Jim' shot two men dead and wounded many more. The house there today looks nothing like the dwelling Tilly and Jim lived in, it having been much changed down the years by renovations, but to this writer (and perhaps anyone else au fait with the goings-on here in the later '20s and the '30s), what remains exudes real menace.

In Nimrod Street, at the top of William Street on the cusp of Woolloomooloo and Darlinghurst, where Tilly once prowled and gangsters lounged in cafés, is the Stables Theatre. There in 1998, Ken Horler's play *Tilly's Turn*, starring Lynette Curran as the brothel-keeper, was staged. Two hundred metres down William Street towards the city is the Strand Hotel, now a watering hole for executives and office workers. It was here that Frank 'the Little Gunman' Green blasted Barney Dalton to oblivion in 1931. The pub has been painted brightly, but its structure is as it was.

Also in William Street, in the Chard building that lately housed the studios of the ABC, Phil Jeffs ran Sydney's most iniquitous drug and illegal liquor den, the Fifty-Fifty Club. The edifice is today in the process of being renovated, but it is the same block that jumped with the jazz of its inhouse combo and the squeals of revellers. Oxford Street, Paddington, one of the hippest shopping precincts in the land, was where Tilly Devine and Kate Leigh once whaled away at each other, Tilly tearing Kate's wide-brimmed floppy hat from her head and Kate flailing at her sworn enemy like a dervish while their curses turned the air blue.

In Palmer Street, Darlinghurst, stands a stylish pub called the East Village. It is fashionably decorated and its buffed waiters serve exotic cocktails, fine wine and good food to the wealthy and sophisticated young business and creative people of East Sydney. But stand outside and look to the top of the building's facade, and see in brick the words 'Tradesman's Arms 1918'. In the 1920s and '30s, the East Village was 'the Arms', a bloodhouse with sawdust on the floor to soak up the spit and vomit, hard stools at the bar and a dozen cheap wooden tables with chairs scattered around. The air was thick with coarse language, raucous laughter and the cigarette smoke pumped out by the Arms's clientele — the factory workers and bakers from the nearby Sergeants pie factory, prostitutes, pimps, pickpockets, muggers, con men, SP (starting-price) bookies and drug dealers. There was a World War I veteran who sat by the door and blew on a harmonica. At his feet was a wooden bowl for the pennies of those who appreciated his energetic, if discordant, renditions of 'The Wild Colonial Boy' and Jack O'Hagan's new bush ballad 'Along the Road to Gundagai'. Pinched-faced children, affecting the silver-screen swagger of James Cagney and Edward G. Robinson, mooched change from drinkers. Cards and two-up were played in a back bar — 'Come in, spinner!' Fights erupted regularly, which was no surprise, for the Tradesman's Arms was the hotel of choice of Guido Calletti, cigarette stuck to his lower lip and his jaw thrust out like Mussolini's. Calletti would case the crowd for victims to befriend then rob. Dulcie Markham, Nellie Cameron, Jim Devine and Frank Green were regulars. Tilly Devine called in to transact business, since the Arms was in the heart of her red-light stamping ground, and just across the street from her brothel and sometime home at 191 Palmer Street, today a popular restaurant, Bonne Femme.

Likewise, Kippax and Forbes streets and Barcom Avenue in Darlinghurst; Woolloomooloo's Brougham and Harmer streets and Butlers Stairs; Darlinghurst and Bayswater roads and Craigend Street in Kings Cross; Kippax and Devonshire streets, Surry Hills (with terrace houses stacked together so tightly that it seemed that if one were plucked from its position in the row, the entire street of dwellings would come crashing down) were mob battlegrounds. Nowadays, all these thoroughfares to a greater or lesser degree have been prettified. They belong to a different, in most ways better, Sydney. But each, in certain corners, at certain times of the day and night, retains a trace of Razorhurst.

But *why* was there unprecedented savagery in East Sydney from 1927 until the outbreak of World War II, the period that encompassed the so-called razor-gang wars? Razorhurst was the result of an ill-starred confluence of between-the-wars social conditions, well-intended but wrong-headed laws, and a truly extraordinary group of ambitious and ruthless crime entrepreneurs determined to cash in on vices beloved of Australians. Given the collision of these elements, Razorhurst could never *not* have been.

Until the early years of the twentieth century, all-day drinking and narcotics use, street prostitution, handgun ownership, off–race course betting and gambling were either legal or tolerated in New South Wales. Then in the fresh flush of the new age, the church, temperance organisations and moral reformers pressured the State Government to cleanse Sydney of vice. The solons who passed the amended *Vagrancy Act* of 1905, the *Gaming and Betting Act* of 1906, the wide-ranging *Police Offences (Amendment) Act* of 1908 and other later laws (including the *Liquor Act* of 1916 and the *Dangerous Drugs Amendment Act* of 1927), banning, variously, street prostitution, gambling, alcohol sales after 6 p.m. and narcotics, failed to understand that indulging these vices was second nature to many Sydneysiders. Eradicating them was as feasible as stopping the breakers from crashing onto the sands of Bondi Beach.

Unwittingly, by their determination to protect the public from itself, the wowsers, and the politicians who appeased them, constructed the legal platform on which syndicated crime was built. There were riches on offer for highly organised criminal entrepreneurs smart and ruthless enough to circumvent the laws, and give the public what they wanted and were prepared to pay for.

When gambling was banned — including the Digger's favourite, two-up — illegal gaming dens, like Thommo's (in operation around Central Station since 1908), proliferated. When off-course betting was made a crime, bookmakers, catering to people's abiding need to gamble on horses, resorted to operating out of pubs and private houses, the wireless and telephone boons to their cause.

In criminalising street prostitution because the practice, as one reformer declared, 'corrupted the sons of Australia and led to the spread of venereal disease', and making it illegal for men (but, as Tilly Devine gleefully noted, not women) to operate brothels, those who passed the *Police Offences (Amendment) Act* of 1908 ignored the reality that there would always be lonely men or blokes on a spree happy to pay for sex (not to mention women keen to cash in by selling it). Ridding the streets of prostitutes, far from stopping the trade, just drove it underground. Streetwalkers flocked to brothel-keepers, like Tilly Devine, who exacted heavy tolls from the sex workers' daily takings for the privilege of allowing them to service clients in her seedy rooms. Out of sight of the police, drug use by prostitutes, violence to them by clients, and stealing (both the prostitute from her client and the client from his prostitute) became rife.

Sly-grogger Kate Leigh's long and lucrative criminal career path was paved by the do-gooders. At the outset of World War I in 1914, the Salvation Army, Baptists, Methodists, Presbyterians and Congregationalists, alarmed at what they believed were escalating levels of public drunkenness and domestic discord caused by the breadwinner spending all his wages on alcohol, combined to serve politicians with massive petitions demanding reduced hours during which 'the demon drink' could be sold. They saw a curfew as the precursor to prohibition. Premier William Holman resisted, mindful of the taxes his government raked in from liquor sales and the popularity of drinking among his constituents, whose goodwill he could not afford to lose. The average Sydney tippler refused to take seriously the reformers' determination to cruel their fun — and ordered another round.

Then, on 14 February 1916, came a godsend for the wowsers when about 5000 Lighthorsemen and other members of the Australian Infantry Forces headquartered at Casula (near Liverpool in Sydney's south-west) went on a drunken rampage. The soldiers were unhappy about harsh conditions and a new training edict that increased their drill hours from thirty-six to forty-and-a-half hours a week. To express their disgust they marched on Liverpool, where hundreds set up camp in the bar of the Commercial Hotel. They drank the pub dry, without paying a penny for their pleasure. The rioters guzzled £2000 worth of alcohol at the Commercial then decamped to the Golden Fleece Hotel and drank that dry too. Soldiers sat sozzled in the street slurping liquor from pots, pans and any other receptacle that did not leak. They then rushed the railway station, planning to catch a train to Sydney, but their officers had posted a guardsman there who repelled the rene-gades with rifle fire. The guard shot one rioter dead and wounded six. The mutineers fell back, then rallied, returning fire. They managed to commandeer a train and steamed to Sydney's Central Station. In the city, with an outnumbered police force powerless to stop the men, the havoc continued. The German Club in Phillip Street was sacked, and Grace Bros department store in Broadway, Kleisdorff's tobacco store in Hunter Street and numerous restaurants and hotels were looted. The soldiers overturned fruit-and-vegetable barrows, and assaulted women and men at random. The bender continued until they dropped in their tracks three days later, exhausted and paralytic with drink.

When the men awoke, they learned that the Holman government had invoked a *War Precautions Act* that enabled it to close indefinitely the doors of every hotel in the metropolitan area. Premier Holman, shaken by the unbridled, booze-fuelled violence, and buffeted by the now more strident than ever anti-liquor lobby, caved in to pressure. Australia being Australia and not America, William Holman was never going to ban alcohol completely, but he did announce that on 10 June 1916 the people of New South Wales would vote in a referen-dum that would determine whether pubs would continue to remain open until 11 p.m. or close their doors at six.

Then, another fillip to the anti-liquor brigade: just three days before the referendum, Britain's Lord Kitchener — the warlord whose stern visage glowered from the famous 'Your Country Needs You' recruitment posters — perished along with his staff when the HMS *Hampshire* was sunk en route to Russia and the Battle of Jutland. The church wasted no time in turning the tragedy to its own end. 'In this solemn hour of the Empire's need every true patriot should vote for 6 o'clock closing!' it intoned. Wowsers urged Australians to 'abstain from all intoxicants, and encourage others to do the same'; 6 p.m. became 'the Patriotic Hour'. At their rallies, the pro-early closing forces would chant a poem entitled '6 O'Clock':

*'Tis after six and he's not in!*
*The children hear her voice grow sad,*
*And wonder if they should begin*
*Their tea — or wait for dad!*

*'Tis pay-day; but despair not yet!*
*She'll keep the good meal warm awhile.*
*But seven strikes, her eyes grow wet,*
*And all have ceased to smile.*

*The children settled safe in bed*
*She sits alone, with fear to start*
*And ev'ry hour, with tons of lead*
*Seems striking at her heart.*

*Then on her knees, distraught in mind*
*She prays, while words and sobs o'er mix,*
*'Oh, God, grant laws of any kind*
*That send men home at six.'*

The publicans and the liquor trade tried to argue that Australian, British and French troops had always fought bravely when issued with alcohol rations. And dedicated drinkers countered with doggerel of their own:

> *Delightful visitant, with thee*
> *We'd hail the time of flowers,*
> *Could you but tell us of a pub*
> *Where they sell grog after hours.*

> *Sweet bird! Thy bower is ever green,*
> *Thy sky is ever clear,*
> *Thy hast no sorrow in thy song,*
> *Thou art not fond of beer.*

> *Oh, could I fly, I'd fly with thee,*
> *With feathered chums to mix,*
> *For this will be a rotten place*
> *With pubs all closed at 6.*

The anti-liquor legions prevailed. At the referendum, 60 per cent of New South Welshmen voted for 6 p.m. closing; just 1 per cent wanted to retain the status quo closing time of 11 p.m. The *Liquor Act* of 1916 was passed. From then until 1955, when the law was repealed and 10 a.m. to 10 p.m. closing introduced, New South Wales pubs were only allowed to serve customers from 6 a.m. to 6 p.m. But anybody keen to drink on after closing time could be assured of a warm welcome at any of Kate Leigh's sly-grog shops.

Anti-drug laws enacted between 1924 and 1927 prohibited narcotics — including the most popular, cocaine, whose users had been able to buy it freely from chemists as easily as purchasing aspirin or toothpaste. Cocaine was mostly used in tiny quantities as a nerve soother, much as Bex, Vincent's APC powders and aspirin were in later years. In 1927, after the passing of the *Dangerous Drugs (Amendment) Act*, 'snowdroppers' could no longer buy cocaine and other drugs from pharmacists and physicians. So drug users turned to organised underworld drug rings.

Another byproduct of laws which created circumstances where underworld entrepreneurs could grow rich on the profits of their illegal enterprises, was the growth of a small army of 'standover' men, who preyed on the earnings of the brothel-keepers, the sly-groggers, the bookies and drug dealers. Unable to complain to the police, most of the entrepreneurs were easy game for these armed and dangerous extortionists. A few fought back. Phil Jeffs, Tilly Devine and Kate Leigh defended their empires, and the bloody gang warfare that stained Sydney was the inevitable result.

The muckraking Sydney weekly tabloid newspaper *Truth*, mindful of the doings of gang lord Al Capone in America, declared Sydney 'the Chicago of the South' and condemned East Sydney as a 'region of bohemia, crime and mystery . . . a breeding place of vice'. In September 1928, when the atrocities had escalated further and the newspaper was leading a campaign to have tough new anti-crime laws enacted, *Truth* unleashed its most purple-hued tabloidese:

> *Razorhurst, Gunhurst, Bottlehurst, Dopehurst — it used to be Darlinghurst, one of the finest quarters of a rich and beautiful city; today it is a plague spot where the spawn of the gutter grow and fatten on official apathy. By day it shelters in its alleys, in its dens, the Underworld people. At night it looses them to prey on prosperity, decency and virtue, and to fight one another for the division of the spoils. The menace increases and nothing is done. Authority sleeps as though the day were not approaching when Underworld Dictators will terrorise the community with threats of certain death at the hands of their bravos.*
>
> *Inadequate policing and an out-of-date Crimes Act are the fertilisers of this Field of Evil.* Truth *demands that Razorhurst*

*be swept off the map, and the Darlinghurst we knew in better days be restored. It demands new laws, and new strength for their enforcement. And it points, for convincing and horrifying evidence, to the crimes already to Razorhurst's discredit . . .*

*Recall the human beasts that, lurking cheek by jowl with decent people, live with no aim, purpose or occupation but crime — bottle men [thieves who bludgeoned their victims, usually from behind, with a bottle], dope pedlars, razor slashers, sneak thieves, confidence men, women of ill repute, pickpockets, burglars, spielers, gunmen and every brand of racecourse parasite. What an army of arrogant and uncontrolled vice!*

*As a result of what goes on daily — thanks to the Crimes Act, thanks to under-policing — Razorhurst grows more and more undesirable as a place of residence for the peaceful and industrious. Unceasingly it attracts to its cesspool every form of life that is vile.*

If there was a symbol for these violent times, it was the razor, adopted as a weapon when handguns were banned. Not that there were no shootings; there were, as we will see. But while most criminals did not carry a gun, they invariably concealed on their person at least one razor, usually a cutthroat blade, honed to hair-splitting sharpness, and, as police and hospital records prove, they did not hesitate to use it. There were a number of deaths by razor, but the implement was also unsurpassed as a weapon of intimidation and disfiguration. An inordinate number of wrongdoers back then wore the telltale mark of a razor attack — an L-shaped scar extending down one cheek then across to the mouth. Like the prospect of a shark attack, or of being gnawed by rats or strapped into the electric chair, the thought of a deep cut with a sharp blade evokes a primeval fear, a response that shivers the skin and tingles the spine.

By the time casualties and a rejuvenated police force ended the hostilities of the gangs of Tilly Devine, Kate Leigh, Phil Jeffs and Norman Bruhn, as many as a score of gangsters were dead and hundreds of others razor-scarred and bullet-punctured.

This is the story of the rise and fall of the warriors of Razorhurst.

# PART 1
# First Offences

# 1

# Slumland

Since the beginning of the nineteenth century, developers had been knocking up cheap, badly designed, haphazardly constructed rows of terrace houses and shacks on the hills and hollows to the east of Sydney Town. The dwellings were for the poor who toiled on Sydney's wharves and in its factories, foundries and shops, and needed to live within walking distance of their workplaces. Many of these houses were unfit for human habitation from the day they were built. Often more than twenty people were crammed together in rough timber-and-brick structures that were refrigerators in winter and furnaces in summer when their corrugated-iron roofs magnified the sun's rays and drove temperatures inside to infernal (sometimes life-threatening) levels. By the early years of the twentieth century, much of East Sydney was a teeming slumland of ramshackle, rat-infested and bug-ridden dwellings, set like rotting teeth in a maw of mean streets and sleazy lanes.

True, there were many fine dwellings in Kings Cross, Woolloomooloo and Darlinghurst, home in the 1800s and the early 1900s to the city's pioneers and those who prospered by dint of good fortune or hard work. A number of these impressive buildings survive gloriously today. But then, in the first fifteen years of the twentieth century, came Sydney's transport revolution, and the 'slumification' of Surry Hills, Darlinghurst, Woolloomooloo, Paddington and Kings Cross was all but complete. With trams, trains, automobiles and improved roads providing quick and easy commuting access to the city from the new garden suburbs of Strathfield, Lane Cove, Hunters Hill, Waverley, Kogarah and Manly, most of the Sydneysiders who could afford to fanned out, abandoning their East Sydney homes primarily to the wretched and the villainous. The evacuees sold their mansions, solid bungalows and terrace houses to developers and slum landlords who divided the dwellings into tiny flats and installed as many tenants as possible. Soon the once-proud homes deteriorated until they were as egregious as any shanty.

In his book *Surry Hills: The City's Backyard*, Christopher Keating cites a 1902 Sydney Municipal Council survey of housing. The survey noted that in those days the Surry Hills area accounted for about 30 per cent of Sydney's houses and that properties in Surry Hills 'exhibited all the old defects characteristic of inner-city rental housing'. Nearly half of the houses in Surry Hills had either defective drains and sewer connections or inadequate sanitary facilities. There were seven times fewer indoor toilets in Surry Hills than elsewhere in Sydney and only 8 per cent of dwellings were properly proofed against rising damp. Rooms were perpetually wet and, usually with tiny — or no — windows, poorly ventilated. Typically, a five-room house in Surry Hills or its neighbouring suburbs had just one tap, and it was in the backyard, by the toilet. There was no garden; no gas, no electricity. Food was cooked on wood- or coal-fuelled stoves. Front doors opened onto the street. Roofs were of slate or iron which rusted and leaked. With inadequate or no sewerage and sanitation, household garbage, dead animals and human waste were buried in the backyard or simply piled up, and, the stomach-churning stench notwithstanding, forgotten. Vermin flourished in the filth. And there were epidemics — notably the bubonic plague of 1900 in which 103 Sydneysiders perished and thousands fell ill.

At various times, well-meaning reformers convinced civic fathers to raze particularly obnoxious East Sydney slums. Sometimes new and better housing rose on the vacant site, but more often a smoke-belching factory or noisy workshop was erected. The residents displaced by slum clearance were forced to sublet rooms from neighbours whose homes had been spared, thus exacerbating the problem of overcrowding.

The poor of East Sydney brightened the gloom of their lives by going to the Rugby League and cricket at the Sydney Cricket Ground, to the boxing or wrestling at the Stadium at Rushcutters Bay, to the Moore Park Zoo, the Domain Baths (with its separate sections for men and women), the White City fairgrounds with their fortune-tellers and merry-go-rounds, or the buckjumping in Hyde Park. The annual Royal Easter Show and a visit by the clowns and acrobats of Wirth's Circus were red-letter-day events.

But for many, fun and games could not assuage their despair, and they took solace in drugs, alcohol and random sex. Consequently, drug addiction, drunkenness and venereal disease were rife. To feed themselves and their families, and also fund a few pleasures, people supplemented their meagre wages earned slaving in machinery shops and arsenic factories, unloading ships, brewing beer and catching and killing rats (the City Council, still traumatised by the bubonic plague, for a while paid six shillings a rodent), by gambling what they could not afford to lose, or becoming thieves and muggers. Women — the widowed, the deserted, the unemployed, those with many mouths to feed, or who needed to pay for their alcohol or drug addiction — became prostitutes. Impoverished parents sent their children to work in factories, and child prostitution was rife.

The death rate in the slums of East Sydney in the early years of the twentieth century was 20 per cent higher than in the rest of Sydney. The *Sydney Morning Herald* branded the area 'a sort of Alsatia for the criminal, the unfortunate and the very poor', and called living conditions in Paddington 'a menace to health and morals'.

Generally, Surry Hills was no better, no worse, than its neighbouring suburbs. It was merely typical. Ruth Park wrote memorably of the Hills in *Poor Man's Orange*, of how it 'clung to the proud skirts of Sydney like a ragged, dirty-nosed child'. A folk poet calling himself 'Bill Rock' captured the essence of the area:

> *Truants scooting wooden slopes*
> *Adventure bound,*
> *Persistent hawkers' raucous hopes*
> *In alleys sound*
>
> *Little shops on little hills*
> *Tawdry array*
> *Pallid plants in pots on sills*
> *Mock dwellings grey*
>
> *Landlords rap and rap for rents*
> *Some quietly*
> *Some blind to tenants' eyes in vents*
> *Fixed furtively*
>
> *Battered belles fill doorway frames*
> *Shifty-eyed*
> *Stare and laugh down seamy lanes*
> *On Surry side*

Of all the wretched traps that festered in East Sydney, the worst was Surry Hills's Frog Hollow, located on and around the sheer cliff that plummeted from the western side of Riley Street, between Ann and Albion streets. In the decade before World War I until the late 1920s, when, mercifully, it was razed, criminals battened themselves to

Frog Hollow like fleas to a rat. The frogs which gave the swampy, crater-like gully in the bowels of the Riley Street escarpment its name sensibly departed to more congenial surroundings sometime in the 1800s, leaving the stinking labyrinth of narrow, dark and airless alleys and higgledy-piggledy, jammed-together hovels to a scabrous collection of blackguards and their barefoot children, mangy pets and vermin. Local clergymen had no trouble evoking a picture of hell for their parishioners — they merely told them take a stroll to Frog Hollow.

There, lawbreakers schemed robberies and murder, lay low from the police, hid their stolen goods, gathered in the notorious Sunbeam Hotel to grow woozy on opium and cocaine and gut-rot booze, suffered the agony of venereal disease, died of plague, and bashed, raped and otherwise abused one another. The area was headquarters for many mobs, and none more forbidding than the Riley Street Gang, whose ruggedly handsome leader, armed robber Samuel 'Jewey' Freeman, lived in a shack there. When he was not robbing people at gunpoint, Freeman's idea of fun was beating senseless the last rag-tag manifestations of the old Surry Hills larrikin youth gangs, namely the Forty Thieves and the Big Seven, who attracted a police presence in the Hills that Freeman (with serious villainy of his own to conduct) could well have done without.

In the late 1800s and the first few years of the twentieth century, gangs of larrikins — called 'pushes' — roamed the streets. The members of Woolloomooloo's Plunkett Street Push, the Rocks Push and Surry Hills's Forty Thieves and the Big Seven were troublemakers and nuisances, but apart from a little mugging for beer and cigarette money they confined their roguery to catcalling women and well-dressed citizens in the street and raising lumps on each others' heads with sand-filled socks. They were often recruited by local politicians to menace rivals' supporters and to swell the numbers at public meetings. These unruly but generally harmless louts were despised and mocked by the district's truly hard criminals, such as Freeman and his Riley Street Gang, and by 1910–1915, the larrikins had been run off.

A frequent ally of Freeman in armed robbery and larrikin-bashing was a weedy con man, safe-cracker and deft picker of locks named Ernest 'Shiner' Ryan. Ryan often dossed in Freeman's lair, and in 1913, the duo was joined by Freeman's latest lover, a wild, thirty-two-year-old thief and prostitute named Kate Leigh.

# 2

# Young Kate

Ned Kelly had been dead just a year when Kate Leigh was born on 10 March 1881 in the cattle town of Dubbo, in central west New South Wales. Near the shanty where she was delivered was a grand new classical court house with a gaol and gallows at the rear. The prison, with its isolation cells and the wooden scaffold that was in use until 1904, fascinated little Kathleen Mary Josephine Beahan — not least because her beleaguered parents often warned the cheeky and wilful child that if she didn't mend her ways, Dubbo Gaol was where they'd send her.

Kate, nicknamed 'Bonnie', was one of thirteen children of Timothy Beahan, an impoverished cobbler who moonlighted as a horse trainer, and his wife Charlotte. Kate and Charlotte were close, but the child was forever at odds with her father. He thrashed her, and punished her by depriving her of food — which only steeled her rebellious streak. From the age of eight, Kate (who in her long life would notch up 107 criminal convictions and serve thirteen gaol terms) was in strife for stealing from her parents and siblings and from local shops, whacking other children and playing truant.

When she was ten, Kate ran away from home and was despatched to Parramatta Girls Home as a neglected child. After four years, she was released and worked as a waitress and in factories in Glebe and

Surry Hills. She was sexually precocious and ran with the wildest youths. Her first criminal conviction was for vagrancy, in effect, being without lawful means of support.

On 2 May 1902, when she was twenty-one, she married a thirty-year-old carpenter, illegal bookmaker and petty crook named Jack Leigh. They had a daughter, Eileen. Jack thought himself a hard man, and was gaoled for beating up and robbing the landlord of their Glebe flat. At her husband's trial, Kate tried to convince the court that Jack had not attacked the landlord in a bid to steal his money, but because he had flown into a jealous rage when he arrived home to find her and the landlord in bed together. She and Jack were so broke, she cried, that she had been reduced to sleeping with the landlord in lieu of paying him rent. The court did not believe her and Kate followed Jack into Darlinghurst Gaol, convicted of perjury and being an accomplice in the assault. It was not the last time Kate Leigh would go down for standing by her man. When Kate and Jack Leigh were released from prison after five years, they parted and, as far as is known, never saw each other again.

For the next few years, from around 1910, Kate provided for herself and Eileen as best she could. She toiled in factories, but soon the long hours and low pay of the straight life grated. She would always deny it in her later years, but police records show that Kate supplemented her legitimate income by running brothels and, in particularly cash-strapped times, prostituting herself on the streets of East Sydney. By 1913, she was strictly illegal. That year, she was convicted of maintaining a house frequented by prostitutes and was placed on a twelve-month good-behaviour bond. By now, good behaviour played little part in Kate Leigh's life.

Those who only knew Kate when she was older and toadlike and blowzy were always incredulous when told that she was the most prized of gangsters' girls before the Great War. She was petite, at 51 kilograms and 152 centimetres tall, and wore her thick, wavy dark hair in a large bun topped with a floppy hat that trailed ostrich feathers. Her small brown eyes twinkled and her handsome face, in spite of the dark and smoky dens she frequented, retained vestiges of a fresh country glow. Brave, anti-authority and usually in high spirits, this 'good-looker' was courted by her criminal peers, both for their own sexual delectation and to snatch a share of her streetwalking takings. Leigh also earned money stealing, fencing and acting as a bail broker. As she had proven in spinning the story that she hoped would get her first husband off his assault charge, she had no qualms about standing up in court and providing false alibis, for which service members of the underworld paid her well.

Kate and Jack would officially divorce in 1922, the year she wed another scoundrel, a Western Australia-born musician named Edward 'Teddy' Barry, on 26 September. That marriage ended when Kate surprised Barry in bed with another woman. She battered them both and banished him from her life.

When Kate and Barry split, she would become the consort of a rogues' gallery of small-time hoods. There was 'Gaol-Bird Joe' Denmead, Len Martin and the charming 'Monkey' Webb, who delighted in climbing aboard trams and appalling the passengers by devouring raw sausages and barking like a dog.

When Teddy Barry died in 1948, Kate attended his funeral in Sydney wearing an unforgiving expression and an expensive silver-fox fur, as if to somehow show the deceased what a bad career move it had been to cheat on her all those years ago. After divorcing Barry, Kate reverted to the surname 'Leigh', which she retained until 1950, when she wed her third husband — of all people, Samuel 'Jewey' Freeman's henchman, Ernest 'Shiner' Ryan.

But in mid-1914, she had been Jewey Freeman's girl for about six months, holed up on and off with him, daughter Eileen and Shiner Ryan in Frog Hollow. And it was there, in East Sydney's most foetid slum, that Freeman, Ryan, Leigh and some accomplices planned the great Eveleigh Railway Workshops payroll robbery.

On the morning of 10 June 1914, payday at Eveleigh Railway Workshops in Wilson Street, Redfern, paymaster Fred Miller and an assistant, Norman Twiss, drew up as usual at the factory complex in a horse-drawn wagon. In the tray of the wagon were two chests, one containing £3696/19/6 and the other £3302/13/6. The pair heaved one box into the main office from where its contents would later be distributed to the workers. Then they returned to the wagon where Twiss began manhandling the second chest off the tray.

Suddenly an old drab-grey car driven by Ryan with Freeman in the passenger seat, both men wearing handkerchief masks and driving goggles, sped up and skidded to a halt in the gravel beside the wagon. Freeman leapt out and, holding a revolver to Twiss's head, barked, 'Don't you move, either of you, or I'll blow your fucking brains out.' He shoved Miller to the ground and ordered Twiss to hand over the cash chest. Twiss did so. Freeman loaded the chest into the back of the car, leapt in and was driven away by Ryan. The car, reported the *Sydney Morning Herald* the next day, 'progressed citywards, and with great speed'.

The daring heist shocked the nation, not least because it was committed in broad daylight, a weapon was used and, for the first time in Australia, a car was involved in its execution. The *Herald* feared it would spark a crime wave and called for more police to be put on the beat to deter potential robbers. 'The Eveleigh holdup is surely unique of its kind in the history of Australia,' noted its editor on 11 June with what sounded like undisguised admiration for the perpetrators. 'For audacity of conception and cool effrontery of execution it could hardly have been surpassed [but had there been a policeman about, the robbers may have been apprehended]. We commend to the Government's notice the increase of the police force.'

Meanwhile, a bystander had taken down the getaway car's licence number — 10297 — and the police traced it to a mechanic named Arthur Tatham, who had reported the car stolen from Castlereagh Street in the city the day before. After grilling Tatham, detectives were sure he knew more about the robbery than he had told them. Then, as the police searched for the thieves, the money and the car, paymaster Miller came to them with his suspicions about his colleague, Twiss. To Miller, Twiss had seemed unusually cool when under the gun and being cuffed about by the thief, almost as if he had expected the robbery and had known no harm would come to him. Miller was convinced Twiss was in cahoots with the thieves, and told police so. But before they could interview Twiss, an informer whispered to officers that the ringleader was Freeman, and police concurred that he was clever and foolhardy enough to attempt such a job. They put Freeman under surveillance and, on 24 June, he was arrested at Strathfield Station, in Sydney's western suburbs, as he was boarding the Melbourne Express. Freeman protested his innocence: on the day of the great heist, he said, he had been at the races. Regardless, he was charged with armed robbery and assault.

Shiner Ryan was confident Freeman would not inform on him and remained in Sydney until he had sent two boxes containing his share of the stolen payroll money to his friend Sam Falkiner, a Melbourne bad-hat. Then he caught a train to the Victorian capital to retrieve it. Sadly for Ryan, his scam unravelled when Falkiner absconded to Tasmania with the cash. A furious Ryan complained to a lover about Falkiner's treachery; she, hoping for a reward, told the police. In early July, fourteen detectives and six uniformed officers surrounded a house in Melbourne's Albert Park and called on Ryan to give himself up. At first Ryan threatened to open fire, but thought better of it, threw his gun into the street and was arrested. Officers found £600 in a glass jar hidden in the chimney of the house. This was the only money ever recovered from the Eveleigh robbery. Ryan was extradited to Sydney in handcuffs. With Ryan and Freeman in custody, the police turned to Twiss, who denied being an accomplice but admitted that he had known Freeman years before and had played rugby with him. The police were certain of his complicity in the robbery and kept him in the cells. Tatham, the owner of the 'stolen' getaway car, was also charged.

At Central Criminal Court, Darlinghurst, in September 1914, Freeman, Ryan, Twiss and Tatham pleaded not guilty to assaulting Fred Miller and stealing £3302/13/6. Freeman also faced charges of shooting and wounding Michael McHale, a nightwatchman who had routed him trying to rob the Paddington Post Office in Oxford Street, just four days before the Eveleigh Railway Workshops job. (Freeman had fired point-blank at McHale, the bullet passing through the man's cheek and wounding a tram conductor on the other side of Oxford Street.)

Twiss was acquitted because of a lack of concrete evidence against him. Elated, he kissed Ryan in the courtroom, waved goodbye and repaired to the Courthouse Hotel across the road in Oxford Street to drown his joy. Tatham was found not guilty of assault and robbery but served three months in gaol for being an accessory to the robbery.

On the witness stand, Shiner Ryan lied outrageously. He portrayed himself as a struggling inventor who had only come to Sydney to find buyers for his invention: a device for automatically coupling trucks. He had checked into a boarding house for his Sydney stay and, lo, Freeman was living there too. Ryan had had nothing to do with the robbery, he claimed, but on seeing a newspaper drawing of a man wanted in connection with it, felt it resembled him rather closely and that he was being framed by somebody, he couldn't say who. So he fled to Melbourne because 'with my criminal record, I knew a long sentence was a formality if, somehow, I was convicted'. He blithely ignored the evidence of the informants, his earlier confession to the crime and the money found in his chimney. Ryan's hunch that he faced a long term behind bars was correct. He was found guilty and sentenced to ten years in Parramatta Gaol. In his first days in prison, he tried to slash his left wrist and ankle with a sharp metal object, but his suicide attempt was thwarted by guards and Ryan served the rest of his time quietly.

It was then Jewey Freeman's turn to test the credulity of the court. Seemingly forgetting he had earlier told police that he had been at the races when the payroll was stolen, he now said he could not have committed the robbery because he had been in bed with his lover, Kate Leigh. When she was called to the stand, a wide-eyed Kate eagerly corroborated Freeman's alibi. Not only that, she embellished it. She swore under oath that after an afternoon's ice-skating together at the Exhibition Rink, she and Freeman went home to Frog Hollow and did not leave the shack for two days. As the *Sydney Morning Herald* noted:

> *Her admission, made in public and on oath, a woman's confession of her own lack of virtue, would have gone far to swing the scales in favour of Freeman. It seemed unbelievable that a woman would publicly parade her shame unless the facts were correct.*

But the jury did not believe Freeman, and it did not believe Kate Leigh. Freeman, like Ryan, was sentenced to ten years in Parramatta Gaol for stealing the Eveleigh payroll. Immediately afterwards, he was sentenced again, for the term of his natural life this time, for shooting Paddington Post Office nightwatchman McHale. The judge asked if Freeman had anything to say before he was taken away. 'Just this,' replied the habitual crook, with a grin, 'do I qualify for leniency under the *First Offender's Act*?'

No one knows if Freeman's facetiousness infuriated the judge, but when he came to sentence Kate Leigh for perjury, he threw the book at her. She would, he said, spend the next seven years of her life in Long Bay Gaol. 'Seven years for stickin' to a man,' Kate muttered sourly. 'I'll swing before I stick to another.'

Early in 1915, after installing teenaged Eileen in a convent, Kate arrived at the new Female Reformatory at Long Bay Gaol, opened just three years before. She was stripped, searched and fumigated before donning a prison uniform and commencing her sentence. As part of her rehabilitation she had to perform daily tasks which required, according to the new prison's charter, 'constant effort'. A good cook since girlhood, she soon gravitated to the gaol's kitchen. Daily exercise was enforced, as was the 'character-building' cold shower she had to endure winter and summer after callisthenics. At all times, she was required to be 'bright and cheerful', exhibit 'self-control' and treat her fellow prisoners with 'politeness and decorum'. When not working, exercising or praying in the prison chapel, she would be confined to her single cell, where she was allowed to read censored versions of letters from the outside and 'suitable literature'. Leigh must have been a model prisoner, for she was paroled two years early, after serving not quite five years.

When Kate Leigh was released from Long Bay in late 1919, the world was much changed. A war involving most of the nations on earth had been waged and won, but at a fearful price. Of the 330 000 Australian warriors despatched overseas from the country's population of 4.9 million, 59 432 had died and 166 819 had been wounded in places named Beersheba, Gallipoli and Pozières. William Morris Hughes was the new prime minister. C.J. Dennis's *Songs of a Sentimental Bloke* and May Gibbs's *Snugglepot and Cuddlepie* were the runaway literary successes. Thousands had perished in the great flu epidemic of 1919. Les Darcy, a young boxer who lived in Paddington's Lord Dudley

Hotel, had looked certain to win the world middleweight title, but he had died of blood poisoning in the United States in 1917, aged just twenty-one. Aviators Ross and Keith Smith had flown all the way from London to Darwin, touching down along the way in Italy, Greece, Egypt, India and Singapore. And, perhaps most interesting of all to Kate, the ALP–Nationalist State Government of William Holman, in response to demands from temperance groups and the church, had decreed that pubs must close their doors at 6 p.m. instead of 11 p.m.

Kate grabbed the opportunity presented by the new laws. For the next thirty-five years, she cashed in by providing illegal liquor, known as 'sly grog', to all those imbibers whom the moral guardians had sought to deprive of a post-6 p.m. drink in a place other than their home. From her savings, she was able to buy a two-storey terrace house for herself and Eileen at 104 Riley Street, East Sydney, just off William Street. She then rented six premises ('sly-groggeries') in Surry Hills, rooms at the back of fruit and grocery shops and in nondescript terraces, and sold illegal beer, wine and spirits in the forbidden hours.

At the height of her career, Kate ran more than twenty sly-groggeries. Some of her sly-grog shops were upmarket and frequented by businessmen; others, said police, 'catered to the worst class of thieves and prostitutes'. On Friday and Saturday nights, crowds of men milled in the street awaiting admittance to 'Mum's', as her establishments were known. Punters could either drink on the premises or take home her booze — albeit at a hefty mark-up on the wholesale prices she paid her hotel and brewery suppliers. (Depending on the groggery's decor and location, this mark-up could have been as much as 100 per cent, costing her customers the princely sum of one shilling and sixpence for a bottle of beer.)

From the early 1920s until the '40s, Kate Leigh, as Sydney's leading sly-grogger and with her income protected by her own combative nature and a team of bashers and gunmen, was one of the wealthiest, and most flamboyant, Sydneysiders. Another key to her success, she always said, was that unlike many of her less-successful rival illicit alcohol sellers, she did not partake of her product. 'I hate the taste of the bloody stuff!' she'd bark while filling a customer's glass to the brim.

Larger than life, greedy, funny when she felt like it and vicious when she needed to be, Kate was like a twentieth-century Long John Silver, a pirate captain aboard the jolly brig Surry Hills. Aside from running the groggeries, she was a standover merchant, a dealer in drugs (for a while she was known as 'the Snow Queen'), a fence for stolen property and, more for sport than anything else, a deft shoplifter who secreted in her voluminous bloomers the goods she removed from the shelves of Grace Bros and Mark Foys.

By the mid '20s, the newspapers would be calling her the 'Most Evil Woman in Sydney'. Leigh liked to sidle up to pretty working girls and try to entice them into her world. She would tell them of the good times, fine clothes and jewels enjoyed by those smart enough to throw in their lot with her, and add with a gap-toothed grin, 'It's a nasty world, so it's best to enjoy it while you can.'

While among the most prominent, Kate was only one of a number of villains who set up shop in post-World War I East Sydney. Sly grog, cocaine and opium, prostitution and gambling formed a lucrative economic base for organised crime. With the onset of the Roaring '20s, the area was the city's criminal kingdom. Newspapers trumpeted a 'crime wave', and with good cause. But compared with the mayhem that followed, to paraphrase Al Jolson, the American singing rage of the time and star of the pioneer talkie *The Jazz Singer* (which had Sydneysiders queuing for blocks around the old Lyceum theatre) the Harbour City hadn't seen nothin' yet.

# 3

# A Camberwell Lass

If Surry Hills's Frog Hollow had a London counterpart it may have been the area bounded by Sultan and Hollington streets in Camberwell, a Victorian suburb in the city's south-west. In his landmark survey *Life and Labour of the People in London*, Charles Booth called these hovel-lined streets 'one of the vilest slums in the whole of London'. In summer's heat or winter's cold, Booth despaired, the children of the area went shoeless and dressed in rags. They ate scraps, committed crimes and died young. Drunkenness was epidemic among women and men, and assaults were common. Booth was shocked by the housing in Hollington Street, in particular. Number 21, for example, was a ramshackle three-storey dwelling of six rooms in which nineteen people, including eleven children, lived. None of the children attended school. Most of the adults were alcoholic. Booth was disgusted by the smells that suffused Hollington Street. There were still piggeries and cowsheds nearby, and linoleum and glue factories, and adding to the industrial effluvium was the reek of rancid fish that locals smoked over open fires in their backyards. Also, wrote local historian Mary Boast in *The Story of Camberwell*: 'Every bit of space was used for stabling ponies and donkeys and storing market barrows. The rotting vegetable rubbish from these added to the sickly atmosphere.'

Tilly Devine was born Matilda Mary Twiss, at home at No. 57 Hollington Street, Camberwell, on 8 September 1900, the year before Queen Victoria died. Tilly's father, Edward Twiss, was a hand-to-mouth bricklayer's labourer and her mother, Alice (maiden name Tubb), a housewife. Tilly Twiss, whose cherubic features belied a crosspatch temper, grew up in abject poverty. Like the other urchins in her street, she froze and starved. Like them, too, her future at best was bleak.

With no fun or distractions to be had at home, Tilly roamed Camberwell and got to know it well. It was an area of amazing contrasts. There were the slums of Hollington and Sultan streets, yes, where she had to return each day from her wanderings, and there was school, which she despised; but Camberwell was also a treasure trove of Victorian delights. In summer, she frolicked at the Camberwell Baths and Leisure Centre, opened in 1891, which resembled a castle in a fairy tale. There was the fortress-like South London Art Gallery in Peckham Road, where poor kids such as she were encouraged to enjoy the great works within. If an employee saw a child peeping into the gallery from the street but too intimidated to enter, the staff member was expected to invite the child inside, make a fuss of them and explain the paintings, so encouraging children to return.

Best of all to young Tilly, were the glittering theatres and music halls where she acquired a love of overblown glitz, ostentatious jewellery and the knees-up, thigh-slapping, handclapping ditties that she would bawl for the rest of her life. One went: 'I'm the Marquis of Camberwell Green/I'm the downiest dude ever seen/I'm a gusher, I'm a rusher/I'm the Marquis of Camberwell Green'. Camberwell boasted the People's Palace of Varieties, Lovejoy's, the Metropole and the Camberwell Palace, where the little blonde urchin craned to catch a glimpse of vaudevillians Harry Tate, Marie Lloyd, Nellie Wallace and Harry Lauder. Experiencing fine buildings, art and exciting entertainers fired Tilly Twiss with a desire to escape poverty and live in a world of wealth, fine possessions and bright lights.

But for the twelve-year-old just out of school, riches and the high life were as attainable as flying to Neverland to romp with the fairies and pirates of *Peter Pan*, the big theatrical event of her youth. Tilly's reality was earning a pound to help her and her family stay warm, clothed and fed. Along the banks of the canal at Camberwell, factories churned out paint, jam, beer and sticky tape, and Watkins & Co. bookbinders bound a million Bibles a year. When she left school, Tilly, like most of the working-class people of Camberwell, slaved twelve hours a day, six days a week in these sweatshops.

Then, epiphany. Just like Kate Leigh 20 000 kilometres away in pre-war Sydney, she came to the conclusion that the straight and narrow was a route for fools. Even a comfortable middle-class existence — let alone the romantic extravagance she demanded from life — was out of reach on a factory worker's wage. So, like numerous young women in her situation, she became a prostitute. As her nephew George Parsons would say more than eighty years later. 'She was a good-looking, smart young girl. She had no prospects. Her only hope of making it was by selling the only thing she owned — herself.'

The young prostitute was 160 centimetres tall and weighed 71 kilos. She was pretty, with big blue eyes, and had a well-developed figure for a teenager. She could play the coquette when it suited her, but was also known in London's West End for her foul language and spitfire temper. She was a street fighter, and needed little provocation to weigh in, boots, nails and all. Her main beat was the Strand, that bustling West End thoroughfare sandwiched between Covent Garden to the north, the Thames to the south, Trafalgar Square to the west and Fleet Street to the east. The Strand was, and is, home to the Savoy

Hotel (whose guests in Tilly's day included the greatest actors and heads of state) and theatres such as Noël Coward's beloved Adelphi and the Savoy, where Gilbert and Sullivan debuted their light operas. The restaurant Simpsons-on-the-Strand served up traditional English fare, and Charing Cross Railway Station swallowed and disgorged thousands of commuters a day, as well as the servicemen on their way to northern France and the horrors of war.

Brassy, blonde Tilly Twiss was ubiquitous in the West End in the years of World War I, spending the day carousing in Soho then hitting the wide footpaths of the Strand at night. There she would solicit with a wink and a smile, and a glance at the bulge of their wallets, the toffs in their frock coats and top hats, as well as joining young servicemen from all over the world in some noisy revelry. In those years when the average wage in England was £2–3 a week, Tilly and her sisters could easily gross £15–20.

The Great War was in its third year when, in 1916, Tilly met and fell in love with an Australian soldier who had fought in the Middle East and was now headquartered at Andover. James Edward Joseph Devine was a tall, hard-muscled sapper in the 4th Tunnelling Company of the Australian Imperial Forces. He was twenty-four, a former shearer, with a criminal record. His hair was brown, his eyes were a piercing, belligerent blue, his complexion was coarse and ruddy. Perhaps it was his blarney that won Tilly's heart, for he told her that he owned a kangaroo farm. Jim and Tilly were opposites who somehow were drawn to each other. He was dour and sullen, she — at least when life was going her way — was flirty, vivacious and always singing. They both liked to drink and gamble and revelled in the criminal milieu of Soho. They fought when they drank, and she gave him as good as she got, although he would settle matters with a slap or a punch. She always forgave him (and would go on forgiving him for the next three decades) and welcomed him back to her capacious bosom. When Jim asked Edward Twiss for his daughter's hand, the doughty south Londoner said yes.

On 12 August 1917, at the modest Church of the Sacred Heart of Jesus in Camberwell, Matilda Twiss married James Devine. Her age on the wedding certificate is twenty-one, five years older than she in fact was. A Canon Murnane performed the ceremony, and Edward Twiss gave his daughter away while her mother Alice sniffled doe-eyed in her pew. An Alice Wesley was bridesmaid and Richard Hirsch, best man. The newlyweds soon had two children: a daughter, who died at birth, and a son, Frederick James.

Jim Devine, known as Big Jim, had many faults. He had a black temper and was violent. He was lazy, dishonest and a liar. He was not blessed with charm, always preferring to snarl than smile, and he used the word 'fuck' as if it was a comma. But let no one accuse him of jealousy. From the outset, he insisted that Tilly stay on the game. He would do all he could for her, give her protection, make sure the money she earned was spent wisely (that is, on him). For her part, she knew prostitution was her ticket out of Hollington Street, and she was an enthusiastic breadwinner.

Acquiring a police record of course came with the territory of her profession, and in the files of Bow Street Magistrates' Court and Police Station, opposite the Royal Opera House in Covent Garden, is ample evidence of her activities. From 1915 onwards, she had spent time in Bow Street court and lock-up for prostitution, theft and assault. On one document it is recorded, in the ornate copperplate handwriting typical of the age, that on 2 October 1918, one Matilda Devine, 'a common prostitute', was arrested by PC Hebbes for 'annoying by soliciting at the Strand'. It is noted on the document that Devine is married, has no fixed abode and that her age is nineteen. In fact, she was just eighteen when she was nabbed. She was given the choice of paying forty shillings or spending twenty-one days in the cells at Bow Street. In the margin it is noted, with a cross, that she paid the money.

Little has changed at Bow Street since the days when Tilly Devine was bundled screaming and kicking into the lock-up. The cells are much the same today as when they were constructed in 1880. They are tiny, have a hard plank bed, cream-tiled floor and walls for easy hosing-out, a small square window to let in a little light, and massive iron doors with a sliding peephole big enough to pass a small plate and a cup through. Virtually the sole difference is that today the toilet is a porcelain bowl in the corner of the cell with interior plumbing. Tilly would have had to use a slop bucket. Oscar Wilde, the World War II traitor William Joyce (aka Lord Haw Haw) and murderers Dr Crippen and the Kray twins are others who have sampled the hospitality at Bow Street down the years.

At war's end, Jim Devine was shipped home to Australia with his fellow Diggers on a troop carrier. His wife followed him a year or so later on the 'war-bride ship' *Waimana*, with scores of other English wives joining their new husbands for a civilian life in Australia. After a six-week voyage, the *Waimana* docked at Circular Quay in high summer, 13 January 1920. Toddler Frederick was not with his mother. In 1943, Tilly would explain to a judge, 'My mother said that I was too young to bring him out to Australia when he was a baby, and he has been with my people ever since'. The boy was legally adopted by Tilly's parents and was known from then on as Frederick James Twiss. (If she ever saw Frederick again, such a meeting is unrecorded. He married and had a son and a daughter, and fought in World War II. It is believed he died in the 1950s.)

Big Jim was at the Quay to meet Tilly when she disembarked, and he whisked her off to his rented flat in Glenmore Road, Paddington. She started work at once. Before they left England, they had decided that she would continue to be a prostitute in Sydney. He would be her pimp and dabble in whatever other illegal opportunities presented themselves. (It is not known whether she asked to see his kangaroos.)

It was 1920, and everyone they knew wanted to party and forget the hell that was the war. The women shortened their skirts, smoked, Charlestoned. The men drank themselves senseless and used opium, marijuana, morphine and the in-vogue drug, cocaine. 'Good-oh' was the catch-cry of the day. Tilly Devine zeroed in on East Sydney like a spider on a particularly exotic bug. For someone like her, who knew no job but prostitution and was bent on making her pile from it, there was nowhere else to be.

There had been a thriving red-light industry in the area since the days of the First Fleet. Throughout Sydney's first 150 years of settlement, males heavily outnumbered females and many of those men not married or in a relationship had no qualms about paying for sex. And, with few legitimate job opportunities for a woman, becoming a prostitute was a means to pay the rent and put food on the table. For many women, selling themselves as a streetwalker or working in a brothel was simply an economic necessity, a job like any other.

Conservative governments wanted to crack down on prostitution, but they were opposed by more liberal thinkers who saw prostitutes as victims, not criminals. In 1908, when the Conservative New South Wales Government attempted to introduce an all-encompassing crime bill that would have lumped prostitutes with murderers and thieves, one Labor member, John 'Red Shirt Jack' Meehan, railed: '[T]he unfortunate women of the streets, I say they are driven there by some of the pillars of society and the church, who rob and sweat unfortunate women and children, and drive them out into the streets, where any person who likes can make use of them'. Another MP, George Beeby, insisted: 'In very rare instances is the woman who is concerned in [prostitution] a woman of abnormal sexual desires . . . 90 or 95 per cent of the women engaged in this traffic are engaged in it as a result of outside pressures of different kinds.'

Enlightened thinkers such as Meehan and Beeby were not referring to Tilly Devine. She may once have been a prostitute out of financial necessity, but by the early 1920s, she had food, shelter, no children to support and a husband profiting from myriad criminal pursuits. With her intelligence, drive and energy she would have always found legitimate work, even in times of high unemployment. Tilly Devine sold herself because it was the best and easiest way she knew to realise her dreams of wealth and power.

In her Sydney streetwalking days in the first half of the 1920s, before she became the ruthless madam of legend, Tilly looked as one might imagine Eliza Doolittle, with her peaches-and-cream complexion; bright blonde hair; bonnets; lacy, high-collared blouses and ankle-length dresses. One policeman recalled her as 'a beautiful young woman with a deep, husky, fascinating voice . . . she had charm and there was something likeable about her. She was recklessly generous, not only to her friends but to anybody who went to her with a hard-luck story'. One observer described her as then having 'a complexion of milk and roses and hair the colour of a hay-rick in summer'.

Annoy her in any way, however, and the sweet illusion would be shattered by a blast of bullocky language and, if her tormentor was particularly unlucky, a punch or a kick. Tilly was just one of hundreds of women in East Sydney out to grab the pounds of randy punters, but she was not fazed by the competition. Attractive, a party girl, and skilled at her trade, she made money from the start. She charged top price, ten shillings or more, and always collected. The foolish few who baulked at paying up after they'd had their half hour with her had the fists and boots of Big Jim to contend with or (maybe worse) the fury of Tilly herself.

Tilly Devine worked all the prostitute haunts: Palmer, Bourke, Forbes and Riley streets and Darlinghurst Road in Darlinghurst; Macleay and Kellett streets and Bayswater Road in the Cross; and Crown and Cathedral streets in the 'Loo. Neild Avenue, running down the hill from Paddington to New South Head Road, was another popular rendezvous for Tilly and other streetwalkers — chiacked as 'inkwells' by cheeky locals, always when out of earshot of the prostitutes' 'bludgers' (pimps) — especially on fight nights at nearby Sydney Stadium, the old Tin Shed with its signs spruiking Laxettes and Penfolds Wines. And William Street, the boulevard of broken dreams that starts at Hyde Park in the city, traversing the northern edge of Woolloomooloo and the southern boundary of Darlinghurst, and on up the rise into the heart of Kings Cross, was a busy place of fun and small business, and a prized position for soliciting. Only the toughest prostitutes backed by fierce pimps and protectors were strong enough to stake a claim there. Tilly Devine made the cut.

Today, William Street boasts office blocks occupied and abandoned, luxury car showrooms, a few coffee shops, general stores, tattoo parlours and pubs, including the lollipop-painted hotel the Strand. The multi-lane road is often gridlocked with the cars and buses of commuters travelling from the eastern suburbs into the city and back again. At night, a handful of prostitutes and bands of carousing youths from the suburbs (spiritual descendants of the larrikins of old, perhaps) loiter on corners. Back then, when Tilly Devine hit town, William Street had recently, in 1916, been widened from a thirteen-metre-wide track to more than twice that width. Cars, omnibuses, horse-drawn carts and wagons jostled chaotically with rattletrap trams and pedestrians for room on the road. (In 1921, thirty-six people were killed by cars in central Sydney; by 1924, the toll had hit 144.)

In the twenty-first century, almost the only remnants of old William Street are the Chard Building, which in the '20s and '30s housed the Fifty-Fifty Club, and the Strand, in Tilly and Jim's day a scabrous saloon where gangsters boozed and brawled (and, at the height of the razor-gang wars, shot each other). In the 1920s, the Strand Hotel's now long-vanished William Street neighbours included Emanuel Berkman's Pawn Shop (there were three other hockshops as well) and the Schibesi brothers' general store. Up and down the street there were gaudy signs for Wolfe's Schnappes, Bushell's Tea, Mother's Choice Flour. Other shopfronts included Misses von Hammer's costumieres; Sing Chong's laundry; Weigzell's Ornamental Hair Works; Isaac Hernandez's oyster saloon; Mrs Peachman's refreshment room; Murphy's wood, coal, coke and bulk supply store; Guy Whar's greengrocery; twenty-nine penny-cheap boarding houses; numerous gambling dens; and bars owned by men named Maloney, O'Shaughnessy, Donovan and O'Sullivan. Tattoo parlours, then as today, abounded. (It's possible Jim Devine was one of their best customers, for he sported a horse's head inside a horseshoe and ribbon, and the words 'Good Luck' on the back of his right wrist; 'Tilly' was indelibly stamped into his left forearm, and on both arms, galleons sailed and flags fluttered. The legend 'Across the Sea' was on his bicep.)

Here in William Street, the heart of East Sydney, Tilly Devine raked in the cash and hoarded it away — in spite of Jim's best efforts to squander it on liquor, cocaine and racehorses.

Until she and Jim made beachside Maroubra their home and headquarters in the late 1920s, the Devines lived in Paddington, Darlinghurst and Woolloomooloo (even then known as 'Woolloomoolethal' and 'Woolloomoolewd'). Their typical digs when they were getting started would have been a dingy circa-1850 terrace house: damp and cockroach-infested, three rooms downstairs, two upstairs, paper-thin walls, reeking open drain and pan-toilet out the back, wooden prop for a clothesline and bathing tub hanging on the paling face. They drank regularly in the pubs in these areas: the Tradesman's Arms; the Strand; Craig's Royal Hotel at Five Ways, Paddington; and the Lord Dudley. Tilly was no respecter of the sexual apartheid then practised in pubs, refusing point-blank to be banished to the ladies lounge.

For a real party, the Devines and their friends went to Kings Cross, with its rakish honky-tonks and gaming dives where men played cards and pool as if fighting war. Also to enjoy there were bare-knuckle fights, gypsy booths and lowlife dance halls where accordians wheezed. Rat pit fighting — where punters bet on how many rats a terrier could kill before being overpowered by the rodents and itself torn apart — had its devotees. Cheap bawdyhouses, known as cock-and-hen clubs, were everywhere. The Cross was a place of clamour and attitude, horror, sleaze and randy charm, all pervaded by the stink of cigarettes, vomit, cheap perfume and frying fish.

Kings Cross was nirvana to Tilly and Jim. They partied there and transacted business in its dives and alleys, Tilly on the game, Jim as a pimp, standover man, mugger, cocaine dealer and occasional hire-car operator. After a night on the tiles, they would head off down the hill to their terrace at dawn, nail a blanket to the window to ward off the sun's rays, and sleep till the late afternoon when they would get up, return to the Cross and do it all again.

In Sydney, Tilly Devine wasted no time in adding to the prodigious number of convictions she had racked up in London. Between 1921 and 1925, she was arrested seventy-nine times for her usual offences — whoring, obscene language, offensive behaviour and fighting. She would have crossed paths, and swords, with Haden Spyer, a constable at Darlinghurst Police Station. As he recalled for Woolloomooloo historian George Farwell, his beat covered Oxford Street, College Street, William Street and Barcom Avenue. He carried a baton and later a firearm. The Woolloomooloo lock-up was most nights full of prostitutes. 'We used to carry drunken women in a barrow if they couldn't walk. From a police point of view we regarded Woolloomooloo as a very low down crowd.'

Usually Tilly was fined; occasionally she was imprisoned for a few days, weeks or months at Long Bay Gaol, where she was known as 'Pretty Tilly'. But by 1924–1925, she was getting into more serious trouble. She served some months in Long Bay Gaol after savagely beating a commercial traveller who reneged on payment after sex. On a charge card dated 11 January 1925, Tilly is described as a 'married woman residing with her husband. She is a prostitute of the worst type and an associate of criminals and vagrants'. Already she bore the wounds of street war, the card noting that she had scars over both her eyes, on her face and chest. And in February of that year she was sentenced to two years at the Bay for slashing a man with a razor in a barber shop. Big Jim hardly got a chance to miss her, for soon afterwards he was gaoled for eighteen months for living on the immoral earnings of a prostitute: his wife. Jim's record by then, too, was burgeoning, with more than a dozen convictions for indecent language, riotous behaviour, assault and larceny.

Like Kate Leigh, Tilly Devine made the most of her time in prison. Always whip-smart and self-aware, she took stock of her life, and in so doing made a vow. She was twenty-five then and had been a prostitute for ten years. It was high time to let others do the dirty work. She knew well that the *Police Offences (Amendment) Act* of 1908, which had made prostitution an offence for the first time, had forced most sex workers off the streets and into brothels, and she knew too of the astounding anomaly in the Act that made it illegal for a male pimp or brothel-keeper to profit from the immoral earnings of prostitutes but not for a woman to do so. Her days of being pawed and violated by sweaty, drunken strangers, she now swore, were over. On her release from prison, she would become a madam, using the money she had salted away to bankroll the biggest, best-organised, most lucrative brothel network Sydney has ever seen.

When freed, she bought a slum cottage in rundown Palmer Street, just off William Street, fitted out its rooms with beds and faux-exotic decor and put a red light in the window. She provided the premises and the women paid her a percentage, sometimes as high as 50 per cent, of their earnings. She charged freelancers who wanted to use her rooms £2 a shift. In her employ at her brothels in Palmer Street, Chapel Street, Woods Lane, Berwick Lane, Burnell Place and environs, were prostitutes of every age and background: seasoned streetwalkers who'd been operating since before the war, hard-up housewives and mothers from the suburbs trying to support their families, lonely and poor young women who had come to the city from the country, or inner-city street kids drawn by danger and excitement and the chance to make more money than they could working in a factory or shop.

Tilly was regarded as a benevolent despot by her workers. If they did their job, paid up on time and didn't try to conceal their earnings from her, she cosseted them. She gave them food and lodging, medical care, clothes and, in the shape of her hired goons, protection from sexually deviant or violent customers or from other prostitution rings out to enlist their services. But if she caught her 'girls' cheating her, she'd sack them — and often beat them as a parting gift. Big Jim sold cocaine to his wife's prostitutes. As discussed further in Chapter 4, it made economic sense for brothel-keepers like the Devines to foster drug addiction in the sex workers: it ensured loyalty and meant prostitutes increasingly preferred payment in cocaine rather than in cash.

As the money rolled in, Tilly bought another house, in Woolloomooloo, and another in Darlinghurst, and another and another . . . By the late 1920s, she had eighteen thriving bordellos. So established, she and Jim paid £1650 cash for a solid red-brick bungalow on the corner of Torrington and Malabar roads, in middle-class suburban Maroubra, and made it their home. Before long, their neighbours' quiet lives were being disrupted almost nightly by the Devines' rough and riotous parties, and their wild domestic arguments, after which Tilly routinely sported facial cuts and black and swollen eyes.

Tilly Devine was on her way to becoming the woman about whom it was written in a police journal article at the end of her long 204-conviction criminal career:

> *She has been in conflict with society all her life. She has fought it with words, with action, with her bare hands. She has held it by the throat and shaken it. She has spat in its face. Her sense of values, her code of morals and of ethics, are her own and she will tolerate no interference. For the average man, her life has held that singular fascination the criminologist describes — the fascination of the thunderstorm.*

# 4

# The Birth of Organised Crime

The 1920s was a decade-long party wedged between the carnage of World War I and the desolation of the Great Depression. In Sydney, as in New York, London and Paris, employment was high and wages were good, and after the tragic attrition of the Great War there was a try-anything spirit in the air that enticed people to live with abandon and for the moment. In East Sydney, criminals took advantage of the prevailing good times. They realised there was big money to be made from workers with more disposable funds than ever before: from the monied classes who came from the prosperous suburbs, and from 'bushies' in town for the Royal Easter Show or the annual Sydney–Country rugby league match.

Especially from 1926 onwards, Sydneysiders had ringside seats for a series of unprecedentedly violent incidents as vice lords and their gunmen, razor-slashers, cocaine and sly-grog sellers, illegal gamblers, pimps, blackmailers, thieves and strong-arm gorillas went to war with each other for a share of the rich proceeds of organised vice. Now, because of the lawbreakers' outrages honest citizens of the city's east had to endure the tabloids referring to their neighbourhood as 'the Dardanelles', 'a vice cauldron', 'a hothouse of crime' and, of course, 'Razorhurst'.

By then, Sydney was no longer a small town but a sprawling

metropolis with a decaying inner city surrounded by middle-class suburbia. In the two decades from 1910, Sydney's population doubled from 630 000 to 1.2 million. As criminologist and author Dr Alfred McCoy has pointed out:

> *In an age when mass urbanism reduced the individual to powerless anonymity, the gangster alone retained the power to rule the city . . . The radiating grids of tram and train drained inner Sydney of its gentility, and the city centre suffered a 10 per cent population loss during the 1920s. As the garden suburbs became the archetype of a life that was both comfortable and moral, the gangster's dominion stood as an inner-city demi-monde of degradation, the antithesis of surrounding suburban propriety.*

The passing of the legislation designed to control or ban all-hours drinking, drug use and dealing, prostitution and illegal gambling did not have the effect the lawmakers desired. Indeed, as stated previously, these vices went underground and into the control of career racketeers, thus becoming more of a problem and harder to police than ever before.

The drug trade, particularly, was out of hand. In the late '20s, police estimated there were around 5000 drug addicts in Kings Cross, Darlinghurst and Woolloomooloo. People smoked marijuana and opium, injected heroin and morphine (one young man set up by night on the steps of the GPO in Martin Place, selling on-the-spot injections of morphine for fifty pence a hit), and drank paraldehyde (one of the many unhappy side effects of which was halitosis for days to come) and chorodyne. But cocaine — or 'snow' — was Sydney's drug of choice. Sniffed, or mixed with water and injected, cocaine induced euphoria, but exhilaration palled quickly and more cocaine was needed to maintain the high. Snow was snorted by the rich at parties, by businessmen in swish 'snow parlours' where each table had a bowl of the drug in the centre, by vagrants in alleyways, by mobsters needing a belt of courage before pulling a job, and by prostitutes seeking fortification to get through a Darlinghurst night.

As mentioned in the previous chapter, prostitutes were often part-paid in cocaine by their pimps and brothel-keepers. Drug addiction, the proprietors knew, kept a prostitute shackled to the game. Selling cocaine to the sex workers guaranteed regular drug sales and, when the women became addicted, the pimps and brothel owners paid them an ever-larger share of their wages in drugs, rather than cash. To sate their addiction, the hooked women had to work more often and for longer. In the late '20s, some 75 per cent of prostitutes were cocaine addicts. In his book on the Australian drug trade, *Drug Traffic: Narcotics and Organised Crime in Australia*, Dr Alfred McCoy cites one once attractive, drug-addicted Surry Hills prostitute whose appearance bore the disastrous effects of cocaine use, and the boracic acid and other impurities used to adulterate the drug. The woman's eyes were sunken, the bridge of her nose had disappeared, leaving the nostrils distended, and her skin was the colour and texture of parchment. The majority of drug busts involved two-bit runners caught selling cocaine to prostitutes, such as this unfortunate, on the streets.

Cocaine was sold to the illicit drug trade by crooked chemists, doctors and dentists, or smuggled into Sydney by sailors from Asia and South America. In 1927, a cache of cocaine-filled wooden pencils was confiscated on the Sydney docks. Cocaine bought by a wholesaler from a chemist for, say, £1, could be bulked up with boracic acid or other adulterating agents, parcelled into tiny 'pinches' and sold by peddlers, or 'runners', on the street for £60 or more.

The first anti-drug laws, enacted in 1924, allowed police to arrest dealers if they caught them in the act of selling but, oddly enough, the lawmakers seemed not to regard possession as a problem, and people apprehended with the drug in their pocket were usually let off if the quantity was small, or lightly fined if it was found in bulk. With organised dealers mainly operating out of guarded premises safe from police surveillance, these flimsy drug laws were never going to curtail drug use.

For a while, the acknowledged czar of the Darlinghurst cocaine trade was Charles Passmore, a faux-genteel habitual criminal with a record predating World War I. Passmore, mainly selling drugs to prostitutes, prospered until coming unstuck in 1928. In 1924, he earned a classic courtroom dressing-down by renowned policeman of the era, Sergeant Tom O'Brien. 'This man,' rasped O'Brien, glaring at Passmore, 'is the representative of all things evil. He is lord and master of a dope combine and has waxed fat and flourishing through the agency of his hopeless clients. You can see him any evening about 11 o'clock standing at the corner of Woolcott and Craigend Streets, Darlinghurst, and its environs, handing out the deadly contents of an innocent-looking package — cocaine — to scores of addicts.' For all of O'Brien's eloquent venom, Passmore was fined just £50.

In August 1927, drug laws got teeth when the New South Wales Parliament passed the *Dangerous Drugs Amendment Act* and Passmore fared less well. The law stated:

> *No person shall manufacture any drug unless he holds a licence. No person shall distribute certain drugs unless he holds a licence. The police will possess power to seize drugs unlawfully in the possession of any person. A register must be kept of all drugs supplied by licensed dealers.*

Passmore was thrown into gaol when police found cocaine in his flat in 1928.

Prominent in the fight against drugs on Sydney's streets was the new two-man Drug Bureau comprising Sergeant Tom Wickham and Constable Wharton Thompson. For a time, their bête noire was the self-professed king of the Sydney dope traffickers, Harry 'Jewey' Newman, a sly, vain and stupid knockabout. While not averse to ordering a henchman to beat up someone who had reneged on payment, Newman lacked the criminal savvy and ruthlessness of a Tilly Devine or Kate Leigh. His modus operandi was to buy cocaine from doctors and dentists at their surgeries for a small sum — he'd often call on them with his young son in tow — then sell it, after cutting the drug by 40 per cent with boracic acid, at Paddy's Market in the Haymarket. Police cottoned on to his activities in April 1925, when they raided the home of prostitute Mary Edwards in Pelican Street, Surry Hills, and she told them that the thirty packages of cocaine in her bedroom were Newman's. Officers now kept tabs on him. They learned that he employed a network of runners, including the convicted criminals Rose Steele, 'Botany May' Smith, James Delaney and Lillian 'the Human Vulture' Sproule. Members of this choice coterie were arrested many times, but always Newman was able to distance himself from them.

It was Newman's rank foolishness that brought him down. Called into Central Police Court on 18 February 1929 on a minor matter, he could not resist big-noting to Tom Wickham. 'I'm taking over Bobbie Carr's fish shop in Goulburn Street, and if I had you fellows with me I could corner the cocaine market, and we could make a packet out of it,' he enthused. 'These fucking women must have snow, you know. In a couple of years you could retire. You'd make a bonzer publican.' As the incorruptible Wickham responded that he was perfectly happy in the force, he realised that Newman had given himself away. From that moment, Carr's fish shop was under permanent surveillance. Five days later, on 23 February, police raided the shop and found eighteen packets of cocaine hidden in a drainpipe. With possession now a serious offence, Newman was gaoled.

In spite of his braggadocio, Newman was no cocaine kingpin. Nor was Passmore. Their turnover was comparatively small and they were constantly bilked by standover men. They were never going to survive. By 1927, the real rulers of Sydney's drugs roost were the highly organised, tough, forward-planning Kate Leigh and Jim Devine. They laughed at standover men, sent them packing with a beating, and they were not intimidated by police, whom they outwitted or paid to leave them alone. Wickham and Wharton were the bane of drug traffickers and made many arrests, but while they rid the streets of a number of small-time pushers, they were, without strong anti-drug laws to support them, relatively powerless against the big-timers.

In the archives of the New South Wales Police Force is this unbylined, curiously colourful description, circa 1927, of Kate Leigh as drug dealer:

> *No more remarkable woman ever strode upon the stage of Sydney's nightlife than this middle-aged, matronly dame who slinks a furtive figure in the background of the drama of real life. A sinister, shadowy character, she plays a dominating part in the tragedy which is spelt with four letters: D-O-P-E. She meets young women in cafés and hotel lounges, and she ingratiates herself with them. Such a nice, steady, agreeable dame! Such a monster in human disguise. For she deals in a commodity that means more than the wrecking of physical health. It means the destruction of mental health, the warping of the moral outlook, the damning of the eternal soul. Clever and unscrupulous enough to know that once a victim is made, she becomes a sure customer for life. To show them the door to Drugland she paints a glowing picture of the joys inside. She conjures up hours of gay, exotic happiness. They open the door, slowly, hesitatingly. She stands behind them and reassures. They enter and find — a living hell. Price is nothing to the*

*victims. They will pay all that is asked. They want more and more and more. If it gets too dear for them, they stop at nothing to get the money. They will impose on their friends, they will steal, and descend as low as a woman can go to feed the ravenous appetite that dope creates. It is a tragic but terribly true thing that a great percentage of fallen women who walk the pavements of Sydney are drug-takers.*

Sly grog was the result of the Holman Government's *Liquor Act* of 1916, which closed hotels at 6 p.m., enshrining the notion that drinkers must be saved from themselves. In spite of the best intentions of the legislators, a (literally) staggering 8896 people faced Sydney's Central Police Court in 1926 charged with public drunkenness. When pub doors clanged shut at six, many drinkers, after knocking off from factory or office at four or five, were just getting a thirst. As closing time neared ('If you can't drink 'em, leave 'em; if you can't leave 'em, drink 'em!' the publican would bawl) they'd guzzle with feverish intensity, soaking up as much as their bladder would hold before they were emptied out onto the street. The notorious 'six o'clock swill' was a Sydney custom until 1955 when 6 p.m. closing was abolished. A visiting British journalist, Arthur Helliwell, was amazed and appalled, as he informed readers of London's *Sunday People*:

*The 5 to 6 o'clock 'beer swill' when hordes of thirsty Diggers invade the pubs for a final hour of frenzied boozing . . . will shock you. You need the physique and constitution of an all-in wrestler to emerge unscathed . . . Elbows, shoulders, knees, fists and feet are all employed indiscriminately as the customers battle for strategic positions near the bar.*

Sly-grog shops were there for those not too battered and bruised by the swill to want to keep drinking into the night.

The quality of illicit after-hours alcohol varied. Well-organised, serious dealers such as Kate Leigh (who fitted out her better grog shops with a lounge, comfortable chairs, card tables, and perhaps a gramophone) craved return visits from their well-heeled customers, so they sold good liquor. Kate did deals with the breweries. She would buy large quantities of Tooth's and Resch's beer and Johnny Walker whisky at wholesale prices, and have it delivered to her network of Surry Hills establishments in trucks and horse-drawn wagons. Flakier operators, whose groggeries, for example, may have been nothing more elaborate than a trestle table set up in a lane with a few unlabelled bottles arrayed upon it and a 'cockatoo' posted nearby to keep a lookout for police or standover men, cut corners. They would make their beer, whisky and gin go further by diluting it with water or tea.

The thirsty public rewarded the sly-groggers' enterprise. Many dealers, none more so than Kate Leigh, grew wealthy and extended their empires; though, to ensure their survival they had to pay off corrupt cops with money and free drinks.

Another unavoidable overhead for sly-groggers (indeed, for almost all underworld entrepreneurs) was the standover merchants out to take a cut of others' ill-gotten gains.

Standover merchants were far more of a threat than police to criminal entrepreneurs of any stripe. Unless racketeers were rich and powerful enough to employ their own gang to defend their interests, extortionist thugs would menace with immunity. Drug-dealing, sly grog, prostitution and illegal bookmaking being strictly cash-only businesses, they were prime targets. If a vice purveyor was being stood over, the police didn't want to know. Their limited resources were stretched protecting the innocent, they protested.

A weekly protection fee, explained the predators to the proprietors, would ensure that other, more unpleasant, mobs would be kept at bay. It would also obviate the mysterious fires, the brawls that erupted from nothing on busy nights (in which innocent patrons were bashed) and the wanton destruction of property that had befallen other sellers who, foolishly, inconceivably, had chosen not to cooperate with them. Most dealers got the message.

As soon as a lawbreaker entered into an agreement with a stand-over team, they became a pawn. In spite of what the protection merchants said when touting for their business, any grogger, brothel-keeper or drug seller paying off one gang was always going to be targeted by a rival mob demanding more. Then the competing gangs would fight each other for the business, with the battleground often their benefactor's establishment. These hard men swarming around the illicit operations were like the grey nurse sharks that feasted on the bloody cattle carcases that in those days were thrown into the Parramatta River from Homebush Abattoir.

Few standover men were as menacing as 'Long Harry' Slater, a pioneer in the practice. The Melbourne criminal moved to Sydney in 1921 and became wealthy ripping off Surry Hills sly-groggeries. Any alcohol seller thinking of resisting Slater forgot about it after Slater's gang murdered the son of a recalcitrant Surry Hills dealer named Monaghan. After three trials, Slater was acquitted for lack of evidence, and cooled his heels in the bush for a few years. But he had set the template, and other hardened criminals followed his lead.

Kate Leigh, however, who by the mid '20s had been a sly-grogger for half a decade, was largely left alone by Slater and those who came after him. Would-be extortionists received the rough edge of her tongue, and often more besides. Kate's motto was 'retaliate first', and she kept standover merchants at bay by hiring her own team of thugs even more formidable than the marauders. Such men as Gregory 'the Gunman' Gaffney and her sometime lover Wally Tomlinson did not come cheap, but with her empire of lucrative grog shops left in peace to prosper, Kate came out way ahead.

'For the first time in its history,' wrote Alfred McCoy in *Drug Traffic: Narcotics and Organised Crime in Australia*, 'Sydney could sustain entrepreneurs who lived by controlling criminals instead of committing crimes.' That's where Kate Leigh, Tilly Devine, and two other wannabe crime bosses named Norman Bruhn and Phil Jeffs came in.

Norman Bruhn was a gunman, thief, standover man and pimp feared for his garrotting skills: one hand tightening a leather thong around the spluttering, purple victim's neck, the other rifling his pockets. He was thirty-two when he arrived in Sydney from his home town, Melbourne, in November 1926, with his wife of six years, Irene, and toddler sons, Noel and Keith. Bruhn had served with the Australian infantry at Pozières in France in World War I and after the Armistice, back home in Melbourne, became a thief, gunman and alley basher, serving time in prison for all offences. He headed north in '26 after absconding from bail while awaiting trial on a shooting charge.

Bruhn installed tiny, dark-eyed dressmaker Irene, one of ten children of a French Creole, and his sons in a rented flat in Park Road, Paddington, and within months of his arrival in Sydney, he was the number-one criminal in Kings Cross and Darlinghurst. (It is possible that it was his Melbourne criminal friend Leslie 'Squizzy' Taylor who encouraged him to go for broke in Sydney. Taylor had tried Sydney on for size in 1924, but found himself under constant police surveillance and soon returned south. 'The Sydney dees [detectives] are too hot,' he grumbled. 'They're a bloody lot of narks, and I'll let them have their

Harbour.') Bruhn's gang included John 'Snowy' Cutmore (who would die just a year later in a Melbourne gun duel with Squizzy Taylor), George 'the Midnight Raper' Wallace and Frank 'Razor Jack' Hayes. The Bruhn mob began rampaging in the Cross.

Phil 'the Jew' Jeffs, bulbous-nosed and thick-lipped, was born in Riga, Latvia, in 1896. His family went to live in London when he was a boy, and, destitute, abandoned their son. The young Jeffs slept on the streets and stayed alive by scrounging in West End garbage bins for food and stealing the clothes of other homeless people. In his early teens, he was employed as a cook's slushy on a tramp steamer bound for South Africa. He lived there for a time, then, in 1912, he signed up for a working passage on a cargo vessel to Sydney, where he jumped ship. Jeffs found a job as a pageboy at the Coogee Bay Hotel but was sacked for stealing from guests. He operated a fruit barrow in Darlinghurst before embracing a life outside the law in the early 1920s.

Jeffs grew into a cocky and super-ambitious young spiv. He affected a bogus urbanity which disguised a brutal soul. He carried a cosh and a revolver, and used them. His dream was to be a rich crime boss, decked in fine clothes and loved by beautiful women. But to see him at work in the early and mid '20s — mugging drunks for a few pounds in the lanes of Kings Cross, slyly exchanging drugs for money in public toilets, working as a cockatoo at sly-grog shops, being an obsequious lackey to crooks more prominent than he — his chances seemed slim.

When chauffeuring a band of drunken mobsters and their girl-friends in the Blue Mountains, west of Sydney, he rolled their car near Glenbrook. One of the passengers, Eva O'Grady of Surry Hills, died in the crash. Jeffs was charged with manslaughter but acquitted. And once, trying to pick the pocket of one William Fisher in the early hours in Palmer Street, Darlinghurst, Jeffs suffered the ignominy of being horsewhipped by his victim in front of a crowd. Jeffs reeled away, then pulled his pistol from his pocket. He fired at Fisher three times from close range, but, as the throng hooted in derision, missed. One of pimp Jeffs's specialities was teaming up with prostitutes to play the 'badger' game. He'd lurk in the street outside the prostitute's flat until he received her signal — the drawing of a curtain, the snuffing-out of a lamp — that she was about to go to bed with her client. Then Jeffs would storm into the room, eyes blazing with outrage, shriek that he was the woman's husband and demand compensation from the hapless john. Desperate to avoid a beating, the sucker would pay up gladly and flee.

All in all, an unlikely beginning, but in time Jeffs would realise his ambition of being a big shot. So much so, in fact, that in Sydney in the '40s and '50s, there was a popular expression, 'As rich as Phil the Jew'.

Aside from Leigh, Devine, Bruhn and Jeffs, there were other criminals who moved in on East Sydney in the mid '20s. Prowling the maze of filthy, scrubby streets and alleys was pimp, gunman, basher and thief Guido Calletti, leader of the feared Darlinghurst Push. Foul-tempered and weasel-faced Frank Green, though then yet to take a life, was snarl and muscle for hire. Beautiful gangster groupie and streetwalker Nellie Cameron was melting the iciest hearts, including Bruhn's. She would later be the lover of Calletti and Green, driving both to murderous jealousy. Jewey Newman and Charles Passmore dealt drugs. Lancelot Saidler worked mostly alone, occasionally for Bruhn, a shadow in the backstreets of the Cross, rolling drunks and prostitutes. And when police hauled in the usual suspects after a robbery or assault, chances were they'd bail up such incorrigibles as Wally Tomlinson, 'Gunman' Gaffney, the Kelly brothers Sid and Tom, Sid McDonald and John 'Chow' Hayes (of whom celebrated policeman of the day Ray Blissett says: 'He was a criminal, a liar and a lair. The world would have been a better place if he had not been born.').

A disparate bunch from many backgrounds, these criminals, reflects Lua Niall, another policeman who patrolled Darlinghurst and Kings

Cross, were typified by a 'sneering contempt for anyone stupid enough to hold a regular job, and they had no qualms about going to any lengths to relieve them of their wages. The criminals themselves were usually unemployed, maybe from time to time working on the wharves or selling fruit from a barrow to tide them over between criminal jobs. Many had wives and children, but they tended not to be family people.'

In 'Choker's Lane', poet Kenneth Slessor vividly evoked East Sydney lowlife as an Antipodean 'Hades'. It is an underworld inhabited by thieves and women whose faces are 'white as zinc', where one can feel 'the breath of beasts decaying in their den' and death with its 'leather jaws' that 'come tasting men'.

Crime fomented through the 1920s, and in 1926, the year before things got truly nasty, there were more crimes committed in New South Wales than ever before. The vast majority of these offences took place in inner Sydney.

# 5

# Blades

Sydney's criminals had always kept handguns and knives in their armoury, but after the *Pistol Licensing Act* of 1927 dealt an automatic prison term to anyone with an unlicensed firearm, many outlaws began carrying another weapon: a cut-throat razor, honed sharp.

Mobsters had used razors as weapons before. In the East End of London in the teen years of the twentieth century, there were gangs that cut marks into their rivals' faces. These mobs comprised Russians who had fled to London after the Revolution. The disfiguration was a punishment, and a warning to those who saw the scars that no one was out of the gang's reach. In the London underworld, the slash was called a 'traitor mark' and served the same purpose as when a Mafia hitman fires a bullet into the mouth of someone who has talked too much.

It's unknown whether news of the East End slashers had filtered to Sydney, but the first recorded use of a razor in a Sydney gang attack was just days after the anti-hand gun law was passed in early '27. In Womerah Avenue, Darlinghurst, a visiting sailor wielded a straight razor in a brawl that broke out in a sly-grog dive. The altercation was reported in the newspapers and members of the underworld, wary now of carrying guns and hugely impressed by the damage wrought by the sailor's blade, began packing razors. Norman Bruhn and his men made the razor their trademark weapon, and became the first 'razor gang' of Sydney. The mobs of Tilly Devine, Kate Leigh and Phil Jeffs followed suit.

A cut-throat, Bengal-style straight shaving blade could be bought for a few pence at a grocer's or chemist's. Razor gangsters carried one or more in their coat or pants pocket. The more serious wielders honed their blade on a sharpening stone. Some crooks carried a more discreet version: a simple safety razor blade embedded in a piece of cork that could be neatly concealed in their fist.

Although they could do horrendous damage, a blade, unlike a gun, was not necessarily used for killing. Many victims of razor attacks did die, but the razor was more often used as an instrument of intimidation and disfiguration. Yet, a sharp and gleaming razor could be as terrifying as any pistol or shiv. Threatened with a slashing by a gangster, the victim would waste no time handing over his wallet, or a prostitute her night's takings. Even the hardest mobster, when bailed up by a razor-flashing rival, tended to do precisely what his enemy demanded.

Sydney's weekly tabloid *Truth* provided an accurate picture of the new phenomenon:

> *The razor is more effective than the revolver as a cash extractor. The sheen of its bright blade close to the cheek puts deadly fear into the heart of the victim . . . Razor gangs are terrorising the underworld of Darlinghurst, that region of bohemia, crime and mystery. The razors its members carry in their hands are feared far more than the revolver of the ordinary crook. Men who will defy the black muzzle quail before the bright blade held threateningly to their cheek. But even with their faces slashed open, victims refuse to speak when questioned by police. They know too well the fate that awaits them once the gang learns that they have allowed resentment to get*

*the better of discretion. So they remain silent, and prefer to attempt revenge in their own way. It is all an underworld affair, to be settled in the underworld's own drastic way and that is why a deep veil of mystery shrouds a carnival of blood-letting. Men have pledged themselves to 'get' each other and there are at least two men who, should they meet face to face in their peregrinations, will stage a combat that should be short, sharp and utterly decisive.*

From 1927 to 1930, there would be more than 500 recorded razor attacks and many, many more where the victims nursed their wounds in private.

In late 1927 alone, in the early days of the razor-gang wars, police confiscated sixty-six razors from suspects searched in connection with crimes. But finding the razor was one thing, convicting its owner of possessing a concealed weapon quite another. All men shaved, so proving that a villain was carrying the razor with bad intentions, and was not merely on his way home from the chemist to shave, was not easy. To make such a charge stick, the victim's blood, literally, had to be on the blade.

A typical victim of a razor attack, such as gangsters Frank Green and Jim Devine, would sport for the rest of his days an L-shaped scar extending down one side of his face to the jawbone, then across the cheek to the mouth. Eyes and ears were occasionally lost in the process. Severed tendons, nerves and muscles resulted in facial paralysis. Thirty to sixty stitches were often needed to close razor-attack wounds.

In those times, Darlinghurst's St Vincent's Hospital and Sydney Hospital in Macquarie Street often tended several victims a week, with the peak slashing periods Thursday night (payday), Friday night and Saturday. In one month in 1927, St Vincent's treated twenty-two razor victims. As reported in a July edition of the *Sydney Morning*

*Herald* after a spate of blade attacks: 'At St Vincent's Hospital several young men were treated for razor gashes and cuts from sharp instruments. None of the men would say how they received their wounds.'

Suddenly, in the wake of the Womerah Avenue razor attack, most lawbreakers carried a razor. On the night of 25 June 1927, an eighteen-year-old razor-man named Harry Griffiths chased wickerworker James Brown 400 metres along Cleveland Street, Chippendale. The pursuit followed a brawl. As Griffiths hared after Brown, he yelled, 'I'll cut your head off.' When Brown collapsed from exhaustion in Buckland Street, Griffiths slashed him across the neck and on both arms. Brown told police in St Vincent's Hospital, where he was treated for massive blood loss, that he would never forget the sight of his attacker's blade gleaming in the streetlight.

Visiting Spanish seaman Joe Sanchez was resting on a wooden bench near the entrance to St James Station in Sydney's Hyde Park on the evening of 31 July when two men, who had been sitting nearby with three women, sidled up and asked him for a cigarette. Sanchez complied, but when delving in his pocket for his packet of tobacco, one of the men drew a razor and slashed Sanchez on the left cheek. The men and women fled. Thirteen stitches were inserted in the sailor's wound, which extended from his eyebrow to his chin. No theft was involved, so police declared Sanchez a victim of mistaken identity.

Just two days later, World War I Digger Harold Ward was slashed in Mary Street, Surry Hills. The blade opened a deep gash across his forehead and almost severed his left ear. Police, who found Ward unconscious and bleeding, did not believe him when he insisted that his injuries had been caused by a fall. Ward, who gave his address as 'anywhere and everywhere', refused to name his attackers.

In October, Guido Calletti slashed one Jules De Flyn in a house in Cathedral Street, Woolloomooloo. De Flyn suffered deep wounds to his throat, right ear, the back of his neck and left arm. After an evening at the cinema with his wife, De Flyn had been eating dinner at the house when a drunken Calletti and three other men entered and, De Flyn said, 'made themselves objectionable'. Calletti tried to kiss Mrs De Flyn and when she resisted he struck her. De Flyn defended his wife, but was held fast by the other thugs while Calletti produced a razor and repeatedly cut the helpless De Flyn, who collapsed, bleeding profusely. The men left, and Mrs De Flyn called the police. Calletti was arrested at a nearby house. He was gaoled, but released after a few months.

That same month, on the 19th, William 'Darby' Lloyd, barber, tobacconist and cocaine peddler, and his sidekick, William Scott, were found bleeding heavily and near death in Crown Street, Darlinghurst. Lloyd's face had been razor-slashed three times, and he had a deep cut on the back of his neck. Fifty stitches were needed to close his wounds. Lloyd told police he could not identify his attacker: 'I don't want any arrest . . . I was drunk, that's all.' Darlinghurst police surmised, correctly, that Lloyd (who had recently been arrested after a fight with a local cocaine addict) had been 'attacked by a member of a razor gang'.

That member, it transpired, was William Smiley, a young thug employed by Kate Leigh, and the lover of Kate's daughter Eileen. Kate posted £400 bail for Smiley. True to the criminal code, the victim Lloyd stood up in court and swore that not only was Smiley innocent, but the two were the best of friends. He and Scott had been slashed not by Smiley but by someone else, someone he did not recognise. Then the Crown produced that rarity of the razor years, a brave and loquacious eyewitness, named Sydney York, who took the stand and told how he had seen Smiley and Eileen Leigh approach Lloyd and Scott in the street and Leigh had pointed at Scott and yelled: 'There he is! Get him.' Smiley, said York, 'hit Scott on the head with what looked to be a bag tied around his wrist. There was a rattle and something shone in Smiley's hand. Scott immediately fell. He was covered in blood. Smiley kicked him several times on the face and stomach. He then stood on his face and jumped on it.' Then, continued York, Smiley attacked Lloyd with his razor and 'Lloyd dropped.'

The jury preferred to believe the evidence of York (who after the trial was terrorised for months by Smiley's friends and forced to quit Sydney for Melbourne) and accepted the Crown's case that Lloyd and Scott were victims of an underworld vendetta by the Kate Leigh gang. The inappropriately named Smiley — though slickly handsome and with luxuriant locks, he wore a perpetual scowl — was sentenced to five years' gaol. 'I believe that you belong to a razor gang,' said Judge Cohen.

When Smiley was released in the early 1930s he took up where he left off, and was a menace on the streets of East Sydney until he was shot and left to bleed to death in Butt Street, Surry Hills, in 1940. A dead cat was found beside his body. Nobody was ever charged with Smiley's murder.

Another example of how razors were suddenly ubiquitous in 1927 unfolded in Surry Hills on the afternoon of 29 December. Les Anderson, a Mosman hotel broker, was drinking alone in a Crown Street wine bar when a local hood named Bill Weldon and a woman entered, and began arguing. Weldon threatened the woman, and she appealed to Anderson for help. Anderson gallantly ordered Weldon to leave. Weldon skulked away, then Anderson comforted the woman and agreed to walk her to her bus stop in case Weldon was lying in wait for her. When Anderson and the woman reached the corner of Cleveland and Crown streets, Weldon leapt upon Anderson from behind and slashed his throat with a razor. Weldon and the woman tried to rob Anderson but he jumped to his feet and, though bleeding and at near collapse, threw Weldon to the ground. Two tram conductors came to Anderson's aid, but Weldon and his accomplice escaped. Later that night, while Anderson was receiving twenty stitches in his throat at St Vincent's Hospital, police arrested Weldon and the woman.

So notorious were the razor gangsters as 1927 drew to an end that they sometimes found themselves scapegoats for crimes they had not committed. On 20 December, after one 'Tassie' Bates presented at St Vincent's Hospital, police were called to inspect an evil-looking gash on his arm. Bates told them how he had been jumped by five razor-brandishing bandits. He had fought the five off, of course, but before they fled howling with fear into the night, one had inflicted the wound that the officers now saw. His tale unravelled when he was confronted by witnesses who insisted he had sustained his wound rather less gloriously. Earlier that evening while drunk he had provoked a fight in a Surry Hills pub. His adversary had picked him up and hurled him through a glass door. The shattering glass had caused his wound.

Suddenly razors and the damage they were wreaking were the talk of the town. Before, when domestic violence erupted, the angry, drunk or unhinged may have lashed out with their fist or boot, reached for a copper stick, wrench, cricket bat or kettle to use as a weapon. Now, they were making for the medicine cabinet and grabbing their razor. In June 1927, Edward Smythe, a World War I veteran and Burwood resident, used a razor to inflict terrible wounds on the face and throat of Elsie, his wife and mother of their five children. He then slashed his own throat with the same instrument. Both recovered, but not before thirty stitches were inserted in Elsie Smythe's wounds and fifteen in Edward's.

# PART 2
# The Razor-Gang
# Wars

# 6

# Storm Warning

By 1927, the cunning, ambitious and ruthless Kate Leigh, Tilly Devine, Phil Jeffs and Norman Bruhn were unchallenged as Razorhurst's major gang bosses. For a while they were content to live and let live. Kate's territory was Surry Hills, where she ran sly grog and dealt in cocaine and stolen goods. Tilly's beat was brothels in Darlinghurst, Kings Cross and Woolloomooloo. Jeffs's specialties were drugs, gambling and sly grog in the Cross and the 'Loo. Bruhn and his razor gang monstered small-time vice purveyors in Kings Cross and Darlinghurst: freelance prostitutes, drug peddlers and low-rent two-up schools and sly-groggers unallied to Leigh, Devine or Jeffs. For a time, none encroached on another's turf or activity. Then in early 1927, the thieves fell out — and hell broke loose.

It was Bruhn who first split from the ranks. Dissatisfied by his takings and hungry to be Sydney's crime kingpin, he attempted to collect protection money from the enterprises of the other three czars. Then, when Bruhn's challenge was repelled, Tilly and Kate declared each other on. In these battles — which became known as 'the razor-gang wars' — screams pierced the narrow, seedy alleys of Razorhurst and the blood of the slashed, beaten and shot flowed in the gutters.

The years 1927–1931 would see the worst mob wars in Australian history. Nothing before or since has approached them for ferocity. By the time hostilities wound down in the early '30s as the Depression imposed austerity on once free-spending Sydneysiders — closing down many sly-grog shops, brothels, gambling dens and drug dealers — and Draconian consorting laws stopped gangs from assembling in the streets, a score of mobsters were dead and hundreds maimed and scarred.

Sydneysiders had much to be concerned about as the clouds of impending gang violence roiled over Razorhurst in 1927. But there were distractions. This was the year when Prince Albert and his wife Elizabeth, the Duke and Duchess of York (he was destined to become King George VI after the abdication of his brother Edward VIII in 1936, and she would become today's Queen Mother) visited Australia. Sydney feted the royal couple when they sailed into the Harbour on HMS *Renown* on 27 March. Before docking at Circular Quay, the duke and duchess inspected the work on the Sydney Harbour Bridge, still five years from completion. 'Every crowd was happy,' next day's *Sydney Morning Herald* declared. 'It seemed as though all Sydney betook itself to the Harbour — until after the landing, one turned to the thronged streets and city buildings. The route of the procession was even more densely populated than the waterfront.'

One of the highlights of Tilly Devine's life was being in the throng at the coronation of the duchess's daughter, Queen Elizabeth II, in London in 1953 so, although there is no record of her being there to wave at the royals in Sydney that autumn day, it's probable she was.

After the idyllic conditions that greeted the duke and duchess's arrival, Sydney's weather deteriorated and, astoundingly, on the day the duke was impressing with his keen interest in the manufacture of cigarettes at a local tobacco factory, snow fell on the streets of Sydney. Fierce storms then lashed the metropolitan area and gale-force winds whipping Bridge Street blew down a large decorative timber arch erected to honour the royals. Eight died in the tempest.

Sydneysiders were appalled when on 3 November, in the biggest disaster to befall their Harbour, the mail steamer RMS *Tahiti* collided with the ferry *Greycliffe* off Bradleys Head and forty-six lives were lost. They were, however, largely indifferent when it was reported that Darwin police chained Aboriginal 'lubras' suffering venereal disease to stakes in their compound. And when Pastor Efon Thomas was stripped, bound with barbed wire and coated with tar for offending local sensibilities in Warragul, Victoria, his plight caused more amusement than fury in the pubs and cafés of Sydney. Both items were barely mentioned in the newspapers.

But the people of Sydney were outraged and reaching for their own barbed wire and tar when local film editor and writer Robert Dexter told a Commonwealth Film Commission conference in Sydney that there was no chance of a viable film industry being established in this country because: 'Beauty is the merchandise of the motion picture, and Australia is practically barren of beauty. Nature made a wonderful job of this continent, but as human beings we are an ugly race.'

In the same month that David Jones opened its luxurious new department store on the corner of Elizabeth, Castlereagh and Market streets in the city ('The finest achievement in Retail Stores within the Commonwealth,' the advertising insisted), fifty-year-old William Alcock drank himself to death in his Balmain shack and when his corpse was found next morning it had been mutilated by rats.

# 7

# The Bad and the Beautiful

Born in 1912, Nellie Cameron hailed from a respectable middle-class home on Sydney's North Shore. By the age of twelve, she was stealing from her parents and local shops, and sleeping with much older men. In 1926, she ran away from home and became a prostitute, cocaine runner and a fence for stolen property. By the age of fifteen, when she met Norman Bruhn, she was a hooker on William and Palmer streets. With her beauty and criminal contacts, she had no need then to enlist with Tilly Devine or any other madam. The teenaged Cameron 'was a very beautiful schoolgirl with a life full of promise,' the top Sydney policewoman of the era, Lillian Armfield, once remarked. However:

> she became a prostitute, for no other reason than she wanted to be one. But she wasn't content with the sordid thrills of the life of a prostitute. She wasn't happy unless she was associated with violent men, and it is beyond any doubt that she encouraged them to violence. And if gangsters held a lure for Nellie, she also held a lure for them, and it turned out to be a fatal lure for some of them. Jealousy over her was responsible for more than one murder.

Cameron was pretty in a wide-eyed, open-faced, toothy way. She had an hourglass figure. Sometimes a redhead, sometimes a blonde, she was noisy, laughed a lot, could fight like a dervish, was a cheap drunk and bathed infrequently. She was brave and never squealed. She always carried a razor, often a gun, and loved to take off her clothes at parties.

Cameron dominated men with her sex appeal, rather than with her criminal clout or overpowering personality, as Kate Leigh and Tilly Devine did. It was said of her that she loved no man, but criminal power was her aphrodisiac. In his book *Wild Women of Sydney*, George Blaikie's pseudonymous protagonist 'Pinto Pete', according to Blaikie a customer of both the young Tilly Devine and Nellie Cameron, gave the points to Cameron: 'Tilly was like a big raw horse [in bed]. Nellie . . . was like a thoroughbred. The Darlinghurst boys used to pay Nellie the high compliment of describing her as a filly that would win at Randwick.'

Throughout her life, Cameron repeatedly took as her lover and pimp the most powerful criminal of the day. Should her man be outdone by another, she dumped the vanquished for the victor. Kenneth Slessor's poem 'The Gunman's Girl' was supposedly inspired by Cameron. His heroine wears 'mother of pearl' as well as 'a coat of real possum'. She carries 'a kiss of a knife' on her neck; her milieu is 'the land where snowdrops blossom', a reference to cocaine.

In early 1927, Bruhn ruled the roost. For a brief while, Bruhn and Cameron were the power couple in the bars and brothels of Kings Cross. Much like Tilly and Jim Devine, it was a case of opposites attracting. His plug-ugliness, querulousness and dour dress sense — suit, white shirt, tie and grey felt hat — were offset by her sunny style and vivacity. Bruhn lusted after her beauty and sexual virtuosity, not to mention the financial benefits she brought him. As well as being Cameron's lover, he was her 'protector', and confiscated part of her earnings in return for safeguarding her against other pimps and giving her a place to sleep and cocaine, beer and cigarette money.

In the late '20s, Cameron charged a minimum of ten shillings for sex (twice that when her reputation was at its height), and accommodated as many as ten customers a day, seven days a week, so before Bruhn exacted his tithe, she was making, at worst, £35 a week tax-free when the basic gross wage was £3. Also, Cameron perfected an age-old game, called 'gingering' in Australia. After soliciting a stranger on the street, she would take him to her apartment and they would proceed to the bedroom. Hiding under the bed or in a cupboard would be her accomplice. When sex was under way, the lurker would stealthily emerge and take the client's wallet from his pants or jacket, which Cameron would have been sure to sling over the end of the bed or a convenient dresser. At that point, coitus would be interrupted by angry banging on the front door by another involved in the scam. Cameron, feigning panic, would exclaim it was the police or her irate husband, and urge the client to dress and depart by the back door. Keen to avoid the embarrassment of prosecution or a beating, the customer would flee and usually not notice until later that his wallet was missing. He couldn't win. To return to Cameron's flat and make a scene would guarantee him a bashing by her pimps or, if he was less than robust, perhaps even by Nellie herself. To press charges with the police would result in his family and friends knowing the circumstances of the sting. Most victims wrote off their gingering as a lesson well learned. Cameron and Bruhn would chuckle as they split the contents of the stolen wallet. Tilly Devine was another adept gingerer and schooled her employees in the practice.

For all Bruhn's pride in being known as Nellie's lover, he beat her throughout their brief liaison, so setting the pattern for her life. She would be kidnapped, bashed, stabbed, slashed and shot by her criminal lovers Frank Green, Guido Calletti, Edward 'Ted' Pulley and Eric Connolly, but somehow outlive them all save Green. Nellie Cameron was known as 'the Kiss of Death Girl'. Once she was asked what she saw in Bruhn. 'When I wake up in the morning,' she answered, 'I like to look down on someone lower than myself.'

At night, Bruhn prowled with his blade-men, George Wallace, Snowy Cutmore and Razor Jack Hayes. On the fringe of this band were freelance hoons who were employed as circumstances dictated: they included Lancelot McGregor 'Sailor the Slasher' Saidler and a gay black man who dyed his hair platinum-white and was known as Nigger. Bruhn found the Kings Cross underworld ripe for exploitation. His modus operandi was simple: he and his men would gorge on booze and cocaine, then bail up sly-groggers, prostitutes and drug sellers in no position to tattle to the police, and demand money. They made it clear that if the money was not forthcoming, the penalty would be at best a slashed face; at worst, death.

George Wallace bore the same name as a popular Australian comedian of the time, but there was nothing amusing about 'the Midnight Raper'. Wallace earned his nickname by sexually assaulting hookers who refused to pay him a cut of their takings. He would often slash their faces for good measure. He was a beetle-browed, cleft-chinned brute who began his criminal career as a member of Sydney's army of pickpockets (memorably labelled by Magistrate McMahon in 1926 as 'dingoes who hunt in packs about the Central Railway Station and ferry wharves'). Wallace soon found drug trafficking more lucrative, then discovered it was easier still to mug other traffickers. His talent for mayhem won him Bruhn's notice.

Snowy Cutmore was a Melbourne bandit who followed Bruhn to Sydney after Bruhn had convinced him that Sydney was an El Dorado for criminals. Like Bruhn, he was an associate of Squizzy Taylor, but had fallen out with the diminutive Melbourne mobster. The fresh-faced Cutmore wore his lank, blond hair long on top and short at the back and sides. Cutmore's go was standover thuggery, dope peddling and sly-grog selling. In 1918, when in his late teens, he shot dead a youth in a Fitzroy, Melbourne, pub but evaded the law. In a precursor to his Sydney work with Bruhn, Cutmore led the so-called Safe Prosecution Gang, which relieved other criminals of their booty. He was renowned for viciousness. In 1919, still years before he turned up in Sydney, he slowly, deliberately, battered a trussed-up rival with an iron bar, stopping only when his victim neared death.

Cutmore was an alcoholic, and in fact was discharged from a 1919 charge of stealing boots from a wagon because a judge deemed him to have been too drunk to be capable of forming intent. Violent — notably with women — at the best of times, Cutmore was homicidal when intoxicated. One such time, the young crook and a friend attended a circus in a field in Northcote. The pair strode past the woman collecting tickets, explaining that the man behind would pay. The manager summoned the police, but before the constabulary could arrive, Cutmore had started a riot, laying into the manager and patrons with fist and boot. When police arrived in force they dragged Cutmore, squirming and lashing out and yelling obscenities, to the lock-up. He accumulated eight convictions in Melbourne, for assault, theft, offensive behaviour and shopbreaking, and notched another seven in quick time in Sydney, principally for assault and battery.

Razor Jack Hayes was a thin, lugubrious scoundrel. He gave his occupation as salesman and, as an habitué of racecourses, a successful punter. What he did best, however, was wield a razor, hence his sobriquet. He was also handy with his fists and was into anything illegal. He was feared, and with good reason, and so was made to measure for Norman Bruhn.

In December 1926, Wallace, Cutmore and three other members of Bruhn's mob were arguing with a young woman on a Darlinghurst street when a promising welterweight boxer named Billy Chambers, no cleanskin himself, chased them off. Word got about that Chambers had routed Bruhn's boys. The mob's reputation was at stake. So on Christmas morning, Bruhn, Wallace and Cutmore broke into Chambers's room in Darlinghurst. The boxer attempted to fight them off, but he was pistol-whipped unconscious. One of the mobsters sliced a long gash down Chambers's leg with his razor, cutting tendons and sinews. They then robbed the helpless pugilist of anything not nailed down. While most Sydneysiders were enjoying their Christmas roast, Chambers had seventy-six stitches inserted into his leg — and would never fight again.

Five months later, in May 1927, two months after Bruhn decided to break the truce and move on the other ganglords' enterprises, Wallace and two other Bruhn men leapt onto the running board of a car driven by a villain from Kate Leigh's firm as the man drove in Darlinghurst. Brandishing a razor, Wallace demanded money. The motorist handed them five shillings each. Not enough. The driver protested, and for his pains he was held firm by the henchmen as Wallace slashed him from forehead to left cheek to chin and across his mouth. Then, with the bleeding man's arms still pinioned, Wallace stole his wallet.

The victim swore revenge and cornered Wallace alone some weeks later in a William Street tobacconist. He levelled his revolver at Wallace's huge belly and announced he was going to pull the trigger. Wallace ran screaming into the street, shrieking: 'Police! Police! He's going to shoot me.' The Midnight Raper, however, had the last laugh. When Wallace found himself cornered at gunpoint again by the scarfaced vengeful man, some weeks later in an Oxford Street, Darlinghurst hotel, he was prepared for the end. The fellow pulled the trigger at point-blank range, but the bullet jammed in the chamber. Wallace whipped out his razor and this time slashed the man's *right* cheek.

The opening gambit in Bruhn's plan to be the unchallenged king of the Sydney underworld was when, in early 1927, he despatched Razor Jack Hayes to deal with Sid 'Kicker' Kelly, one of the infamous Kelly brothers, hard men whom Bruhn knew were friends and allies of Phil Jeffs. Hayes slashed Kelly's throat, but Kelly survived. Retribution was inevitable. One night not long after, Sid Kelly and his brother Tom followed Hayes and Bruhn into Mack's, a sleazy cocaine and sly-grog den run by Joe McNamara, in Charlotte Lane, Darlinghurst. There they goaded Hayes and Bruhn into a fight, and the Kellys gave them a severe walloping, followed by a kicking. Bruhn and Hayes were hospitalised.

Starting in March that year, Bruhn, unfazed by his beating, targeted Jeffs's, Devine's and Leigh's establishments in a series of hyena-like hits that left his enemies' operatives bruised and slashed. Bruhn's attacks began to bite into the others' revenue as patrons, fearing serious trouble, began to stay away from their establishments. It's not known if Jeffs, Leigh and Devine gathered for a council of war, but they did stock up their arsenal and plotted how to destroy the Bruhn gang without drawing police attention to themselves.

Police knowledge of the escalating war was sketchy due to the criminal code of silence. But they, like reporters on the crime beat, sensed that something nasty was brewing in Razorhurst. *Truth*, in an article on the razor gangs, fretted sensationally:

> *And so . . . the vendetta gets fiercer . . . Its climax may come in a wild campaign of shooting any night, as the mystery gangsters, once elusive, shady and unknown, are now easily identifiable by those who have sworn to 'get' them. The 'Midnight Raper' has other names, ordinary names, but they do not count much, as a criminal changes his title about five times a week if it suits him. There are others identifiable by nicknames, too, one of them of snowy white locks who is called 'Nigger', and yet another who is referred to more often than not as 'The Jew'. The reputed leader [of the worst gang] is a Melbourne man who absconded from bail and bolted for Sydney after he had been committed for trial . . . And so, known to the police and known to their victims, the gangsters prowl through the shadows, and even into the light of day, spreading supreme terror as they go, and never fearing that the processes of the law may be set against them.*

Bruhn's fate was sealed when in May he and Hayes held up a sly-grog shop, in Liverpool Street, Darlinghurst, in which Phil Jeffs held a major financial interest. As Bruhn knew it would be, the audacious strike was interpreted by Jeffs as a direct and personal challenge. To avoid being branded a coward and losing his underworld credibility, Phil the Jew had no choice but to lash back at Bruhn.

In the early evening of 6 June, Bruhn's man Razor Jack Hayes was gunned down in Liverpool Street, Darlinghurst. Passing taxi driver Jack Edelman told police he saw two men arguing on the footpath. One, he said, drew a revolver from his coat and shot the other in the chest. Edelman had seen the gun flash and heard a 'pop'. The shot man fell into the gutter. The shooter climbed into a large, dark limousine, which turned into Bourke Street and sped towards William Street. Edelman pursued the limousine and took its number, then returned to where the victim lay unconscious and bleeding. He lifted him into his cab and drove him to St Vincent's Hospital. For days, Razor Jack was not expected to recover. The bullet had entered his upper-right chest, passed through his body and emerged from his back. It had missed his heart but blood loss was heavy. Although Hayes refused to name his attacker, police, acting on Edelman's information, traced the getaway car and charged Tom Kelly with malicious wounding.

By the time Kelly's trial began, at Sydney Quarter Sessions on 28 July 1927, Hayes had recovered. In court, he heard the accused admit to shooting him only in self-defence after Hayes had threatened him with a razor: 'I'll cut your ears off!' Fearing a reprisal from Hayes's mates nearby, Kelly claimed, he'd then sped off in his car.

When Razor Jack took the stand, his was a virtuoso performance. Both Kelly and cab driver Edelman were confused or lying, he declared. He said that he knew Tom Kelly, but he had never quarrelled with him, and certainly Kelly was not the man who shot him. Hayes's version of the incident was that he had spent the day at

Randwick racecourse and was standing outside a Darlinghurst tobacconist's when summoned to a nearby car. He approached the vehicle then felt a pain in his chest, but remembered nothing more until waking in hospital the next day. And, he told the Crown prosecutor, he had no idea who was in the car or why anyone would want to shoot him. Yes, he knew Norman Bruhn, but he was not a friend. He and Bruhn had never held up anyone nor slashed them with a razor. It was not true that people had been afraid to report him and Bruhn for assault because they were terrified of retribution. Hayes *did* know a barrowman in Oxford Street, Darlinghurst, named Ellis, but no, he had never slashed Ellis with a razor while Bruhn pinioned his arms. He did not have a razor in his pocket on the night he was shot, and was not, as far as he knew, known as 'Razor Jack'.

Hopelessly confused after hearing three differing versions of Hayes's shooting, the jury acquitted Tom Kelly, and on 28 August he strode jauntily from the court. Perhaps his spirits were bolstered by the knowledge that he would never be called to account by Norman Bruhn, at least, for shooting the feared gangleader's trusted henchman. For, by late August, Bruhn himself had been dead almost two months.

# 8

# Norman Bruhn's Death Wish

Bruhn seemed unperturbed by the 6 June shooting of Hayes. Far from curbing his attacks on the other crime leaders, he escalated them.

While Hayes was recovering in hospital, Bruhn and his gang stormed into one of Kate Leigh's sly-grog shops in Liverpool Street and, razors flashing, took her proprietor's night's takings, £100 of the man's own money and a stash of jewellery. A few nights later they returned to Liverpool Street and lay in wait outside the home of a well-known thief, knowing he had recently pulled a job but had not yet unloaded the loot to Kate Leigh. When the thief arrived home they hustled him inside his house and demanded his cache. The thief did not resist, and handed it over. When she learned of the heist, Kate totted up the money Bruhn had once more cost her and seethed.

Next, Bruhn and Wallace even held up Mack's, Bruhn's old stamping ground in Chalmers Lane, another dive in which Phil Jeffs had a stake. They took money and a quantity of five-shilling deals of cocaine. Bruhn, Wallace and Cutmore then raided a number of Tilly Devine's brothels, assaulting prostitutes and patrons alike. Bruhn was out of control.

All day Wednesday, 22 June 1927, Norman Bruhn drank in the Courthouse Hotel, Darlinghurst, with a young horse trainer from Melbourne named Robert Miller; Jim Hassett, a professional punter; and a man named Dick O'Brien. As trams clattered up and down Oxford Street outside and the wheels of justice turned at Central Criminal Court across the road, the four grew drunk and rowdy, and Bruhn argued with Hassett and O'Brien. At closing time, 6 p.m., the four staggered out of the pub into the chill of a winter's night and weaved up Oxford Street toward Paddington Town Hall.

Bruhn's wife Irene was not surprised when her husband did not come home for dinner. Thanks to Nellie Cameron, Bruhn's appearances in their seamy little flat at 21A Francis Street, Darlinghurst (just around the corner from Mack's) were rare these days. Although, from her later comments, it seemed Irene had no knowledge of Bruhn and Cameron's affair. Irene Bruhn fed herself and her sons and went to bed about 9.30 p.m. An hour later she was awakened by three loud bangs — gunshots — but was assured by a neighbour, 'Oh, that's only backfiring from the taxi garage.' Shortly afterwards, she later told the police, someone from Mack's came in and said, 'Norman has been shot.'

The usual silence descended on Razorhurst after Bruhn's death, and the mystery of who killed him has never been solved. What *is* known, from police reports and witness statements at the 25 July inquest at the City Coroner's Court, is that at about 9.45 p.m. on 22 June, Bruhn, Miller and two other men hailed a checker cab outside Paddington Post Office in Oxford Street. The taxi driver, Noel Infield, told the coroner that all four were drunk. Bruhn ordered Infield to drive them to the Best Hole Cafe in Chalmers Street, Surry Hills. The four entered the cafe while Infield waited in his cab. After a short time the men returned to the taxi and Bruhn told Infield to take them to Mack's in Charlotte Lane. 'Now,' snapped Bruhn to Infield when they arrived there, 'hop out and knock at the door.' When a man opened it, Bruhn, Miller and the two other men went inside.

Infield noticed that Mack's was very quiet. After a while, he left the cab to stretch his legs with a stroll in the pitch-black lane. Suddenly two men appeared from the shadows and asked him how many people had just entered Mack's. 'About five,' Infield replied and, unsettled, walked away. A minute or so later, he saw a number of dark figures in the lane outside Mack's. Suddenly, the cabbie said, he heard four gunshots (Irene Bruhn said she heard three shots, other witnesses recalled five) and saw men scatter in all directions.

Then Infield heard a wail of agony — 'Help, I'm shot! Oh, I'm shot!' He ran to where a man lay writhing on the ground. It was Bruhn, and he had been shot twice in the stomach. His clothes were blood-soaked and there was blood and foam pouring from his mouth. He continued to scream, 'I'm shot! Help, I'm shot!' Infield, and a beat constable who had come running when he heard the gunfire, tried to make Bruhn more comfortable. When Bruhn recognised Infield, he gasped: 'Bring your taxi, quick. Get me to a hospital. I'm shot.' Infield and the constable lifted Bruhn, still writhing and 'swearing terribly', into the back seat and Infield drove to Sydney Hospital. On the way, the constable repeatedly asked the semi-conscious Bruhn his name but received no cooperation from the dying man. Detective Sergeant Miller interviewed Bruhn at about 11 p.m. as his life ebbed away. He introduced himself. 'Yes, Mr Miller,' whispered Bruhn, 'I know you.' But to the sergeant's questions as to the identity of the gunman came the all-too-familiar Razorhurst reply: 'I won't be a copper. I wouldn't shelf anybody. Go away, I'm too sick. I don't want the police to interfere.'

Irene Bruhn was with her husband when he died in the early hours of 23 June. Later, Detective Sergeant Miller asked Irene if her husband had told her who shot him. 'No,' she snapped. 'And I wouldn't tell you if he did.'

Bruhn was buried at Rookwood Cemetery in Sydney's west, with only Irene and his two brothers from Melbourne at the graveside.

After the killing, his lover, Nellie Cameron, and henchmen, Wallace, Cutmore and Hayes, went to ground.

In the days after Bruhn's funeral, his widow spoke at length with reporters. 'These things they say about Norman in the newspapers are wicked lies,' she sobbed. 'God knows, if he had been as they say, I should have discovered it, for I had been married to him for seven years. I married him when I was sixteen and he was twenty-six, and to me he was a good husband and a good father to his children.' (What Nellie Cameron must have thought when reading this can only be imagined.) 'He had his faults,' Irene went on, 'but despite what everyone says, I never knew him to carry a razor or a gun. Norman fought in the War, having enlisted with the 6th Battalion. He was severely wounded with shrapnel, and those were the marks they saw on him at the morgue.'

To Melbourne's *Truth*, she claimed that in his final moments, Bruhn had whispered to her the name of his killer and had told Irene: 'He did not intend to shoot me. It was somebody else he was after.' And, before he expired, Bruhn had made her promise never to reveal the identity of his slayer. She said that prostitutes who gathered in Charlotte Lane after the shooting also assured her that the killer got the wrong man. The reporter asked Irene Bruhn why she would not want to help bring her husband's slayer to justice. '*I* don't want to be shot,' she replied.

The police did their best to catch the killer of Norman Bruhn. Police Commissioner Mitchell declared that he had given the force definite instructions and drastic action would be taken to apprehend the gunman or gunmen. In spite of copious evidence to the contrary, Mitchell declared that he did not believe Bruhn was the victim of an underworld vendetta, and added that, to his knowledge, only a few local hoodlums had been fighting among themselves. Superintendent Tom Mankey, head of the Criminal Investigation Branch (CIB), was placed in charge of the manhunt, headquartered at Darlinghurst Police Station. 'We will get the murderer,' Mankey's second-in-command, Officer Pattison, assured the public. 'We might come up with him in less than a week.' They didn't, and today, seventy-three years later, Bruhn's murder remains unsolved.

Certainly the authorities got no help from Robert Miller, Bruhn's drinking companion who was at the scene of the crime, nor Joe McNamara, the proprietor of Mack's. At the coroner's inquest, Miller seemed terrified, at times to the point of hysteria, that he would say something to incur the wrath of whoever killed Bruhn.

A study of the court transcript that icy July day reveals that Coroner H.F.W. Fletcher and Detective Sergeant Miller could hardly have found a more unreliable and uncooperative witness than Robert Miller. Fletcher began the questioning. No, Miller remembered nothing of the 22 June drinking session and its aftermath, apart from being with Bruhn in the hospital that night ('I was drunk all day'); but then, yes, he did remember walking with Bruhn in Charlotte Lane and that shots were fired. When reminded of the statement he gave to the police the same night, he could not now recall who he was walking with — in fact he didn't even know Charlotte Lane at all. Yes, he remembered telling the police officer that there were four men on the corner and that one of them pushed him away; but when asked who else was there that night in Charlotte Lane, replied 'Nobody'.

Detective Sergeant Miller then took over the questioning; the witness, according to court reports, now fidgeting and sweating profusely. This time around, Robert Miller could at least shed some light on the drinking session before the shooting: yes, he recalled that Hassett and O'Brien were present. And then the self-contradictions continued. No, he wasn't drunk after a session alone in a Dowling Street pub prior to going to the Courthouse Hotel. So he was sober on entering the

Courthouse? No, he was drunk — and had been for three days. Did he know Mack's? No, he'd never been there. So could he swear that he wasn't at Mack's earlier in June? No, he couldn't remember. And when asked by the detective sergeant, exasperated no doubt by his witnesses's alcohol-fuelled memory loss, 'Look, Miller, are you always drunk?', he replied (truthfully perhaps for the first time), 'I've been drunk ever since I came to Sydney last Easter!'

When Joe McNamara, thin, shabbily suited and with his hair greased and parted down the middle, took the stand, he took his inter-rogators inside his den on the night of the shooting, but could not (or would not) unmask the culprit. Curiously, he said a man named Snowy was with Miller and Hassett when he opened the door to let them in. However, when pressed by Detective Sergeant Miller, he said he did not believe it was the man he knew as Snowy Cutmore. And when Jim Hassett was paraded before the inquest, McNamara offered that the Hassett standing before him was not the Hassett with Bruhn, Miller and the mysterious Snowy on 22 June. At the end of the inquest, exasperated and stymied, Coroner Fletcher pronounced that Norman Bruhn had been shot to death by an 'unknown murderer'.

On 23 June, the day after the shooting, taxi driver Infield was called to a police line-up to try to identify any of the men who scarpered by him in the dark of Charlotte Lane. In the line-up were Tom and Sid Kelly, Frank Green, Gregory Gaffney and other denizens of the under-world whom police had rounded up overnight. Infield could make no positive identification. That night he was sitting in his cab in Oxford Street when a man he described to police as 'thick-set, with side-levers [sideburns] and a dark grey suit' spoke to him. 'It's just as well you didn't recognise anybody in that lineup today. Be equally as care-ful tomorrow, or you'll find yourself in hot water.'

The feisty Infield turned on the threatener. 'How come *you* know so much about it?'

'That's all right,' smiled the man. 'Remember what I've told you,' and walked away.

At another line-up of local crims the next day, Infield again could be of no help to police, but he told them of the stranger's words the night before and assured them he had not been influenced by them.

So who killed Norman Bruhn? Did Miller, Hassett and O'Brien lead him into the Charlotte Lane ambush? Did McNamara kill Bruhn to pay him back for earlier trashing and robbing Mack's? Was Bruhn's death, as Irene claimed, a case of mistaken identity? Author Hugh Anderson in his biography of Squizzy Taylor, *Larrikin Crook*, raises the possibility that Snowy Cutmore killed his boss to avenge a friend who had been robbed by Bruhn. (One theory goes that Cutmore's slaying of Bruhn incensed Bruhn's old partner-in-crime Taylor and it was bad blood over this that led to Squizzy and Snowy's fatal rendezvous four months later in Cutmore's mother's house in Barkly Street in Carlton, Melbourne.) Did Tilly Devine or Kate Leigh have Bruhn murdered to stop his invasion of their territory?

Policewoman Lillian Armfield, in Vince Kelly's biography *Rugged Angel*, said she believed that Frank Green shot Bruhn. Green could have done so at the behest of his boss Tilly Devine, or he might have killed Bruhn to win Nellie Cameron, to whom he was attracted. Did Phil Jeffs kill Bruhn, or have him killed? A Jeffs hit seems probable. Did he set the Kelly brothers onto Bruhn? Or go further afield? It *is* acknowledged that Melbourne standover man and killer-for-hire Harry Slater, a man well known to Jeffs (and Bruhn), was in Sydney shortly before the slaying.

# 9

# And Then There Were Three

Bruhn's murder left Jeffs, Leigh and Devine at the pinnacle of Sydney crime. Bruhn's razor gang disintegrated.

Razor Jack Hayes took his bullet-scarred carcass to Germany after being once more badly injured, this time in a street affray in 1928, and was never heard from again. For so long a feared menace, George 'the Midnight Raper' Wallace became a figure of fun. Wallace was in Brisbane when Bruhn was shot, and shortly after his return in early July '27 he ran into Tom Kelly in Victoria Street, Darlinghurst. It is not known what started the fight, possibly recriminations over the shooting of Razor Jack Hayes, or Wallace may have accused Kelly of killing Bruhn, but it was quickly settled. When Wallace shaped up to Kelly in a boxer's stance, Kelly picked up a hammer from the doorway of a hardware shop and hurled it at Wallace's head. The direct hit made Wallace flee.

Then on 23 July, Wallace, drunk and addled with cocaine, was again humiliated in a fracas he started at a cafe in King Street in the city. Wallace had barged into the Plaza Cafe nightspot without paying the five-shilling cover charge for supper and cabaret. Manager Harry Murray approached and told Wallace he would have to pay the cover charge or leave. 'If I do leave,' snapped Wallace, 'I'll do some damage before I go,' and punched Murray in the face. Murray fought back and the pair grappled as customers ducked for cover. When Murray began to get the upper hand, Wallace slashed him on the head with his razor. Then, as Murray lay bleeding, Wallace, bellowing with rage, upturned tables and threw glasses. Seizing a heavy coffee pot, he hurled it at a waitress, hitting her on the head.

While Wallace was wrecking the place, staff locked the doors and called the police. Wallace saw he was trapped and attempted to escape, but his way was barred by staff and customers. The gangster slumped disconsolate and near tears onto a chair, and this was how Sergeant Dennis found him. At first Wallace claimed he was the victim, that for no reason he had been set upon by the crowd. This was met by a chorus of incredulous denial by diners. Dennis handcuffed Wallace and led him to the police station as patrons heckled and jeered the deflated thug.

Facing court over the brawl, Wallace threw himself on the jury's mercy: 'I've got a wife and a child five weeks old, and I've got a job in the city and I'll guarantee not to make a slip again.' He was found guilty, fined £2 and a further £3 to pay for the Plaza's damages.

Soon after, Wallace left Sydney for good. His guarantee to the court was worthless, for his criminal record shows many subsequent convictions for assault and robbery in Brisbane, Melbourne, Perth and numerous country towns along the way. On 23 November 1948, Wallace was stabbed to death in the toilet of the European Club in Perth. He was forty-six. A miner, Leonard Levy, whom Wallace had robbed of £140, ended the life of the Midnight Raper with a butcher's knife.

Snowy Cutmore, his wife Gladys and a friend of Phil Jeffs named Herbert Wilson (aka Roy Travers) returned to Melbourne in mid October 1927. Curiously, there to meet them were the ubiquitous Kelly brothers, Sid and Tom, who had dealt with Cutmore's cohort Hayes and were suspected by some of killing his boss Bruhn. (Cutmore's rendezvous with long-time adversaries Wilson and the Kellys just months after Bruhn's murder adds weight to theories that Cutmore had betrayed his leader.) In Melbourne, Cutmore renewed his feud with Squizzy Taylor, badmouthing him to any associate who would listen. After a riotous day at Richmond racecourse with Wilson (Cutmore's behaviour and reputation saw him warned off the course by detectives) and a round of welcome-home booze-ups at which he was at his obnoxious worst, Cutmore fell ill with influenza. He took to his bed at his mother's home, where he and Gladys were renting a bedroom, at 50 Barkly Street, Carlton.

On 26 October, just as Cutmore's mother was cooking her bedridden son a dinner of roast lamb and peas, Squizzy Taylor came calling. He burst into Cutmore's bedroom. The two argued and twelve shots were fired in rapid succession. Herbert Wilson and Cutmore's mother, who was wounded in the shootout, later took police to the bullet-riddled room. There, her son's perforated corpse lay sprawled and stiffening on the bed. There was a bullet in his heart and his right-hand little finger had been blasted off. Squizzy Taylor, also shot numerous times, had staggered from the death house but died of his wounds half an hour after being dumped at Melbourne's St Vincent's Hospital by a hire-car driver. Police arrested Wilson and the Kelly brothers and questioned them at length over the deaths of Taylor and Cutmore, but the Sydneysiders were soon released.

Sometime Bruhn mobster, the floridly named Lancelot McGregor 'Sailor the Slasher' Saidler — small, pale and obstreperous — continued after Bruhn's death as a lone-wolf standover merchant targeting the bars and clubs of Glebe and the section of Elizabeth Street (near Central Railway and the Toohey's Brewery) known as 'the Barbary Coast'. At 3 p.m. on Saturday, 13 September 1930, he stalked into Ernie Good's wine bar in Elizabeth Street, near Central, a watering hole frequented by police and crooks alike, and demanded five shillings protection money. Good was a man not easily intimidated, and he told Saidler to leave. Saidler threw a glass of wine in the proprietor's face. He then drew his razor and growled: 'I'll carve you up. I'll slice off your smeller with this little beauty!' As Saidler ranted and waved his blade in the air, Good calmly reached into his drawer, took out a pistol and shot the razor-man dead. Police charged Good with manslaughter but he was acquitted on grounds of self-defence.

An interesting insight into the private life of a razor gangster came to light in late September, when Saidler's grieving widow, Lallie Brown, whom he had married when she was fifteen, went to Good's saloon and, with a penny, scratched a message into the woodwork on the front door: 'I'll kill you for killing Sailor.' For reporters, she then painted a picture of her happy life with Saidler.

He wasn't a gangster, she insisted, just a 'wild boy', a 'daredevil'. He kept a house full of cats, and he pulled the noses of Chinese children in Surry Hills until they squealed with delight. He was kind and thoughtful and, why, he was so concerned for her welfare that he had even dissuaded her from smoking. 'We were sitting at a table in a wine saloon,' she fondly recalled, 'and there were other girls there, all of them smoking. I picked up a cigarette that one of them had placed on the table, and put it in my mouth. Sailor said, 'Do you want to be like these other girls?' and I told him I wanted to learn to smoke. He plucked the cigarette from my mouth and thrust it back in again, only he put the lighted end in first. It burnt my tongue and blistered my mouth inside, and I had to cry out. He asked me if I would ever smoke again. I was wild with him and I said I would if I liked. He stood up and hit me in the eye. You see, he always tried to look after me and keep me from being like the other girls. He was wonderful.'

If Nellie Cameron mourned her lover Bruhn at all, she did not do so for long. Within weeks of his demise, she was arm in arm on the streets of Razorhurst with Frank 'the Little Gunman' Green.

# 10

# Razor-mania and the Campaign for Law and Order

Scarcely a night passed without a slashing in Razorhurst. If straight society prayed that the street mayhem of 1927 was an aberration, and that the demise of Norman Bruhn and his gang would see the streets of East Sydney safe once more, a spate of violence in the first weeks of 1928 dashed their hopes. While Leigh, Devine and Bruhn circled each other warily, preparing to strike before they were struck, crime's lower echelons went at each other with razors. 'Following on the operations of the notorious [Bruhn] razor gang at its zenith have come a crop of desultory slicings, and stabbings and hackings,' noted *Truth* on 1 January 1928. The paper declared there could be no doubt that the blade was quickly gaining favour over the 'old-fashioned bare knuckle fist when it comes to settling underworld squabbles or even to holding up honest citizens.'

On 17 January, Woolloomooloo prostitute Dorothy Roberts, known to her friends as Black Dot, took umbrage at a sailor customer from HMAS *Sydney* who ran off after sex without paying her. Roberts, twenty-one years old and described as 'short and stubby with a mop of black hair, black eyes and heavy black eyebrows', ambushed the sailor, Victor Kelly, and razored him from groin to knee. On 25 March,

Sam Barker, a young Darlinghurst crook, stormed a Newtown cinema with fifteen henchmen looking for a rival named Billie James. After the brawl, the police tracked Barker down, and found in his pockets a revolver and three razors.

Also in late March, Judge Herbert Curlewis sentenced Gordon Barr, described by one courtroom observer as 'a mean-looking, flashily-dressed mockery of a man', to five years in prison for slashing the face of prostitute Betty Carslake in Darlinghurst. As Barr whimpered and cowered in the dock, Curlewis thundered that the prison sentence was scant punishment for 'one of the most poisonous and loathsome creatures on the face of the earth'. Curlewis regretted being unable to order that Barr be whipped. Nevertheless the sentence imposed was enough to unhinge a group of women in the gallery. Barr's mother wailed, 'Oh, no! Don't!' while Barr's present and former wives, Dolly Barr (aka Diamond Dolly) and a woman named Tremaine (aka the Flying Angel) hysterically abused the judge and were escorted from the premises by police.

Months after he shot an underworld figure named Alphonso Clune, gangster Norman 'Mickie' McDonald was himself blasted twice in Surry Hills in March and even while he was being treated and refusing to name his attackers to police, two of the men who had shot McDonald were themselves shot and a third razor-slashed. In November, in Surry Hills, William Dillon (aka Darkie Davis) was shot in the face in a revenge shooting that followed Dillon's slashing in Darlinghurst of a member of a rival gang. Dillon wouldn't name his attacker.

In a domestic argument, this time played out in broad daylight at Central Railway Station, Betty Honeyman slashed an eight-centimetre gash in the neck of her husband Jim. As he fell to the ground bleeding, Jim Honeyman screamed: 'This woman is one of the razor gang! She has slashed me with a razor!' In court, Betty was found guilty of grievous bodily harm, but no evidence was produced to support her husband's claim that she was in cahoots with Phil Jeffs, Frank Green or Guido Calletti. Jim Honeyman, like other Sydneysiders that year, was under the influence of 'razor-mania'.

There were also more than twenty gang-related shootings in the lanes and alleys of East Sydney in 1928. Notably, in March, Lawrence Tracey was gunned down on the corner of Goulburn and Riley streets, Surry Hills. He died without squealing. On 7 April, again at Surry Hills, extortionist Tom O'Brien was shot in the stomach; but when police arrested three local hoodlums on the most incriminating evidence, O'Brien refused to identify them.

Phil Jeffs spent 1928 setting up a string of cocaine and after-hours sly-grog clubs in Kings Cross, Woolloomooloo and Darlinghurst. He was making enormous sums from drug trafficking, and extorting from drug dealers, illegal bookmakers and prostitutes. He also set up brothels in Kings Cross flats. He was as capable a criminal as either Tilly Devine or Kate Leigh, but on 5 March 1928, his burgeoning career almost came to an end.

Around 11.30 p.m., Ida Maddocks, twenty-eight, of Darlinghurst, a married mother of two babies, staggered hysterical with clothing askew into Darlinghurst Police Station. She said that two hours earlier she had been walking down Bayswater Road, Kings Cross, when two men emerged from a lane. One had whispered to her, 'Hello, love,' and the other hissed, 'Come here, dear.' Maddocks said she quickened her step but the two men and another who had appeared from the shadows grabbed her by the shoulders and skirt, and dragged her down a passageway and into a side door of a block of flats named Kings Lynn. In a bedroom there, she was raped by her three abductors and another man who was in the flat.

Maddocks told police, 'I said, "For God's sake, let me go home to my husband and children."' One of the rapists had snapped back, 'You'll go home when we're finished with you.' A fifth man, this one small and swarthy, entered the bedroom. One of the men addressed him. 'Phil, this is our little sport. I've given her £2 for the night. Will you make it three?' The man named Phil had said, 'Certainly,' and sent the others outside, locked the door of the bedroom and, said Maddocks, 'threw me onto the bed and assaulted me'.

The next day the police arrested Phil Jeffs, Ernest Wilson, Fred Payne, Les Heath and Herbert Wilson (the same man involved in the Snowy Cutmore–Squizzy Taylor shootout in Melbourne) and charged the five men with rape and assault. If found guilty, they would hang. The crime, which became known as 'the Darlinghurst Outrage', was front-page news for weeks, and when Jeffs and his cohorts arrived at court to be charged, a crowd of citizens and pressmen milled in the road for a glimpse of them. When questioned by police, Jeffs snarled brazenly, 'What you say and the questions you ask don't interest me.'

At Darlinghurst Criminal Court in May, the accused men's defence team attempted to discredit Maddocks's story. She was a woman of loose morals, they sneered, whose own husband had recently threatened to razor-slash her face 'from ear to ear' when he learned she was working as a prostitute. On the night of 5 March, Jeffs's lawyers told the court, Maddocks had been soliciting in Bayswater Road when she was approached by a group of men and she had agreed to have sex with them all for £5 at Kings Lynn flats. At the flats, she had, for reasons known only to herself, become distraught and ran to Darlinghurst Police Station where she accused the men of raping her.

Further, the lawyer continued, the five fellows in the dock may not even have been the men with whom Maddocks had willingly had sex that night. Fred Payne swore he was drinking wine with a woman named Fifi in the park opposite the Watsons Bay Hotel when the alleged attack was taking place. Les Heath claimed he had been at a Kings Cross cinema enjoying a crime double bill, *The Underworld* and

*Tell It To Sweeney.* Jeffs, too, had an alibi: clad in an expensive white fur, Olive Reynolds, a barmaid at Kings Cross's Temple Bar Hotel, told the court she had spent the day and evening drinking champagne with Jeffs and other friends. The jury took just thirty minutes to acquit the defendants.

Police were furious at the acquittal, and for the next few months kept Jeffs under constant surveillance, desperate to catch him committing an offence so they could haul him back to the cells. On a number of occasions, he was arrested and charged with having no lawful means of support, but each time Jeffs beat the vagrancy rap. Once, he said he had a half-share in a ham and beef shop and when police asked its location, Jeffs chuckled, 'That's what you're paid to find out.' On another time, he claimed he was paid £4 a week for tending William Archer's Hot Bath House in Crown Street. He told one officer who tried to 'vag' him that he was a pastrycook, and another that he had 'a half-interest in a bookmaker's bag'.

Charged yet again with vagrancy, Jeffs boasted to prosecutor Constable Stinson that he was a man of many, many talents, but dealing in drugs and peddling illegal alcohol were not among them. 'Do you support yourself by assisting in sly-grog selling?' Stinson demanded. 'I do not!' barked Jeffs, his face twisted with mortification at the very suggestion.

'He's discharged!' said the magistrate.

The almost daily violence was decried in the press, in parliament and from the pulpit.

From the outset, *Truth* led the pack. Every time it covered a Razorhurst crime in salacious, gloating detail, as it had the Bruhn killing and the serial offences of George Wallace, its circulation soared. For a time it was unchallenged as Sydney's chronicler of the underworld, as its crack court reporters and police roundsmen luridly described every shooting, beating and slashing. 'Truth existed on the fears of men and the tears of women,' recalls old-time policeman Lance Hoban.

But Truth was also capable of switching from being a voyeuristic vulture to a moral guardian in a flash and without a qualm. Amid its ads for Akubra hats ('There's personality in an Akubra!'), Clarke's Blood Purifier and the movie version of For The Term of his Natural Life (offered 'with Magnificent Atmospheric Presentation', at the Crystal Palace), it would declaim against slumland conditions and weak laws that bred the crimes it so enthusiastically headlined and cashed in on. In a series of articles in 1928 — under such titles as 'Wipe Out Gang Terrorism!', 'Gaol Dingo Packs That Are A Canker in City's Heart!' and 'Flogging For Razor Slashers!' — it harangued politicians and police to stamp out the mobsters and street thugs of Razorhurst.

Truth was determined to stir the 'lethargic' public conscience and to keep stirring the government until the city could tell the world it had its gangs of criminals in hand. 'To the man who returned to Sydney this year after a couple of years' absence, [it] must have appeared . . . a veritable jungle abounding with human wolves and tigers' whose utter contempt for any law was being fearfully demonstrated as each week brought its fresh list of atrocities.

Truth's legion of detractors were on safe ground when accusing the newspaper of hypocrisy and scaremongering, but the paper can claim credit for goading politicians into action and helping to create a social climate a couple of years later in which new laws could be enacted that helped bring the gangs to heel.

On 15 January 1928, the newspaper crowed that on its urgent representations the Minister for Justice had called for immediate reports on the crime wave sweeping the state.

*This is the hour of the glistening blade and crimes of vio-*
*lence — particularly razor slicings — are part of the daily*
*increasing carnival of bloodletting. It is no longer possible for*
*decent citizens to walk the streets of Sydney without fear of sud-*
*den and terrible attack . . . The harvest of hackings and slicings*
*and stabbings is being garnered in all parts of the metropolis.*
*The razor has found its place in the pockets not only of the*
*original razor gang, but in the hands and thoughts of hundreds*
*of nondescripts who have found that a well-honed blade is a*
*weapon that strikes terror into the hearts of innocent victims.*

Years before the establishment of 21 Division and the consorting laws, the tabloid called for the establishment of 'a special vice squad — backed by an effective vagrancy act — to clean up the meandering, prowling degenerates and social parasites who hunt in packs around sordid Darlinghurst's flatlands'. In the same article, on 11 March 1928, it decried the fact that in New South Wales there was only one policeman for every 700 citizens and demanded the recruitment of more. As a result of *Truth's* hectoring, New South Wales Police Inspector General James Mitchell agreed that 'the *Vagrancy Act* has for a long time needed stronger amendments' and promised the public 'legislation that enables the police to deal more effectively with criminals under that Act'. That day, too, Chief Secretary Bruntnell announced that a further 200 police would man the metropolitan police district.

All year *Truth* pounded away at Premier Thomas Bavin, who had campaigned for office on a law and order platform, to give the vagrancy laws the added teeth of imprisonment and flogging for razor carriers, and for the establishment of an anti-vice squad and consorting laws that would gaol known criminals if they were caught associating with each other. In September, its campaign, which reflected the sentiments of an increasingly frightened public, bore fruit when State Parliament's Upper House passed Attorney-General

Boyce's Crimes Amendment Bill, which decreed a six-month sentence 'for those found in possession of a razor, razor blade, or other cutting instrument who cannot satisfy the justice that their purpose is lawful'. People convicted of assault with a razor would be jailed for a longer term, and lashed if the magistrate so deemed. Well and good, but many months of debate were yet to come before the amendment became law as parliamentary committees sweated over the fine details.

While the politicians dithered, street violence not only continued but worsened. By year's end, advocates of reform who had long supported the conservative government called for a halt to the Bavin government's procrastination. 'Stop This Dilly-Dallying,' demanded *Truth*: 'Amendments of Crimes And Vagrancy Acts Must Be Made Law: Attack That Cancer Of Crime'. The paper declared it was up to Premier Bavin to 'shake himself from his lethargy' and protect the 'law-abiding sections of the community'. 'It is useless blaming the police force; they are doing their best under awkward conditions . . . The Bavin Government has been appealed to again and again to amend the laws but always something happens to save the artists of the underworld from the treatment they merit.' *Truth* noted the amended Crimes Act had not been heard of for months. 'It is a certainty that we shall not get this legislation this year. Meanwhile, the criminals . . . aware of the ineffective state of the law and the powerlessness of the police under the present system, will make hay during the Christmas and holiday season.'

What *Truth* and the Bavin government's other accusers didn't know was that, far from sitting on his hands, Bavin had co-opted the hard man of Darlinghurst Police Station, William Mackay, to advise them on the practicalities of enforcing consorting laws. Mackay, characteristically, threw himself into the task. By 1930, due in large part to him, it would be a gaoling offence even to be in a known criminal's company. The Draconian legislation, enforced down the years by elite police officers such as Ray Blissett and Greg Brown, would go far to cleaning up the razor gangs, but, as 1929 dawned, the Consorting Law and the anti-razor Crime Amendment Bill were simply dreams on a drawing board. The twelve months until their enactment would see the bloodiest criminal conflict in Australia's history.

# 11

# The Sly-grog Queen and the Battle of Blood Alley

The year 1929 was Sydney's worst for shark attacks, and there was a spate of maulings on metropolitan beaches. A lad named Colin Stuart was savaged while standing waist deep in the surf among a crowd of bathers at Bondi. He died of horrific wounds the next day. Another youth was mauled at Maroubra Beach, and yet another died when attacked while swimming in the Parramatta River at White Bay. Then a girl was maimed at Collaroy Beach.

The human sharks of Razorhurst were tearing and ripping too. Throughout 1928 and the early months of 1929, as the lawmakers squabbled and prevaricated, casualties mounted. On 18 February 1929, Alice Preston was slashed to death by her lover Charles Wilson, who then took his own life with the murder weapon.

Ne'er-do-well William Thompson was badly wounded in a gangland shootout outside Darlinghurst's Frisco Hotel on 21 February. Guido Calletti was one of a number of locals questioned by police, but although it was well known locally that Calletti and Thompson had been feuding for months, Thompson insisted he had never before laid eyes on Calletti.

That day, too, Ellen Kelly was slashed by a man with a razor in

Crown Street, and the next day on the same street another citizen was the victim of a knife attack. It was Joe Ryan's turn on 28 February: he was sliced up in Kippax Street by a mystery razor-man.

Next came two dreadful domestic assaults. On 1 March, Hazel Sly was fatally slashed by her husband at Five Dock in Sydney's west, and on 4 March, May DePena needed multiple stitches after being cut by her husband at their Redfern home. Then, in an horrific razor attack in Francis Street, East Sydney, Roy Watson, an old adversary of Norman Bruhn, was slashed on the face, neck, shoulders and chest by a gang of three blade-men. Only a rush trip to St Vincent's Hospital prevented Watson bleeding to death on the ground where he lay.

Kate Leigh and Tilly Devine were consolidating vice empires that would endure for decades. Because both had clawed their way to the top in a hard man's milieu, they had to be tougher, smarter and nastier than the male of the species. Neither woman hesitated to use violence to protect what was theirs or to add to their fortune. Indeed, as police records attest, they delighted in doing so. As nabobs of crime, only Phil Jeffs was in their league.

Nearing fifty at the end of the 1920s, the handsome looks of Kate Leigh's youth that had had men queuing for her favours were gone. She was now squat and puffed up, her big face leathery as a saddlebag. Kate's nose was broken and a pronounced gap split her brown, tombstone-like front teeth. A one-woman hullabaloo, she swore, threatened and gave orders in a voice that was a gravelly blast. 'I'll tell ya *what*, luv!' former policeman Greg Brown recalls her bellowing. 'When she'd show her granddaughter around Surry Hills, she'd say, "Look at me little baby here, love. Doncha love her, *hey*!"'

The alcohol Kate sold was not the adulterated swill — notably 'pinkie', new wine fortified with cheap spirits that hospitalised many imbibers — on offer in so many other sly-groggeries. As stated previously, hers was premium-quality beer, wine and spirits purchased from breweries or hotels. In David Hickie's biography of the criminal John 'Chow' Hayes, *Chow Hayes — Gunman*, the old lag recalled how when he knew her in the '30s and '40s, Kate would buy beer in 200-dozen lots. If the beer cost one shilling and twopence a bottle, she'd pay the supplier one shilling and sixpence and this would include delivery of the beer to her sly-grog shops in Surry Hills. Her customers would pay her three shillings for the privilege of buying a bottle after hours. Drinkers obviously didn't mind the mark-up, because, as Hayes told Hickie, cabs and cars would be lined up for blocks around her grog shop in Lansdowne Street, their occupants waiting to gain entry. Hayes claimed that Kate paid off police to leave her alone. As former policeman Lance Hoban recalls: 'If it suited the police, they'd raid her, confiscate the liquor from the premises, and charge her. Then when she was released, it would start all over again.'

Kate was fearless and always carried a small pistol in her handbag in case she landed in strife. Although she would assault an enemy with whatever was handy. 'She wouldn't think twice about hitting a bloke over the head with a tomahawk,' laughs Ray Blissett. She was also known to use bricks and sticks on her victims' skulls. She often resorted to her fists, and was said to have a punch like a mule's kick.

Her favourite spectator sport was attending trials. She would sit in her seat at the front of the public gallery, sometimes peeling vegetables, and, like Madame Defarge in Dickens's *A Tale of Two Cities*, heckle the judge and prosecutors, and comment noisily on the defendant's chances or a witness's veracity. Her asides and bawdy quips occasionally led to her ejection, but more often reduced the courtroom to gales of laughter. Offensive behaviour was second nature to Kate Leigh. As policewoman Lillian Armfield recalled in the '50s, in Vince Kelly's *Rugged Angel*:

*She was one of the toughest to be found in this or any other country. She grew up hating the police, and particularly police-women after we were appointed, but I must say she was invariably polite to me. She was particularly sour on the Drug Bureau men because they spent a lot of time trying to catch her in possession of cocaine, which they knew she was handling, and cocaine was a dreadful social menace at the time . . . she was so cunning and experienced in every police tactic that it seemed we would never catch her with cocaine.*

Kate Leigh's gang in the late 1920s was a colourful crew. Her team included Gregory 'the Gunman' Gaffney, Bernard 'Barney' Dalton, Leigh's bodyguard and lover Wally Tomlinson, Mona Woods, May Seckold, Ivy Ryan and Vera Lewis, all of whom had been in trouble for prostitution, drug and sly-grog selling, offensive behaviour and robbery. Bill Flanagan (aka the Octopus) was her knuckle-man and chief 'chucker-outer' when sly-grog customers became unruly. Another acolyte was Bruce Higgs, a nattily dressed, baby-faced, hapless youth, who was her errand boy and chauffeured her around in her tanklike Studebaker Director car. Some said Kate had a crush on Higgs.

In November 1928, Higgs and his brother Hubert had been charged with being accessories to the murder the previous month of retired grazier Ronald Leslie near Valley Heights in the Blue Mountains. The pair's other brother, William, was charged with shooting Leslie in the back with a revolver. The siblings, who denied the charges, had been seen with Leslie on the day of his death and William Higgs's bloodstained jacket was found hidden in a log. William claimed he had lost his coat the day before. Because nobody witnessed the shooting, the charges could not be proved and the brothers were discharged.

The following February, when Bruce Higgs appeared in court to face a vagrancy count, Kate, in what would seem a dubious favour indeed, spoke up for him. Higgs was her chauffeur, she said, and for that she paid him £7–8 a week depending on any overtime he worked. He had no knowledge of her business, Kate went on, but simply drove her where she instructed him. He was a respectable young man and, she wanted the court to know, he respected his parents. When the prosecutor accused Higgs of living off the proceeds of crime, Kate exploded: 'Don't you say that! If you do, I'll stick a knife right through your heart. He's my boy.'

Higgs was let off in spite of Kate's colourful advocacy — but warned by the magistrate to find a different occupation before he found himself in truly serious trouble. But Higgs had no intention of seeking other employment, for days later he and Kate were arrested after police found them with loaded revolvers in Kate's car at 1 a.m. in Palmer Street, Darlinghurst.

On 9 February 1929, Kate, Higgs, Woods, Seckold and Flanagan were arrested in a property rented by Kate (27 Kippax Street, Surry Hills) and she was charged with 'being the keeper of houses frequented by thieves'. These houses included nos 25, 27 and 31 Kippax Street, and a house in Barcom Avenue, Darlinghurst. In court, police accused Kate of luring men to 27 Kippax Street on the pretext of selling them alcohol then doping them with spiked drinks and robbing them. (Flanagan would live up to his nickname of 'the Octopus' by picking up the slumbering men bodily and dumping them in a nearby lane.) Kate, said the police, was caught in the act when they raided no. 25 on 9 February, and she and the other accused attempted to flee by running out the back door and climbing through a hole in the fence to no. 27. As the gang piled into the house, police were waiting and nabbed them. Constable Fischer said that when he surprised Kate, she had said, 'What do you fucking-well want in my place, Fischer?' When Fischer reminded her that he had warned her many times about having undesirables such as Seckold and Woods on her premises, Kate snapped, 'It is my place, and I will have who I fucking-well like here.'

At her trial in June, as she was wont to do all her life, Kate made her accusers work hard for a conviction. 'You will admit that you are a reputed thief?' said a Sergeant Dennis.

'No, I am a person of good repute,' Kate insisted, whose criminal convictions were now approaching sixty. 'No one can say that I am a woman of ill-fame.'

Dennis tried again. 'Are you a truthful person?'

'I know what you are going to say, that I once did five years for perjury,' Kate declared, 'but anybody could make that mistake.'

In spite of her Bradman-straight bat, she was sentenced to four months' imprisonment, and Woods, Seckold and Flanagan to three. Kate appealed, but although represented by the astute and expensive Clive Evatt, Mr Arnott SM upheld the sentence and she took up residence in Long Bay Gaol from June until September.

Phil Jeffs ignited the so-called 'Battle of Blood Alley' in Eaton Avenue, Kings Cross, on 7 May 1929. Jeffs had long been tempting fate by heavily cutting cocaine with boracic acid, while charging customers the full price of the pure drug. When one Woolloomooloo gang realised Jeffs was robbing them, they challenged him and his gang to fight.

Like some wild west showdown, the two heavily armed groups gathered for battle soon after 10 p.m. in Eaton Avenue, an ill-lit lane off Bayswater Road. Locals referred to it as 'Blood Alley' due to the many muggings that took place there. (These days Eaton Avenue serves as an enclosed courtyard between blocks of flats.) For a hair-raising thirty minutes, until the police arrived in force, the gangsters went at each other with guns, razors, clubs and boots.

No brawler escaped unscathed. Jeffs's friend William Archer, proprietor of Archer's Hot Bath House in Crown Street, Woolloomooloo (where Jeffs claimed to tend baths to escape a vagrancy rap) fared worst. He was shot in the leg by one Charles Sorley and when, bleeding profusely and weakening fast, he tried to flee the melee by leaping onto the running board of a passing car, Sorley dragged him off and kicked him unconscious. At that, Jeffs and his men leapt upon Sorley and battered him. Archer was later treated at St Vincent's Hospital but when interviewed by police said he had no idea who shot him, nor did he recognise a single one of the combatants in the Eaton Avenue rumble.

When police finally arrived, Jeffs was one of a number of men arrested. At Darlinghurst Police Station he was charged with assaulting one Frederick Johns then released on £100 bail. He caught a cab to his luxurious Kensington home and went to bed.

At dawn next morning, passers-by heard groans and found Jeffs sprawled on his front lawn, bleeding from bullet wounds in his shoulder and chest. Near death in St Vincent's Hospital, he was grilled by police. Convinced that his remaining hours were few, he broke the code of silence and told the officers he had been shot by a man named Jim Taylor. Taylor and one Bill Clark, said Jeffs, had smashed in his front door while he was in bed at about 5 a.m. and demanded money. When Jeffs had refused to pay up, Taylor shot him twice. Jeffs told the police he had chased the men but collapsed on his lawn from his wounds. Taylor, short and heavy-set, and Clark were quickly arrested. But by the time of their trial, in June, Jeffs had recovered and now had a different tale to tell.

He took the stand, a jaunty gamecock in a purple suit topped by a blue overcoat. No, he swore, he had never named Taylor as his attacker to police. Those police had lied. Neither Taylor nor Clark was at his home on 8 May. What *really* happened, he said, was: 'I arrived home at 3.30 a.m. after being held at Darlinghurst Police Station. I went to bed and later was awakened, and I could just see the vision of a man standing over my bed. Two shots were fired at me, which doubled me up, and I rolled over in bed. I saw the man jump through the window. I could not say who he was, but he was tall and thin.'

Inevitably, the case was dismissed and Jeffs retreated to the New South Wales Central Coast town of Woy Woy, where he had invested in property, to recuperate from his bullet wounds. One local police-man noted wryly that since Jeffs's arrival in the holiday burg, the streets and pubs had been filled with sinister-looking men with thick necks, bent noses and dark suits.

Two months later, bullets again ricocheted on the streets of Razorhurst, this time in Darlinghurst. As far as the police could determine, a small-time crook named Joe Messenger was caught stealing from one of Kate Leigh's sly-groggeries and Kate exacted harsh punishment. A group of her gorillas, including Wally Tomlinson and, for some reason, Phil Jeffs's friend William Archer (just recovered from his Eaton Avenue licking), cornered Messenger and beat him up. With Messenger curled on the ground, trying to ward off the kicks of a dozen men, a young police constable named Jackson waded in and grabbed two of Messenger's assailants. One was Tomlinson, who did not resist arrest. The other man pulled free, drew a gun and shot at Jackson. Still gripping Tomlinson, the policeman drew his own gun and returned fire, narrowly missing William Archer, who was quickly arrested by Jackson's partner Constable Naylor. The mob, which had turned tail when Jackson arrived, now doubled back and advanced on the two constables. Jackson fired again and Charles Thompson, another of Kate's thugs, fell to the ground, his shoulder shattered. A red mist had descended on Razorhurst.

# 12

# Madam

The shrewd (and shrewish when she had to be) Tilly Devine was continuing to buy and rent premises in Palmer Street, Darlinghurst, and thereabouts, then installing hand-picked sex workers in them. In her heyday in the 1930s, she would preside over between twenty and thirty bordellos.

Typically, she'd sublet the basement, the ground floor and bedrooms upstairs to her prostitutes as places of business, but also rent at least one room to a law-abiding person so that, in a pinch, she could claim that she and her employees were not vagrants with no lawful income, but landladies. Because of the violence that regularly erupted as a result of customers' drunkenness, unfulfilled sexual expectations and gingering, Tilly had the doors and ground-floor windows of her brothels steel-reinforced to stop forced entry, and she insisted that there be at least one loaded gun at each brothel to discourage protection-mongers and aggrieved customers.

The latter included a labourer from Bathurst named Robert Powell, who told the police in January 1929 that Tilly had gingered him at a brothel in Alberta Street, Surry Hills. He claimed that while he was having sex with one of her employees, he saw Tilly sneak into the room, take his wallet from his trousers and open it. He called out to her to drop it and she fled, but later Powell discovered three £5 notes missing. At Darlinghurst Police Station, Tilly lost her temper when she heard Powell's charge. 'Do you say I robbed you?' she howled at him as he stood dumbstruck. 'You dirty, greasy mongrel! I never robbed you, and I'll not stand being pinched for it!'

Darlinghurst policewoman Maggie Baker knew Tilly and Kate. 'Kate tried to get on with Tilly,' she says today, 'but Tilly was a spiteful person. Tilly would lie. Kate never lied. If you found her out, she'd admit it. Tilly never admitted anything.'

Tilly Devine swore inventively and incessantly in a South London accent she never lost in fifty years in Australia. She was a gaudy dresser who sported twice as many rings as she had fingers. 'Aunt Til was never one for sartorial subtlety,' recalls George Parsons. Once or twice a week, she would have her hair permed into an elaborate curlicued confection that sat atop her now-hard face like a fluffy animal. She chain-smoked and consumed large amounts of liquor. Although never an alcoholic, she often drank straight from the bottle in the street and at the races at Randwick.

Tilly and Jim lived together in their Maroubra home at the corner of Torrington and Malabar roads, which was protected at all times by an armed bodyguard and Tilly's squad of yappy Pomeranian dogs. The handsome brick home was richly appointed with expensive dark wood furniture and sumptuous lounges, chairs and beds. Australian landscape paintings festooned the walls, and a chandelier sprayed sparkling showers of light on the dining table. A sideboard yawned with myriad bottles of spirits and sweet wine and cut-glass decanters, bowls and wine and spirit glasses. There was fine china in the chiffonier and the lounge room boasted a gramophone, grand piano and a £200 wireless.

Tilly's beloved Pomeranians had the run of the house, and one guest recalls seeing her blow cigarette smoke into the animals' mouths. The language she used when at her Maroubra residence was considerably more restrained than in her other, less lovely, Razorhurst haunts, where the banshee in her personality prevailed. At Torrington Road, she affected refinement and style, living out her Camberwell childhood dream of wealth and sophistication. As a boy, George Parsons often visited his aunt there and says he never heard her swear.

Today, the bones of Tilly's house remain on that corner block, but over the years subsequent owners have renovated it until it now bears no resemblance to the dwelling of Tilly's day. The original bungalow has grown a storey and the whole structure has been encased in cladding. It is almost as if the old house has been sentenced to wear a hairshirt as penance for the sins it once hosted.

As well as their Maroubra home, Tilly and Jim owned a terrace house, 191 Palmer Street, which, while never used as a brothel then, was a convenient headquarters and depository for the night's prostitution takings. At the end of their shifts her sex workers would come to Tilly's terrace to pay their boss her percentage. The prostitutes entered the backyard of 191 Palmer Street from a lane, took a key from a secret hiding place and entered what was to all intents and purposes an airlock. Not until the reinforced outer door was shut and locked behind a sex worker, would the cockatoo or lookout open the door leading into the house proper. This system ensured that police or standover men could not gain entry to Tilly's house by barging in with one of her employees.

Although not a heavy woman until late in life, Tilly was physically strong and did not shy from physical violence. Good with her fists, boots, razor and, on at least one occasion, scissors, she was arrested many times for brawling in the street with other criminals — male and female — barrow men, fish sellers, police officers and passers-by guilty of nothing more than letting their eyes linger upon the notorious Tilly a little too long. In a vicious fight with Kate Leigh's friends Elsie Kaye and Vera Lewis in a courtyard off Central Criminal Court early in 1929, she all but bit off one of her adversaries' fingers. All three women were arrested, charged and fined.

Another dust-up, with her local butcher in Maroubra, also ended with Tilly before a judge. After William Ashcroft inadvertently sold one of her lackeys rancid meat in February 1929, Devine went to his shop, plonked the chops or sausages on the counter and demanded the return of her three shillings. 'What do you mean by sending me this stinking meat?' she cried. Ashcroft insisted there was nothing wrong with the meat. Devine was not placated and threatened to take the offending produce to the Board of Health and have the butcher gaoled or fined.

Ashcroft toughed it out. 'Then bloody-well take it to the Board of Health!' he retorted. 'Now, get out of my shop and don't make a scene here.'

By now, Tilly's temper was sizzling and sparking like a loose power line in the night. 'I'll clean your place up!' she shouted, and hurled the meat at Ashcroft. She then grabbed a large, sharp knife from Ashcroft's chopping block and jabbed it at his chest. 'Give me my fucking money back, or I'll put this knife through your fucking heart.'

Ashcroft, now white with fear, handed over the three shillings but by then that was never going to save him. 'She retreated to the door,' he later told police, 'then threw the knife that struck the ice chest two feet from me.' When Tilly left the premises, the shaken shopkeeper called the police. Tilly was arrested and charged with assault with a deadly weapon. The case never came to court.

Less serious was her January 1930 altercation with a heavyweight beat sergeant named Henry Ham. The officer had had the misfortune to pass Tilly in the street and, as she usually did when she encountered a policeman, she had let fly. Ham claimed in court that Tilly's obscenity-packed harangue had ended with her bawling: 'I have diamonds and property, and a Straight Eight [Hewlett-Packard car], and I didn't get them from working either. I got them from stealing!' Ham had arrested her for offensive behaviour. Tilly, when her turn came, told Magistrate McDonald that Ham was making up the whole scenario. She had merely passed the time of day with the policeman in the street, and her parting shot, in fact, had been to remind Ham of what a good day they'd had when last they'd met, in Windsor, 'where Henry had a couple of bottles of beer with us!' Nevertheless, she was fined £1.

Tilly Devine was an implacable enemy. Once she took revenge on a corrupt policeman attempting to extort protection money from her. She arranged a fake cash drop in a public toilet in a park in Woolloomooloo. When her henchman arrived, the officer was waiting inside the toilet cubicle, as arranged. However, it was no packet of money that the lackey dropped over the toilet door, but a balloon filled with petrol. The balloon burst when it hit the floor, drenching the policeman with the inflammable liquid. Tilly's man, as she had instructed him to, then lit a match and tossed it into the cubicle. It is unknown how the policeman explained his burns to colleagues.

Although Kate Leigh's and Tilly Devine's criminal activities rarely overlapped, the former concentrating on sly grog and cocaine and the latter on prostitution, the women despised each other. Kate and Tilly's enmity was not totally professional, but also borne of fierce personal rivalry. As the only two female arch-criminals in Sydney, each strove to outdo the other, to be richer, more powerful, more feared, dress more lavishly, and get more and bigger headlines in the papers.

Policewoman Maggie Baker recalls one of her first assignments: 'Right after I started at Darlo, Miss Lillian Armfield said to me, "I want you to find out all you can about Kate Leigh and Tilly Devine." Out I went. I'd only ever come across Kate once before, although I'd heard about her for years. The first time our paths crossed was when I came upon an argument on the street in Darlinghurst, and of course it was Kate shouting and swearing at another woman. I said, "Hey you two, cut it out," and Kate glared at me and said, "Listen, be a bright copper. You'll live a lot longer if you piss off back to the station." Then, just days later, Miss Armfield detailed me to put Kate and Tilly under surveillance.

'In a lane near Palmer Street I came face to face with Tilly. She was blocking the footpath, preventing me from proceeding. She said, "You're the new copper, aren't you?" I said, "I'm a *policewoman*, and I'm new on this beat." She said, "Well, you're not comin' down this bloody street." I said, "I am." She grabbed me and started shaking me. Next thing, a woman wearing a great big black hat got off a tram. It was Kate Leigh. She came up to where Tilly was shaking me like a rag doll and, without a word, she king-hit Tilly Devine and then sat on her in the street. Then Kate, cool as you like, looked up at me and said, "Go and do what you gotta do love, I'll be here when you come back." By that time half of Darlinghurst was on the scene. All the standover blokes too. "The next time you declare her on," Kate said to Tilly, "I'll give you a second helping."

'But Tilly could handle herself, no fear. She was a dirty fighter and very strong. I saw her and Kate have a blue in Oxford Street one day. Kate was a big woman, very fat. Tilly had Kate's hat off and was pummelling her on the ground. Kate got much the worst of it. I said, "If you don't stop fighting at once, I'll sling you both into the police van and run you in."'

Mirroring the bosses' mutual hatred, Tilly and Kate's gangs disliked each other intensely. Just as violence, certainly verbal and usually physical, would ensue whenever the two women's paths crossed in Razorhurst, there would be a fracas when the foot soldiers happened upon each other. Often one henchman would make some wisecrack at a rival. That putdown would lead to a bashing which would be avenged by a slashing which would be repaid with a bullet.

In the hammer-and-tong years from the late 1920s until the early '30s, when the Leigh and Devine gangs called a truce of sorts, Kate would still send her razor crew out to disfigure Tilly's prostitutes, and Tilly would hit back by despatching her men to slash the faces of the women Kate paid to pose as prostitutes while selling cocaine. In particularly heated periods, Kate protected her street sellers by stationing rifle snipers on Surry Hills rooftops to repel Tilly's attackers. (These shooters seemingly were largely for show, for there is no record of anyone ever being shot by a rooftop marksman.) Tilly ordered squads of warriors to smash the contents and customers of Kate's sly-grog shops, and Kate's men trashed Tilly's brothels. As the battle raged, the women ratted on each other to the police, like two kids poking tongues and tittle-tattling in a hellacious schoolyard.

# 13

# Green and Calletti

Though Tilly Devine was eminently capable of taking care of herself and her business, she, like Kate Leigh, surrounded herself with a gang of hardened criminals, led by her husband, Big Jim, to safeguard her interests. The most terrifying thug on her books was Frank 'the Little Gunman' Green who, by the start of 1928, had been Nellie Cameron's lover and pimp for five months. Green's pale complexion, long face and shock of black, brilliantined hair, his hyperactive lope and rapid speech, marked him out as a distinctive Razorhurst figure. His refusal to consider the consequences of his actions was matched by a boundless delight in doing bad things.

Francis Roland Green was born in 1902 and his first recorded offence was in 1920, for using indecent language. Green was a small man, but he had an explosive temper and was lethal with gun and razor. Part of Green's terrible aura was that no one ever knew quite how far he was prepared to go to win a fight. The fact was, he would do whatever it took, up to and including murder.

In one photograph taken by a police photographer when he was in custody in the late 1920s, he wears a dark suit, white open-neck shirt and a snappy felt hat. His killer's eyes are narrowed, as if indicating to the photographer that unless he takes his bloody picture quick-smart, something unpleasant is going to happen. Green's face was scarred by razor slashes. The worst, which had required sixty stitches to repair and resulted in a lifelong L-shaped scar on his right cheek, was inflicted by a man who, Green unconvincingly told police, he knew only as 'Daring Bill'. When Green died, the coroner was shocked to find his body riddled by bullet wounds.

He was proud of the woman's breast tattooed on his right upper arm. Though he was a psychopath, drunkard and cocaine addict, women were attracted to Green and he was rarely without a lover, his most notable being Nellie Cameron.

Green strongarmed money — he called it 'paying your subscription' — from sly-groggers, prostitutes and drug traffickers. He liked to cruise in a taxi, ordering the driver to let him out at illegal betting joints and relieving the gamblers therein of their takings at gunpoint.

In Vince Kelly's *Rugged Angel*, Lillian Armfield said of Green:

> *He was the terror of a lot of Sydney's prostitutes. He wouldn't hesitate to bash up a prostitute if she didn't hand him a cut of her immoral earnings. He would cruise around brothels, illegal gaming houses, sly grog shops and SP shops, and demand a toll at revolver point from people who were reluctant to report the hold-ups to police, partly because they themselves were breaking the law, but chiefly because they dreaded the vengeance that would follow the tip-off.*

Until their bloody falling-out in the early 1930s, Green was used by Tilly to protect her brothels. Employing the Little Gunman was sure protection indeed.

Green's great rival was the equally formidable Guido Calletti. The pair, the two proud young bulls of the Sydney underworld, butted horns for the affections of Nellie Cameron for more than a decade. For years she cuckolded one suitor with the other, driving them to jealous furies, depending on whose underworld stocks were higher at that moment. Should Green be in gaol or lying low from the police, she was Calletti's girl. Should Calletti be recovering from wounds or a guest of His Majesty, she was Green's.

Green despised the foul-mouthed, garishly dressed Calletti, and the feeling was mutual, not just because of their rivalry for Cameron. To each, the other stood in the way of his being the most feared man in Razorhurst. The main difference between the two was that Green preferred to be a hired hand, part of a team, in the pay of a Tilly and Jim Devine, whereas Calletti aspired to be his own boss. But while — with Green — he was Sydney's wildest villain, Calletti was not quite savvy enough to be a gang lord. He had their propensity for violence, but lacked the tactical flair and organisational skills of Jeffs, Leigh and Devine.

Evil-tempered, swaggering and squat (he was 86 kilos and 160 centimetres), Calletti split his time between operating alone as a one-man crime wave — pimping, 'protecting' and extorting from tin-pot gamblers, sly-groggers and drug pushers, conning and mugging ordinary citizens — and leading his gang, the Darlinghurst Push. Small-time compared with the organised syndicates, which largely left the innocent public alone, Calletti's mob comprised street brawlers and standover gorillas not fussy about where they made their pile.

Calletti was capable of unrestrained ferocity. He lived to fight and was cruelly capable with any weapon — he could wield a razor with blinding speed, throw a knife accurately up to twenty metres and reputedly shoot the ash from a cigarette — not least his fists. One of his *pièces de résistance* was to join a drinker in a pub, tell a few jokes and buy him a beer or two then talk his newfound friend into accompanying him out into the night in search of more alcohol, drugs and women. The friendship would last until Calletti found a dark and deserted area. He would then attack his mark and steal his money.

Calletti, tagged in the *NSW Criminal Register of 1934* as a 'robber, gunman and gangster . . . of drunken habits and violent disposition', travelled by taxi like Green, but rarely paid. At his destination he would do a runner, or if he was feeling especially malicious, he would produce his razor then smirkingly dare the cabbie to ask for his fare. His heartland was Woolloomooloo, Kings Cross and Darlinghurst, especially Palmer Street, where most of Tilly Devine's brothels were clustered. When they passed in the street or the Tradesman's Arms Hotel, Calletti and Tilly may have nodded icily, but generally they kept out of each other's way.

Of Italian heritage, but born in Australia in 1902, Calletti grew up at Eastwood, north-west of Sydney. He was christened 'Hugh' but an uncle nicknamed him 'Guido' when he was a toddler and the name stuck. He never learned to read or write. From the age of eight, Calletti's antisocial behaviour saw him sentenced to terms in reformatories in Mittagong and Gosford, and at age thirteen he was classified 'uncontrollable' by a children's court.

Calletti wed while still a teen and fathered a son, but the marriage broke up. At twenty-two, he was confined to Gosford Farm Home for carrying an unlicensed pistol. By age twenty-five in 1927, he was leading the Darlinghurst Push, whose fifteen to twenty razor-carrying members bowed to his superior skills as gunman, garrotter and razorman.

When police cracked down on Calletti, he moonlighted as a labourer, fished for prawns or picked peas in then-rural Eastwood until the heat was off. For years, he shared a Darlinghurst fruit barrow with fellow no-good Scotty McCormack (later to die, like many others, romancing Dulcie 'the Angel of Death' Markham). The arrangement worked well. When Calletti was in prison, McCormack donned the fruiterer's apron, and when McCormack was incarcerated Calletti manned the barrow.

Early on, Calletti recognised the profits to be made from pimping, and 'represented' a number of prostitutes. 'Pay me money and I'll protect you from other pimps, and if you refuse *I'll* bash you,' he said. Calletti made it his business to know all about the women of the streets, and before approaching them he'd assess their potential for making him money.

As his success with the coveted Nellie Cameron attests, Calletti, like Green, was a successful womaniser, in spite of his chronic bad temper, alcoholism and cheap, showy clothes. He was an accomplished dancer in an era when waltzing and foxtrotting to live combos or gramophone recordings of the Paul Whiteman Orchestra playing 'Whispering' and 'Deep Purple' was a popular pastime of Sydney's young dash-abouts. But Calletti was rarely content to dance the night away. Dance hall proprietors knew that if he was on the floor there'd be trouble sooner or later. He amused himself by singling out an attractive woman, then insulting her dancing partner, leaving the unfortunate man with the choice of backing down in humiliation or challenging Calletti to fight. The latter option ended with the fellow bleeding in the alley outside.

Although operating on a smaller scale than Jeffs, Leigh and Devine, Calletti enforced his rule, as did they, with violence. He swiftly dealt with gangsters from other areas who sought a piece of his action. The Ultimo Push once ventured into Darlinghurst and robbed some of Calletti's prostitutes. The following day, Calletti and fifteen henchmen arrived at the Ultimo Push's favourite hotel and beat and slashed the rival mob in the bar.

The late 1920s was a purple patch in Calletti's criminal career. In 1929, he was charged with razoring a man named Curran in a Darlinghurst alley, but denied the charge. In court, Calletti laughed in the face of the prosecutor, saying he'd had a punch-up ('fair and square') with Curran, but he had not slashed him. Curran's terrible facial injuries, smirked Calletti, were just scratches caused by 'a ring I used to wear in them days'. Calletti was not punished for cutting up

Curran, principally because Curran, after a visit from Calletti, decided not to testify. Curran later told how Calletti knocked on his door, a wide grin on his usually dour face. The thug had extended his hand and chuckled, 'Now, I don't suppose you're going to make it too hard for me, are you, Curran? I want you to go to the police and say it wasn't me who attacked you. Tell them you mixed me up with somebody else. Someone with a name that sounds like "Calletti".' Curran said Calletti left him in no doubt about what would happen to him if he did otherwise.

While he was on bail for the Curran assault, Calletti found himself in more strife when he brawled with two policemen. He king-hit one and ran off, but the officers tracked him down and hoisted him from his hiding place. As they were escorting him to Darlinghurst Police Station, Calletti bit one's finger to the bone. When he faced that charge, Calletti called the officer a liar. 'The policeman's finger was cut,' he said, 'when his fist made contact with my teeth while he was assaulting me in custody.' Calletti's skilled lawyers were able to stir up sufficient doubt in the jury's mind to get their client off lightly.

Then Calletti fell out with another criminal, named Eric Connolly, who had made the mistake of falling in love with Nellie Cameron and living with her briefly. On 16 February 1929, a slanging match between the pair turned violent, and Connolly fired five bullets into Calletti. Amazingly, none caused serious damage. Cameron bandaged Calletti's flesh wounds, and the following morning, at 2 a.m., he went to a party in Womerah Avenue, Darlinghurst, called Connolly outside, and shot him down. Connolly was rushed to hospital for emergency treatment for a bullet wound in his stomach, and Calletti returned to his flat in Barcom Avenue, Darlinghurst.

At eleven the next morning, police officers, acting on information received from two friends of Connolly (one a street singer with a withered arm named Hardy, the other Eadie Hudson), burst into Calletti's apartment. Inspector Lynch later claimed he saw Calletti fumbling with a revolver on the lounge, trying to hide it under a pillow. When Lynch accused Calletti of shooting Connolly, Calletti denied it, said he didn't even know Connolly had been shot. He said he had returned at 4 a.m. from a party at Kate Leigh's daughter Eileen's house and gone straight to bed. At this point, recalled Lynch, Nellie Cameron came into the room in a sleep-dishevelled state and announced to the officers that she could explain everything. She had found the gun, she said, a six-chambered revolver with five live bullets in it and one discharged shell, in the street wrapped in brown paper and had planned to hand it in to police later that day. Lynch, skilled in forensics, knew at once that the gun was the one that had been used to shoot Connolly.

In spite of Cameron's alibi, police arrested Calletti and took him to Darlinghurst Police Station. There, after Hardy and Hudson, seemingly unaware of Calletti's underworld standing, testified against him, he was charged with shooting Connolly with intent to murder. When the detectives had laid the charges, they left Calletti alone for a moment. That was all it took. He approached Hardy and Hudson and threatened their lives. The frightened pair left the station. With no witnesses for the prosecution — the badly wounded Connolly, of course, didn't squeal — the case against Calletti collapsed.

By the time he was shot dead in 1939, Calletti would have appeared in court in New South Wales, Queensland and Victoria fifty-six times for a variety of crimes, most often assault and consorting. Police believe he may have killed as many as four men.

# 14

# Shootout at Maroubra

At 10 p.m. on 17 July 1929, Tilly and Jim Devine were driving in Oxford Street, Paddington, when they were hailed by a man named George Gibson who told them that Frank Green, whom the Devines were due to meet in half an hour, had been shot and wounded earlier in the evening by Kate Leigh hireling Gregory 'the Gunman' Gaffney (aka George Gaffney and Raymond Neill). Gibson had taken Green to Sydney Hospital to be patched up. Then he ran into Gaffney who told Gibson, 'I shot the bastard and I am going out to go on with him and Devine tonight.' Devine was incredulous, but, Gibson assured him it was no empty threat. 'He's got an automatic and he means business.'

The Devines then drove to Brasch's Corner in Woolloomooloo where they had arranged to meet Green and their bodyguard Sid McDonald (known to the police as 'a very violent man'), who was living with them at Maroubra. Green and McDonald were waiting, and when the pair climbed into the Devines' car, Green collapsed. He gasped that he had been shot in the shoulder and was weak from blood loss. He was sure that Gaffney, twenty-five, a brown-haired, blue-eyed desperado with a badly broken nose, would make a second attempt on his life that night. It was decided that Green should lie low at the Devines'.

On the drive to Maroubra, Green explained that the trouble had started two days before when Nellie Cameron had brawled with another woman in the grounds of Central Police Court. Green had stood up for his lover and found himself in a fist fight with Leigh's man Gaffney, who happened to be the boyfriend of Cameron's adversary. The fight had been broken up by police and the combatants dispersed, but not before Green and Gaffney vowed to take vengeance on the other. Gaffney had struck first, ambushing Green and Sid McDonald in Woolloomooloo that evening. As the pair had walked along Nicholson Street, a car stopped beside them. Gaffney and another man sprang out. Gaffney had shot Green at point-blank range while his partner had knocked McDonald to the ground and kicked him in the stomach.

En route to Torrington Road, Jim Devine stopped at an associate's home and emerged with a short-magazine Lee Enfield .303 service rifle and a handful of steel-jacketed bullets. His own arsenal, that he kept cleaned, oiled and loaded at Torrington Road, had been confiscated just the previous day by the police (who fined him £50 for having no firearms licence).

Meanwhile, Gaffney had learned that Green had gone to the Devines' home to recuperate. Knowing that as soon as Green was able he would come gunning for him, Gaffney collected Kate Leigh's lover and bodyguard, the tall, horse-faced, mushroom-haired Wally Tomlinson, and Bernard 'Barney' Dalton, another Leigh gang member, then hailed a taxi and set off for Maroubra to finish the job.

At about midnight, Tilly and Jim Devine, Green and McDonald were talking and drinking and listening to the wireless in the Devines' living room, waiting for the attack they knew was coming. Suddenly the Pomeranians howled. Then a gruff voice rang from the street: 'Come outside!'

Jim Devine grabbed his gun and said to McDonald, 'Switch the lights off. This might be the team now.' McDonald did so. Grasping his loaded and cocked rifle, Devine stepped onto his front verandah and peered under its canvas blind, straining to see who was outside. As Devine's eyes grew accustomed to the gloom, he saw a figure, whom he recognised as Gregory Gaffney, brandishing a pistol.

Gaffney bawled, 'I want Green's blood,' and started to clamber over the front fence.

Devine shouted, 'Don't climb over that fence or I'll shoot.'

'Go on, shoot, then,' retorted Gaffney. 'I've got plenty of mates with me.' He kept coming.

McDonald would later tell the Coroner's Court: 'Devine fired and I looked under the canvas blind and saw a man stagger away from the fence. He had a pistol in his hand and he fell down on the road.'

Gregory Gaffney lay groaning, a pool of blood widening around him. Tomlinson or Dalton shot at Devine who returned fire, ripping off another seven shots in their general direction. The street resounded with the pops and cracks of revolver and rifle fire. There was another cry, followed by pained cursing. Devine had hit Tomlinson in the arm. Dalton fled.

When it seemed safe to do so, Jim Devine and Sid McDonald went outside to inspect the carnage. 'Don't go,' cautioned Tilly. '[Gaffney] may be kidding, and let one go at you when you get close.' Still, the two men, with Tilly and Frank Green at their rear, ventured out of the front gate.

They found Gaffney with a gaping wound in his chest. McDonald told the police later that he offered Gaffney a sip of brandy. Gaffney thanked him and said that he wouldn't tell the police who shot him: 'I'll be solid.' The police arrived, summoned by the Devines' terrified neighbours, and found Gaffney mortally wounded. True to his word, he told officers neither his name nor who had gunned him down before he slipped into unconsciousness. In a house down the road, Wally Tomlinson lay on the kitchen floor with a bullet in his arm. Tomlinson recovered. Gaffney died in hospital at 4.30 that morning.

The broadsheet *Sydney Morning Herald*, then a staid newspaper of record, had never reported crime in *Truth*'s florid style, but its account of the 2 August inquest into Gaffney's death, at which both the Devine and Leigh factions gathered to glower and catcall at each other, could have been ripped straight from the yellow pages of the tabloid. Under the heading 'Scenes at Gang War Inquest', the *Herald* reported:

> *Evil-looking men with battered faces rubbed shoulders with bejewelled women in fur coats at the Coroner's Court yesterday when Mr May inquired into the gang duel which occurred at Maroubra on July 17. Seldom have so many criminals convicted of serious offences, some of them with a notorious police history, assembled in the public portion of the Court. Factions between them were noticeable. Belligerent glances were freely exchanged.*

Tilly Devine stole the show. She took the stand dripping with jewellery and decked in rich shades of brown. Giving evidence, she gesticulated showily to ensure that the throng got an eyeful of her ring-laden fingers.

'What was the state of your nerves at the time of the shooting?' one lawyer asked her.

'I was excited, more than frightened,' she beamed, as she recalled the mayhem.

Coroner May found Jim Devine had a case to answer and had to stand trial for slaying Gregory Gaffney. But at his murder trial, Big Jim was found not guilty on the grounds that he was defending himself, his wife and his home. He, Tilly, McDonald, Green and Nellie Cameron and more than 100 well-wishers partied at Torrington Road that night. They consumed chicken, ham, beer and French champagne, then danced and sang till dawn.

August 1929 was not an auspicious time for Kate Leigh. She was still languishing in Long Bay Gaol after the Kippax Street bust, and was seething over the murder of her man Gaffney and the wounding of Tomlinson by the Devine mob. With their enemy on the backfoot, the Devines went for Kate's jugular.

On the afternoon of 8 August, members of Tilly's gang armed with guns and razors converged on one of the Leigh stamping grounds, Kellett Street, Kings Cross, then a reviled strip row of hovels, dingy tenements and bawdy houses. The opposing forces eyed each other in a goading way. They lurked in doorways, and sat in the gutter drinking from bottles and snorting cocaine.

As the chilly afternoon turned to a freezing night, the tension mounted. Tilly's mob's jibes and threats were returned by Kate's men. Bottles and rocks were hurled. By 10 p.m. a pitched battle between the drunk and seething gangsters, now spitting and snarling at each other like alley cats, was inevitable. One gutsy Kellett Street resident, J.C. Bendrodt, called from his first-floor window for the men to kindly stop their vile language and breaking bottles and to please go away. Bottles rained upon him. Bendrodt ducked away from his window then returned with a revolver which he fired over his tormentors' heads. The mobsters shot back. Their gunfire lit the fuse, and the forty-odd mobsters of the Leigh and Devine crews then tore into each other with razors, guns, fists, boots, bottles and rocks.

In a premeditated attack designed to hit hard at Kate Leigh, a bunch of Devine men ganged up on Kate's young driver and confidante, Bruce Higgs, during the skirmish. Two held Higgs by the arms while others sliced him with their razors. Higgs received slashes over each eye, four on his forehead, one on each cheek, and his arms and hands were shredded. The injuries he received were so bad he would carry them for the rest of his life, but still he refused to name his attackers when later questioned by police in hospital.

Higgs was the major casualty but in all more than a dozen, from both factions, were badly wounded in the Kellett Street riot. Not one, however, identified their assailant to police. In the wake of the battle, one senior detective opined, 'The police force would welcome a solution of the problem of how to break down the wall of silence that invariably surrounds underworld crimes.'

# 15

# 1929–1930: The War Gets Personal

As they licked their wounds after the battle of Kellett Street, the Leigh and Devine camps continued to exchange threats and insults. Both sides stockpiled firearms and itched for an opportunity to use them. The word on the street was strong that Kate Leigh had offered Wally Tomlinson and Barney Dalton many thousands of pounds to kill Jim Devine and Frank Green as payback for the murder of Gregory Gaffney.

On 5 September 1929, the police, fearing new blood-letting, raided the Devines' home and confiscated a cache of revolvers and rifles. The Devines' bodyguard, Sid McDonald, was still in situ, shacked up on the verandah of the Torrington Road house. Frank Green was living in a back bedroom. The streets of Razorhurst crackled with the anticipation of gangland Armageddon. The inevitable happened on 9 November, and the instigator was Frank Green, who, having recovered from being shot by Gaffney, had made it his mission to destroy Kate Leigh's gang.

At about 4.30 p.m., Tomlinson (whose own arm wound from the Torrington Road shootout was also on the mend) was drinking with Dalton, and their cohorts Edward Brady and a razor-man named

Charles Connors, in Sharland's Strand Hotel on the corner of William and Crown streets. Also in the bar were Phil Jeffs's friends the bathhouse proprietor William Archer and Tom Kelly, Razor Jack Hayes's nemesis. Green entered the saloon alone. He sauntered up to the bar and ordered whisky. Then, with a murderous leer, he rounded on Tomlinson and Dalton and declared loudly that he was happy to accommodate trouble if anyone cared to give him any. Furthermore, he said, Big Jim Devine was outside and ready to back him up. The Leigh men were unsettled by Green's bravado and backed off. Green left.

At closing time, the drinkers were shunted out onto the footpath. When Tomlinson and Dalton emerged, Green, who had been lurking outside with Jim Devine in the early-evening shadows, walked briskly to within a metre of Kate's men and yelled, 'Cop this, you bastards!' He fired his long-barrelled revolver three times at Tomlinson and Dalton.

Dalton, shot through the heart, screamed and crashed to the ground, where he sprawled dead. Tomlinson did not seek cover but ran to where Dalton lay, making himself an easy target for Green. 'You cop this, too!' snarled the Little Gunman and shot Tomlinson, who, once more, took a bullet in his left arm. He went down. Green wasn't finished. He stood over Tomlinson and levelled his revolver at him. Tomlinson looked up at Green from the gutter and gasped, 'Have another go.' Green obliged, and shot Tomlinson in the chest. Tomlinson, his right lung punctured, spluttered blood and lay still.

Green and Devine tore from the scene, Green throwing his gun over the back fence of a house in Palmer Street. Police arrived, and took Tomlinson's dying deposition. Believing himself mortally wounded and with reprisals the least of his worries, Tomlinson named Green as the man who had shot him and Jim Devine as his accomplice. Tom Kelly drove Tomlinson to St Vincent's Hospital where, to the amazement of all, he pulled through. For the next weeks, Kate Leigh was often at St Vincent's, clucking over her recuperating henchman.

Barney Dalton's wake was held at his Woolloomooloo home a couple of days after his death. Family and friends gathered to eat and drink to his memory. There was little show of sadness as the mourners convivially helped themselves to bottles of beer and port, and sandwiches. Their children sat around eating corned beef and drinking lemonade. In an adjoining bedroom, visible from the lounge room, Dalton lay in an open coffin, his face rouged a weird pink.

The day after the Strand Hotel shooting, Jim Devine was arrested on the Princes Highway, near Waterfall, south of Sydney. He denied involvement, 'I'm not mixed up with gangsters. I come from a respectable family,' he protested, but allowed that he did know the shooting was 'on'. Devine was charged with the attempted murder of Tomlinson and refused bail. A police dragnet scoured Green's haunts, but he had gone to ground.

One officer was detailed to follow Green's lover Nellie Cameron, and the shadow was on the job when, on 3 December, Cameron, carrying a suitcase, caught a train to the southern Sydney beach suburb of Cronulla and stumbled furtively through scrub to a shack at Boat Harbour where she remained for some hours. When the police tail reported her movements to headquarters, detectives surmised she'd been taking provisions to Green. That night, a squad crept through the undergrowth to the shack. They banged on the door. 'Open up! It's the police,' shouted Inspector Lynch.

'Don't shoot, we have no guns,' called Green from inside.

Moments later, Sid McDonald opened the door, and he and Green were hurled to the floor and handcuffed.

While Green was in Long Bay Gaol awaiting the January coronial inquiry into Dalton's death, Guido Calletti, as if unwilling to be upstaged by his sworn enemy, muscled *his* way onto Sydney crime's centre stage. In the early hours of Christmas morning, 1929, a prostitute named Maisie Wilson was walking in Palmer Street when she was approached by a group of men who asked her to accompany them to a nearby house for a drink. When the tiny blonde refused, the men dragged her into a derelict house, beat her, then raped her.

When they had gone, Wilson staggered out of the house into a lane and collapsed. A cruising taxi driver saw her lying on the ground and rushed her to hospital. Witnesses to Wilson's abduction identified Guido Calletti, Sid Kelly and a young crook named Aubrey Cummins as her attackers. The trio was rounded up, charged with indecent assault and faced court in the first week of the new decade.

By then, however, Maisie Wilson, the chief prosecution witness, had vanished. In her absence, the case collapsed and Calletti, Kelly and Cummins walked free. As the trio left Central Criminal Court, a newspaper photographer tried to take their picture. Calletti, and Sid's brother Tom grabbed the photographer while Sid tore the man's expensive camera from his grasp, threw it onto the footpath and jumped upon it. A photo, snapped by another pressman, captures Calletti and the small, sharp-featured Kellys wearing well-cut light-coloured suits, high collars and snappy fedoras, manhandling the photographer in the clear light of day in busy Oxford Street.

When the intrepid *Truth* tracked down Maisie Wilson, lying low in Brisbane, she left its reporter in no doubt that Calletti and Kelly had warned her of the consequences of testifying against them. 'I came to Brisbane to be out of the way,' she said when doorstopped by the reporter. 'I don't want to be slashed. I know a certain mob, and you don't. I don't want to go back. They'll kill me. Oh God, they'll get me if I say anything. Before the case I got whispers of what they'd do to me if I gave evidence.'

Unfazed, Calletti and Sid Kelly continued on their nefarious way. The Kelly brothers' dealings took them to Melbourne and it was not long before they were in more strife, the consequences of which left

Sid Kelly wishing he'd never ventured south of the border. On 30 August 1930, Kelly's lover Poppy Kirdy argued with a man named John Penfold in Albert Street, Melbourne. Penfold slapped Kirdy's face and she told Kelly, who went after Penfold. The two men fought, and Penfold knocked Kelly down. Picking himself up off the ground, Kelly snarled, 'I'll fix you for this!'

And he did. That night, just before midnight, the Kelly brothers, a musclebound friend named Joe Sinclair and two other men broke into Penfold's home in Young Street, Fitzroy. The Kellys beat Penfold and held him down. Sinclair then razor-slashed a twelve-centimetre gash across his face.

Penfold reported the Kellys and Sinclair to police. Tom Kelly and Sinclair were convicted of assaulting Penfold and fined, but the instigator, Sid Kelly, said Magistrate Book at the men's trial, had committed 'one of the cruelest outrages that has ever come before the Criminal Court. Having been worsted in a fight with Penfold, you threatened to "fix" him later. What you did was not in the heat of passion. After calm and deliberate thought you went with other men to the house in Young Street for the purpose of seeing Penfold.' As the magistrate lambasted him, Kelly grinned defiantly. But what Book said next cracked the criminal's composure: 'Sidney Kelly, I sentence you to five years hard labour . . . and fifteen strokes of the lash.' The gangster swayed in the dock, his face suddenly parchment-white. Had police not seized him and led him away, he would have fallen.

At the inquest into Barney Dalton's murder at a packed Sydney Coroner's Court in January 1930, Wally Tomlinson nervously confirmed to Coroner E.A. May that Frank Green had killed Dalton. But Devine, he had now decided, was not at the scene. From across the room, Green fixed Tomlinson with his trademark laser glare, the one he usually reserved for those he was about to maim.

Inevitably, Coroner May announced, to whoops of joy from Tilly Devine (dressed in vibrant green, her fingers a-flash with diamond rings) that because Jim Devine could not be positively placed at the scene of the shooting, he must go free. Why other witnesses of the shooting were not called as well to place Devine at the scene is unexplained.

Not all the sensations were confined to the courtroom. During the hearing, as Tomlinson left the court for a lunch break, he was attacked by Green and Sid McDonald. Green was furious that Tomlinson had squealed only on him and not Devine. Police dragged Green and McDonald away before they could do much more than inflict a few bruises on Tomlinson's face. The Leigh henchman, however, knew that from now on he was a marked man.

The coroner found that Green must stand trial for murder. Things looked grim for the Little Gunman because as well as Tomlinson's incriminating evidence against him, a Constable Mills had overheard Green bragging to another prisoner while in custody on 3 December. 'That bastard Tomlinson picked me today,' Green had said. 'He never hesitated. It's a pity I didn't get him as well as Dalton while I was at it.'

While Green, scowling in handcuffs, was returned to Long Bay Gaol to await his trial, Jim Devine strutted from the court grinning broadly, Tilly clinging to his arm. One reporter noted that Big Jim had an angry crop of boils on his thick neck.

Frank Green's murder trial began in March. It was played out before an overflowing gallery, which included Kate Leigh, released from Long Bay the previous September, and her daughter Eileen, other underworld figures and the curious public.

Though he feared for his life, Tomlinson, having come so far, had no choice but to testify against Green. He told the court, 'I heard Green say to Dalton, "Cop this, you bastard!" and he then shot him down in cold blood. I went to pick him up and got shot myself.' But again he insisted that Devine was not present and added, contradicting the evidence of years of violence between them, 'Jim and I have always been the best of friends.'

This was too much for one lawyer defending Green: 'Tomlinson has been identified as one of a number of men who set out to kill Devine at his home last July, and when he tells the court that he and Devine are the best of friends, he makes such an inroad on our intelligence that it makes us wonder if we are in Callan Park or a court of law.'

Green's legal team's strategy was to destroy the credibility of the chief prosecution witness. Green's chief counsel, Mr Windeyer, described Tomlinson as 'a man of low criminal cunning'. And, it seemed, the Devine camp had called in favours or splashed around money on Green's behalf, for appearing for the defence were William Archer, Edward Brady, Tom Kelly and Charles Connors — who wore a high-collared coat in the dock to cover an ugly razor scar on his neck. Though men of the worst character, they managed to impress the jury. Each said he had been drinking in the Strand Hotel when Green stalked in and on the street when the shooting took place. Each swore on the Bible either that the shooter was not Frank Green but someone they couldn't recognise, or that they hadn't seen who had fired the bullets.

When he took the stand, Green, who would hang if convicted, gave the performance of his life. Like an actor in a high-camp silent melodrama, he wrung his hands and swooned histrionically, and swore to God he didn't shoot either Dalton or Tomlinson. The policeman Mills had made a mistake, he insisted. What he'd told the prisoner on 3 December had not been 'It's a pity *I* didn't get [Tomlinson] as well as Dalton,' but 'It's a pity *they* didn't get him . . . ' He didn't know for certain who killed Dalton, but he *had* seen the murder weapon before.

'Where?' demanded the prosecutor.

'At the Devines' home,' said Green.

This last-ditch attempt to get off the hook by creating the impression that Jim Devine may have been the shooter had the desired effect on the jury and helped save Green from the noose, but, whether in his desperation he realised it or not, his words made instant and implacable enemies of his old friends. At the end of the trial, the jury, confused by the wildly conflicting evidence, could not reach a verdict. They were discharged and a new trial set for June. It was back to Long Bay Gaol for the Little Gunman.

Meanwhile, although feeling that Green had doublecrossed them, the Devine camp had made it clear that for shelfing the Little Gunman Tomlinson had to die. It was openly acknowledged in Razorhurst that there was a contract out on Kate's man. Even the press knew. *Truth* ran an article headed 'Is He Marked For Death?':

> . . . *The chief witness for the Crown is Walter Tomlinson. It has come to the knowledge of* Truth *and the police that he will be done away with before the trial comes on. As chief witness in a case where a man is arraigned on a capital charge, this must not be permitted to happen. The threats — no idle threats either — constitute such a sensational possibility that the police must take the utmost precautions to ensure his safety in the interests of justice.*

The tabloid's fears were well founded. Just days after the stalemate of Frank Green's first murder trial, a gang began a series of attacks on Kate Leigh's home at 104 Riley Street, where, it was widely believed, Wally Tomlinson was hiding. In fact Tomlinson was elsewhere — at Cronulla in a friend's house. On 20 March 1930, four men burst into

Kate's house and demanded that she lead them to Tomlinson. When she replied that he was not on the premises, they punched her and smashed her furniture. Kate did not report them to the police, but did buy a new rifle and twenty cartridges.

On 26 March, the gang returned. Roused from her sleep by the din of someone trying to kick in her front door, Kate flung open her bedroom window and demanded to know who was there. A voice rang out: 'I'm going to kill Tomlinson. Fetch him out.'

Kate bellowed that he wasn't there and furthermore she had a gun, 'and if you come near me, I'll use it'.

'We want Tomlinson!'

'I won't tell you again. If you come into my house, I'll shoot you. Now, fuck off!' In reply, the marauders threw rocks at Kate's window and fired a shot into the air. This time, she called the police, who all the next day cruised Riley Street on the lookout for her tormentors.

It is unknown whether the gang who took on Kate Leigh — John 'Snowy' Prendergast, his brother Joe, Ed Runnails and Fred Lee — were in the pay of the Devines or Frank Green. It is possible that they were, because Snowy Prendergast, twenty-six, the leader, was friendly with Green. Yet it is possible, too, that the Prendergast outfit was trying to make a name for itself and ingratiate itself with Green and the Devines by punishing an underworld pariah. Prendergast was a Kings Cross hoodlum who bored his associates rigid with his constant skiting that he was afraid of nothing.

On 27 March, the young braggart found himself fatally out of his depth. At around 7 a.m., Prendergast and his men battered in Kate's reinforced back door with a large piece of timber, and piled into the kitchen, where they smashed and upturned more furniture. With pistols drawn, they then approached the stairs that led to the first-floor bedroom where they believed Tomlinson was hiding. Suddenly, Prendergast came face to face with Kate Leigh. She was standing on the third step of the stairs in her nightdress, and her rifle was cocked and aimed at Prendergast. 'If you come another inch,' she rasped, 'I'll shoot you.'

Prendergast laughed at her and advanced. There was no second warning. Kate shot Prendergast in the stomach. He fell heavily. Ignoring their boss's pleas that they take him with them, his henchmen fled into the dawn. Prendergast managed to pull himself up off the kitchen floor slippery with his blood and, clutching his stomach, staggered out the back door and into a lane, where he collapsed again.

When the police arrived, summoned by neighbours who had heard the rifle blast, they found the gut-shot bandit writhing in agony, gasping that he would murder 'bloody Kate Leigh' for what she had done to him. The object of his ire stood calmly by in the lane. She told the officers: 'This is one of them. I shot him. They tried to get into my place. Look what the bastards did. They broke up all my furniture.' Then, to Prendergast, 'I shot you down, and your mates deserted you.'

Barely conscious now, Prendergast whispered to her, 'Finish me off, you bastard. I'm dying.' And indeed he was.

Kate was arrested and charged with murder at Sydney Quarter Sessions. She pleaded not guilty. It had been a matter of self-defence, she said, she was protecting her life and property. Besides, she'd not meant to kill Prendergast, just incapacitate him by shooting him in the leg, but her aim had been bad. To no one's surprise, the jury acquitted her.

At the end of her life, Kate would muse: 'I've never been proud of shooting that chap and I've never stopped saying a prayer for the repose of the blackguard's soul. That's because I'm religious, I s'pose.'

Frank Green's second trial for the murder of Barney Dalton began on Monday, 9 June 1930. He entered the court thin and sickly-looking after his months in prison. In the public gallery was his wife Dolly, mother of his infant daughters Eileen and Norma. Dolly Green had been given the week off from her job at a Woolloomooloo custard-powder factory to provide moral support for her husband. Again, Tomlinson took the stand for the Crown and repeated his version of the events of 9 November. Green's lawyer, Mr Windeyer, told the court he thought it strange that 'of all the persons in a position to see who did the shooting, Tomlinson is the only one to blame my client.'

Green, in the dock, contradicted Tomlinson's every charge. 'On my word of honour, gentleman,' he lied in a strong voice that belied his wasted appearance, 'I was not in the hotel after 4.30 p.m.' He went on, his voice quavering with emotion, 'I don't know why Tomlinson has given this evidence against me. I don't think he knows himself. Unless it is because of a woman . . . a woman with whom he has lived, a woman who hates me. Kate Leigh.'

Summing up, trial judge Justice James expressed his hope that the underworld war of the past two years would end. Addressing the large number of criminals in the gallery — Tilly and Jim Devine, Kate Leigh, Sid McDonald, Tom Kelly, Nellie Cameron — he implored: 'Do something to clean this thing up. If you have a quarrel amongst yourselves, then get together and settle it. If it is necessary to fight, fight with your fists.'

At this, Green, the most lethal gunman in Sydney, piped up, 'I *have* always fought with my fists, Your Honour.'

Justice James, noting that 'it is very difficult to convict in a case like this,' acquitted Green.

Next morning a reporter from *Truth* called on the Green family at their flat at 21 Harmer Street, Woolloomooloo, where in years past the poet Henry Lawson had lived. With mind-rattling hypocrisy, the reporter from the paper which prided itself on being the scourge of the criminal classes fawned on the killer, razor slasher and pimp of Nellie Cameron:

> Truth *found a happy family reunion at the little terrace house in the little side street. The principal figure, the acquitted man,*

*who, if the verdict had gone the other way, would at the hour have been standing at the brink of Eternity, seemed just as much at his ease as anyone else.*

*Since his incarceration seven months ago, he has lost considerable weight. In his crumpled morning suit for home wear, collarless, but shaved and groomed, he was breakfasting in royal style on much bacon and many eggs. A veritable swarm of children climbed all over him, and he gave the impression, at first glance, of a young professional man lolling in the seclusion of his home.*

*For a few minutes, he got rid of the kiddies when an 'apple on a stick' man trundled his cart past the door. He shouted apples on a stick for the crowd, and returned to his breakfast. 'It's wonderful to be back again with the kiddies,' he said, 'and I did not really realise before what a grand little mate I had in my wife who kept her end up all that while on her own. Jobs aren't too plentiful, but I hope to land one soon.' 'And they have been wonderful to me at the factory, too,' said his wife. When Green returned home on the previous evening and the kisses were over, his daughter's first question was, 'Daddy, are you going to buy me those Zu-Zus [a popular sweet of the day] now?' At that,* Truth *left them to their various contentments.*

To the surprise of few, the newspaper's saintly depiction of Frank Green left it, like the breakfasting mobster, with egg on its face. Within months the Little Gunman was back on the rampage.

# 16
# The Law Fights Back

The year 1930 was one of legendary feats, a year when Sydneysiders seemed always to be throwing their felt Akubras into the air. They threw them when British aviator Amy Johnson touched down in Darwin after her epic solo flight from London. They threw them when Australia won the Ashes series against England after a succession of massive scores by Don Bradman. Up went the hats again when the north and south spans of the Sydney Harbour Bridge kissed in August. And when Phar Lap won the Melbourne Cup on 4 November despite having been shot at by hoodlums and being loaded with a 9.12 pound (4.1 kilogram) race handicap, he received a telegram from fans: 'If you could only stand up on your hind legs and talk, we'd make you prime minister of Australia.'

In January 1930, beleaguered Sydneysiders had something else to cheer about. The *New South Wales Vagrancy (Amendment) Act 1929* was passed with bipartisan support and came into operation. To the people of Sydney, perplexed and frightened by the unprecedentedly high level of street crime in general and the tit-for-tat violence of the Leigh–Devine gang war in particular, the Act was welcomed much as settlers in the Old West under Indian attack welcomed the arrival of the cavalry.

The Consorting Clause, a part of the Act, was formulated to clear the East Sydney streets of gangs. It specified heavy penalties — including six-month gaol terms — for anyone who 'habitually consorts with reputed thieves, or prostitutes, or vagrant persons who have no visible or legal means of support'. If criminals were prevented from associating with each other, they could hardly form a gang. Villains did not even have to be committing an offence. In effect, a policeman coming upon two or more citizens of proven bad character chatting on a corner or in a pub about Easts' chances against the Newtown Bluebags on Saturday, or last night's radio quiz, could, if he wished, haul them to gaol. The mere suspicion that a person was a vagrant was good enough reason to make an arrest.

'The Consorting Clause was the best thing ever,' says former detective Bill Harris. 'It broke up the razor gangs, because we'd see these criminals going about, see them together or even near each other, and we could say, "I'm booking you for consorting." But while it stopped the street crime, it didn't stop criminals getting together in private and planning their schemes.'

The Consorting Clause gave New South Wales police almost unlimited powers to arrest, and judges to imprison, any person who met with associates of whom an officer disapproved. It was one of the most authoritarian measures taken against organised crime in a Western democracy. Under supporting clauses of the Act, police testimony of such associations or lack of lawful income constituted prima facie evidence of illegal activity and could stand as the basis for conviction.

The government gave the new law bite. Also enacted in 1930 was the *Crimes Amendment Bill*, which provided for automatic six-month sentences for anyone unlawfully possessing a razor. Those convicted of using that razor as a weapon would be gaoled *and* flogged. Tom Wickham and Wharton Thompson, the overworked two-man Drug Bureau, got much-needed reinforcements. A special vice unit, which would evolve into Frank 'Bumper' Farrell's legendary 21 Division, was created to put the boot into sly-groggers, illegal gamblers, drug barons and their distributors, prostitutes and their pimps. At last, the politicians had given the police the ammunition they required to quell the criminal rampage.

And the Consorting Squad was formed. It was a crack force of streetwise cops who, like Ray Blissett, who would one day head the squad, were hard-headed, hard-fisted policemen, generally as tough as the gangsters they targeted. 'We'd go out with our notebook and make a note of where the criminals were and who they were with,' Blissett says. 'And then we'd come down on them. We could bust them on the spot, but generally, six bookings in a statutory period of six months and they'd go to gaol. It was very effective. We were allowed a lot of liberties in those days. I don't believe in violence, but you met fire with fire. To be a good copper around Sydney then, you had to be able to beat your weight in wildcats.'

Blissett's partner was Greg Brown, now eighty-three. Brown joined the force in the early '30s and worked in the gazette room at the CIB in Central Lane where they compiled the criminal registers. 'We would go through the discharge list of gaols and put together a profile dossier on these offenders. I did that for two years. Then I was posted to Darlinghurst Police Station. I went on to work with Ray Blissett on the Consorting Squad. Being gaoled for doing nothing was the worst thing that could happen to those fellas. Getting six months just for talking! Those blokes were ropable. We could use the new law as a lever to obtain information. We'd see a bloke and say, "Look, you've got six bookings, mate, we could arrest you and put you inside." Then we'd hit them for information. Intelligence about underworld goings-on was the street policeman's lifeblood. Often these criminals, rather than be charged with consorting, would give us information that we could use against other gangsters in our district or pass on to other police.

'Our threats didn't always work. Many times when I told a fella I was going to charge him with consorting, he'd tell me to go and get stuffed! Occasionally there'd be violence if he and his mates had had a few drinks. We didn't mind violence. If we knew there was a mob of criminals in a room somewhere, we'd go in. We didn't worry about the door being closed in those days.'

'The Consortos', as the Consorting Squad enforcers were known, enjoyed immediate success. In 1930, their first year on the beat, they arrested fifty-four males and sixty-two females, and of these, sixty-eight went to gaol. In 1931, sixty-eight men and eighty-one women were nabbed, and 121 of them were imprisoned. 'The reign of terror is ended,' exulted New South Wales Police Minister Chaffey only months after the Consortos set to work. 'The Consorting Clause gave the police more power than they sought, and the results certainly exceed anything I expected . . . no other Act of Parliament has been of such assistance in ridding the city and streets of undesirables.'

Chaffey's boasting was justified, to a point. Ostensibly, East Sydney was suddenly a safer, less rambunctious place. The street mobs, such as Guido Calletti's Darlinghurst Push — which had wrought havoc on the streets, defying police, press and public censure — were forced to disband, leaving the likes of Calletti as lone operators. The Leigh and Devine teams tended not to prowl in public en masse any more, though they continued to gather in private. There were fewer prostitutes openly plying their trade (the new laws forced them off the streets and into brothels — which suited madam Tilly Devine). And the traffic in cocaine that fuelled much gang warfare decreased (although by then the Depression was entrenched and many Sydney 'snowdroppers' could no longer afford drugs).

But while Tilly and Kate suffered setbacks because of the police crackdown — each would serve time in gaol under the new laws — their illegalities continued apace, if conducted a little less brazenly than when Sydney was a wide-open crime town. The two women, Calletti, Frank Green, Nellie Cameron and a newcomer to the underworld, 'Pretty Dulcie' Markham, and, when he returned from his self-imposed exile in Woy Woy, Phil Jeffs, would all be active for years to come. Consorto Greg Brown recalls: 'We kept arresting Tilly and Kate, they'd be fined or do some prison time, and as soon as they were back on the street it would be business as usual. While they were [in gaol], their mobs carried on their operation.'

The 1920s and '30s boasted many formidable and dedicated police officers: William Mackay, boots 'n' all beat cop Ray 'the Blizzard' Blissett, Lillian Armfield, drug-squadders Wickham and Thompson, and undercover man Joe Chuck. But for all the forces aligned against them, lawbreakers held sway in the 1920s.

It took only a few corrupt and on-the-take officers to counter the toil of the straight arrows. As well as the bad apples within, the police force was still nobbled by a weak *Crimes Act* and was undermanned and ill-equipped; not surprisingly, with its long hours and scandalously low wages. In 1927, the Police Association was in the Industrial Court trying to make the State Government increase the minimum pay of a policeman to £1 a week.

When Superintendent John Parmeter, who patrolled Darlinghurst and Kings Cross in the 1920s and '30s, retired from the force in 1960, he reflected that Razorhurst 'was a policeman's honeypot'. Some 95 per cent of the city's criminals lived there, and whenever an interstate criminal arrived he headed straight for the Cross. 'Those days, you'd strike more crime in Kings Cross in one night than in all of Sydney in a month today. It was against departmental orders to patrol there at night without a mate. There was no police radio then, so you couldn't call for a fleet of cars to back you up if you got into trouble. It was you against the mob.' Parmeter said that to get a crook to the police station an officer had to run a gauntlet of the arrested man's family and friends 'who would follow you along the street, cursing and spitting at you'.

Car accidents kept police busy, and no resource was spared to catch the individual violator — the murderer, the rapist, the safe-cracker. But organised crime — defined as 'a continuing and self-perpetuating criminal conspiracy that operates for a profit motive and which thrives on fear and corruption' — was largely left alone by the police. This was because organised crimes such as prostitution, sly grog, narcotics and gambling were usually victimless and popular with the people. And even when police did happen to arrest and charge a racketeer (as Kate Leigh and Tilly Devine proved time and again in their long criminal careers), they got off lightly because they could afford the best legal defence, and also count on unofficial help from political and judicial contacts, and their many powerful customers, to minimise the damage to their illegal concerns. It was usually only when organised crime resorted to violence against the public that the police reacted with heat. If the bloodshed was confined to warring gangsters, police were delighted to turn a blind eye.

Weighing against the lawmen, too, of course, was the Sydney gangster's version of the Mafia code of *omerta*. 'One reads with amazement,' mused Sydney daily newspaper the *Sun* in 1929, 'that individual after individual, sorely wounded, brutally battered, or shot in cold blood, refuses to disclose to police the names of his assailants.' Nobility had little to do with the outlaws' silence. Any 'shelfer' who identified their assailant to the authorities, of course, paid dearly. Reprisals against them, their family and friends were inevitable, swift and deadly. If a victim wanted revenge against a rival, they would have to mete it out themselves. Police were powerless when a victim refused to cooperate. 'What can we do?' worried one in August 1927. 'The victims won't talk. We seize a suspect. Often we are sure we have the right man, and he is arrested. Then he is discharged when his victim won't testify. And that's the end of it.'

Greg Brown, now living on the north coast of New South Wales, has wonderful recall of the era and its personalities, bad and good:

'The main trouble spots were Darlinghurst, the 'Loo, Surry Hills. They were lucrative patches and that's why the gangs fought each other so ferociously to run their piece of turf. There was cocaine in those days, maybe not as much as there is today, but it was everywhere in East Sydney. Criminals used to snort it before a job. That was the big thing. They thought it would give them courage.'

As well as being the recognised queen of sly-groggery, Kate Leigh was a major receiver and seller of stolen property. Thieves would make a beeline to Kate with their stash, she'd inspect the goods with a hard eye, pay a pittance for them, then sell them to a warehouse for a profit. 'If there was a big robbery,' says Brown, 'Kate would be the one the robbers would come to see first to unload the goods. She'd sell that stolen property in a flash. She was a rough, tough old bird. I could never warm to her, although many in the force liked her. When I first started in Darlinghurst, there was a young copper who used to patrol near a pub called the Pottery. It was a hangout for crooks. The Pottery was only about thirty metres around the corner from one of Kate's sly-grog shops. One day a gang of hoodlums got stuck into the young constable. Kate came storming out of her house with a gun tripped for shooting. She said she'd shoot the mob unless they let the policeman go. She saved that young man's life.'

Brown had many clashes with Guido Calletti. 'Guido was vicious. He was stocky and an extremely aggressive street fighter. The word around Darlo was: don't cross Guido. I ran into him in Palmer Street once in the mid '30s and he gave me a bit of lip so I charged him with using obscene language. He was a standover man and ran prostitutes and tried to ally himself with Tilly and Kate. He was also associated with Nellie Cameron and "the Angel of Death", Dulcie Markham. Every bloke who got mixed up with Dulcie got murdered. She was a good-looking bird, too. I saw her early in the piece before time damaged her and, I tell you, she was a particularly good-looking girl. She could look and act beautifully and you'd never pick her as a prostitute and gangster. But she certainly had a foul mouth when it suited her. The swearing was the same as today, the F-word and the C-word.'

Brown looks back on his career with pride. In the early 1940s, he was promoted for chasing and catching two escaped Long Bay convicts single-handedly. His act of bravery made all the front pages of the day. 'It was such a good life, so interesting. I'm sure I could have got another job that paid more, but I loved the work.'

More than any other single police officer or politician, William Mackay was responsible for the jihad on Razorhurst. Mackay, known to his men as Billy, was born in Glasgow in 1885, the son of a prominent policeman, named Murdoch. He followed his father into the Glasgow constabulary in 1905, and such was his aptitude for policing he spent only about two years in uniform before being made a detective and cracking some major cases, many involving murder. Glasgow then, as now, was a violent city, and it was there, wrote police historians Lance Hoban and Bruce Swanton in the *NSW Police News*, that beefy, two-fisted Mackay 'learned the hard way policing's most basic rule — run to a fire but walk to a fight'.

In a portent of the controversy that would dog Mackay's Australian police career, he resigned from the Glasgow force in acrimonious circumstances. A murderer he had arrested was freed on a technicality. An angry Mackay then applied for the reward that had been offered for the suspect's capture and when he was offered a fraction of the sum, just £68, in disgust he decided to emigrate with his new wife to Canada. However, when he learned that it cost only £52 to book passage to Australia, he and his wife sailed to the southern hemisphere instead. The Mackays docked in Sydney on 1 April 1910 and moved into a small house on the north shore. Mackay bought a shovel and found work as a labourer, then became a clerk in a city office.

Days after starting at his new job, Mackay made a citizen's arrest of two pickpockets at the corner of Pitt and Market streets in the city. He beat up both men when they resisted. A plain-clothes officer who helped Mackay frogmarch the thieves into custody suggested he was wasting his time working in an office and that he should join the New South Wales Police Force. Mackay was sworn in as a probationary foot constable in June. After an office stint, he shed his uniform and worked in plain clothes on the vice beat.

A rising star, Mackay was posted to the Metropolitan Superintendent's Office, the administrative nerve centre of the force. There he learned the idiosyncrasies of policing Sydney and, being personable, ambitious and smart, he was befriended by senior officers. His most influential champion was fellow Scot James Mitchell, who, in 1914, was appointed metropolitan superintendent and the following year inspector-general of police in the state.

During the war, with many officers serving overseas, Mackay (whose application for military service had been rejected on essential service grounds) took on a backbreaking administrative workload. Nor did he grumble when at weekends he was sent to quell brawls in the Domain in Woolloomooloo and to keep an ear out for any subversion in the speeches of the soapbox orators there. Mackay became a sergeant (first-class) in 1917, and in 1923, he was placed in charge of detectives at Clarence Street Police Station. There he concentrated on policing sly grog, vice and graft, and fought successfully to have patrol cars fitted with wirelesses.

In 1927, just as the razor gangs were honing their blades, the now-Inspector Mackay was supervising police arrangements for the New South Wales tour of the Duke and Duchess of York and their opening of Parliament House in Canberra. On the royals' departure, he was relocated to Sydney's hot spot, No. 3 Division, Darlinghurst Police Station, to do battle with Bruhn, Jeffs, Leigh, Devine and their foot soldiers. After a period in the Razorhurst trenches, often working closely with Tom Wickham and riding in the sidecar of the division's only motorcycle, Mackay was made head of the CIB in late 1928. Soon after he was one of a group of senior police sent to England, the Continent and America to study new police methods, including the effects of consorting laws and special vice squads on street and organised crime. His findings led to the formulation of the Consorting Clause.

Mackay became a favourite of New South Wales Premier Jack Lang, whose Labor Party won office in October 1930. With the far-right-wing organisation the New Guard a thorn in the side of the government, Mackay made it clear to Lang that it would be a privilege to take on the rabblerousers.

'Mackay's an interesting bloke,' says George Parsons. 'He got the police commissioner's job, as I understand it, because the existing commissioner wouldn't sort out the New Guard, and Jack Lang said, "This is no good, now who are the brightest young people on the force?" And Mackay was among them. Lang called Mackay in and said, "Do you want to be commissioner?" Mackay said he did, and Lang said, "Right, then, sort out these New Guard bastards for me." Mackay drafted all the working-class cops he could find and sent them out on the streets to combat the New Guard. He gave them instructions to "belt the bloody heads off the Guardsmen". After Mackay cowed the Guard, Lang said to him, "You'll do," and, in time, he was made police commissioner.'

Mackay's troops were fond of him, too — as praise from Greg Brown shows: 'The best police commissioner I ever worked under was Billy Mackay. He was a policeman's man, rather than someone who tried to please the politicians at our expense.' Brown insists that Mackay had no great love of politicians, and in fact kept a dossier on them which listed their foibles or misdemeanours and could be used to control any politician trying to make Mackay's working life difficult. Maggie Baker says: 'Mr Mackay's door was always open to us.'

Mackay was made metropolitan superintendent in March 1932,

and found himself again in the national limelight on the 19th of that month when at the official opening of Sydney Harbour Bridge he arrested a leading light of the New Guard, Irish-born antique dealer Captain Francis de Groot, after de Groot galloped in to sabre-slash the commemorative ribbon before Lang could snip it with his ceremonial scissors. 'First to reach de Groot was Superintendent Mackay, chief of the CIB, and with brisk agility that officer pulled him from the saddle and flung him to the ground,' reported the *Sydney Morning Herald* next day.

(Poor de Groot wouldn't have known if he'd been shot or stabbed when, a short time after being bulldogged by Mackay, he collided head-on with Tilly Devine. De Groot's appearance on 5 April at Central Police Court to face charges of offensive behaviour on the Harbour Bridge coincided with one of Tilly's regular appearances there. Seeing de Groot at the court, Devine, who — says George Parsons, for all her airs and graces and love of the monarchy, was in fact a socialist at heart — buttonholed de Groot. 'You are a basher,' she growled at him. 'Wait until the [left-wing] Nationalists get back in. You'll starve then. You would not give a dying man a feed!'

By now, William Mackay was the obvious choice to succeed his friend James Mitchell as inspector-general, and he oversaw many landmark innovations. The old Central Barracks had become the headquarters of the CIB in August 1930 and the state's most effective officers were employed there. Crime-scene examination became an art, modus operandi and property tracing sections were established, and consorting, fraud and motor surveillance teams recruited. The Special Squad (later known as 21 Division) was employed. These officers used the *Vagrancy Act* to pressure criminals, prostitutes and vagrants. Call-boxes popped up all over inner Sydney and later, in 1935, the police cadet scheme was introduced. Mackay upgraded police communications, especially radio, and during his reign, New South Wales police had one of the world's most sophisticated police wireless infrastructures.

Later, Mackay, who, almost inevitably, became police commissioner in 1936, introduced the Police Rescue Squad, the Air Wing and Police–Citizens Boys Clubs. He also knew the value of good publicity, and so ordered spectacular police entertainments each year at the Royal Easter Show. A favourite was the chariot race using police motorbikes, and long queues formed at the Police Exhibition, where bullets, razors, mug shots and the odd pickled hand fascinated young and old.

Mackay's was a glittering career, though controversy brought on by his increasingly dictatorial ways and love of a drink — Hoban recalls seeing him falling-down drunk — tarnished his reputation. The 1937 Royal Commission into SP Betting found him to be 'impetuous and impulsive'. In the 1940s, Mackay's health deteriorated and he suffered a hernia and an eye haemorrhage. He was forced to take sick leave, but never really recovered. He died of a coronary occlusion in 1948.

If William Mackay was the brains of the New South Wales Police Force, Ray Blissett was the muscle. 'The first I ever heard of Ray Blissett,' recalls Lance Hoban, 'was when I was young, in about 1930. I read in the paper how Ray had arrested a fellow after he hurled his baton at the fleeing miscreant and felled him cold. I said to my dad, "My, he must be a pretty fair shot." I got to know Ray as a good and loyal friend.'

Blissett's Consorting Squad colleague Greg Brown remembers one night when he and Blissett were in Woolloomooloo and a local rough-nut named Geoffrey Robinson and his cronies decided to test Blissett's reputation as a hard man. 'I didn't even get a chance to help him. He cleaned up the entire gang. He had a very heavy punch. You see movies where the hero knocks a baddy out with a single blow and you laugh and say, "That's impossible." But Ray, who was a woodcutter, could do it. If he hit you, you stayed hit.'

Blissett, rugged and incorruptible, was feared and respected by the underworld, and his deeds did much to swing the balance of power between the police and criminals back to the lawmen. After becoming a feared uniform and plain-clothes cop in Glebe and East Sydney, the stocky bruiser was a Consorto and, in 1953, as a detective sergeant, became chief of the Consorting Squad. The year before he retired in 1968, Blissett won the Queen's Police Medal for distinguished service.

Funny and smart, Blissett, now ninety-two, lives in a neat brick bungalow in the western Sydney suburb of Abbotsford, with his wife Elva, a fine pianist. Their son recently retired as a senior magistrate and their grandson is a solicitor. 'The law is in our blood,' Blissett quips.

When interviewed for this book, Blissett was not as hale as he may have wished, and walked with a frame, but he laughed often as he recalled his beat days, when he was paid five shillings a week and found all the excitement he could handle. 'One day I went to the wedding of a cousin. His father, a policeman, was there in uniform. Over the keg I said, "You fellas have got an easy job." They said, "Well you're big enough, why don't you join us?" I was only nineteen.'

As soon as Blissett turned twenty, in 1928, he joined the police force and was posted to the Regent Street Depot, the training centre, at Redfern. 'My first day on the job, they brought in what we used to call a "sword swallower", he'd been caught behaving indecently in a park or public toilet. He was complaining about the way he was being treated so a sergeant knocked him down. He got up and complained some more and the sergeant knocked him down again. Regent Street was the busiest police station in Australia. I learned my trade there. I was soon sorting out the razor slashers, the pickpockets and bashers. Like with the sword swallower, you knocked 'em down and if they got up and complained, you knocked 'em down again.

'The original razor gang was Norman Bruhn's mob and the other razor mobs followed Bruhn's lead. He came from Melbourne, and he and Snowy Cutmore and their gang were carving blokes up and getting carved up themselves. Slashing and shooting. They were cruel bastards. Sydney's major crime in the '20s and '30s was assault and robbery, but there was plenty of sly grog — the chief librarian at Sydney Town Hall had a sly-grog shop at Glebe. There was cocaine in Darlinghurst and Kings Cross, and I was always raiding the Chinese opium dens at the Haymarket. Rounding up the illegal gamblers kept me busy. Mostly the gangs kept to their turf, and other gangs didn't try to encroach. But when one gang strayed into another's territory, there would be trouble.

'The best informant the police ever had was Kate Leigh. When I came to Regent Street, Kate had a sly-grog shop behind Toohey's brewery in Foveaux Street, Surry Hills. Jack Aldridge, one of the best detectives Sydney ever knew, read the lesson for Kate when she died. But he didn't tell the truth. He didn't tell what she was really like. She was an old bitch, she really was. She'd hit you with an iron bar as soon as look at you.'

Blissett worked from 1 to 9 p.m. every Friday at Central Police Station, and was well located to roust shoplifters at the big department stores that dotted that end of Sydney in those years. He was often summoned to Snows, Mark Foys or Anthony Horderns when the store chose to press charges against a shoplifter, shop pilfering being epidemic in those days.

'Out I'd come to take the shoplifters to the cells. One night, Eileen Leigh, Kate's daughter, was caught stealing a fur coat, so I went down. There was a lane in George Street just below Liverpool Street where all the employees gathered. I took Eileen out there and in the lane in front of all these people she threw herself on the ground and said, "He's assaulting me!" Sydneysiders have always had a natural antipathy towards the police, except when they need us, so these employees all started calling out to me to leave her alone. Eileen wouldn't get up so I grabbed her by the hair and I dragged her across the street on her backside, and I took her to the police station, where she was charged and ordered to appear in court on Monday morning. Outside the court on Monday, bright and early, Kate marched up to me and said, "I want to see you, Blissett. You hurt my daughter, I *love* my daughter." "Yes," I said, "and I suppose that's why you made a moll out of her, Kate. Now, if you don't clear off, I'll lock you up too."'

The first time Blissett clashed with Tilly Devine was in 1929. 'On a Sunday afternoon, the prostitutes would be on the steps of Mark Foys on the corner of Elizabeth and Liverpool streets like ants. I'd go up there to clear them away. This day, there was five or six prostitutes in a doorway at Foys and with them was a blonde woman who was showing off her silk stockings to the passers-by. I went up and said, "Come on, bugger off, get out of here. My sergeant is complaining."' But the blonde was unintimidated: 'Oh, come back when you grow up, sonny,' Tilly said to Blissett.

In 1930, Blissett was posted to the Consorting Squad to police the new provisions. 'I ended up in charge of the Consorting Squad. I worked all hours and loved it. Shifts didn't matter to me. In those days there were so many crooks about you could stick your hand out the police station window and pull in a thief any time. If I believed a man was guilty, I'd "vag" him. We were allowed liberties then. One of the best cops I knew was Martin Fisher, a big, strong fellow. Molls used to battle around Elizabeth Street and Railway Square to sleep with Martin before they started their work for the night.

'I was religious in those days. A Catholic. Then a bloke came in to be in charge of detectives at Regent Street and he was a big shot in the [anti-Catholic] Masonic Lodge, and that was the end of my detective career at Regent Street. At twenty-three, in 1931, I was an ex-detective. They put me to working traffic outside Grace Bros at Broadway. I said, "This is no good. Can you send me to Glebe?" So they sent me there as a probationary constable to replace Colin

Delaney, a Glebe detective who had been transferred to the CIB and later became police commissioner. I worked the beat at Glebe. I was a terror there. My nickname was "the Blizzard". I never walked around a hooligan, I walked *over the top* of him. I found it was very effective. My reputation preceded me.'

Blissett says if he wanted a quiet Saturday afternoon in Glebe, he'd jump onto the running board of a tram, ride it down Glebe Point Road to George Street and back, and word would get out among the hooligans who roistered in the pubs in Glebe that Blissett was on duty. 'Nobody would start trouble, because they knew if they did I'd crack 'em. I caught more than my share of thieves and bashers. I never had a moment's trouble with Chow Hayes. I'd say, "I want to see you at the station, Johnny." I never called him Chow, always John or Johnny. He'd be there, don't you worry.

'Norman Connolly, he was a bad man, a thief around Glebe in the early '30s. I pinched him once for stealing the false teeth from some bloke who was having an epileptic fit. He'd stand on the corner and rob kids of their pocket money and on pension day he'd rob old people coming out of the post office with their money.

'I was in uniform at Glebe. I had a couple of years' experience behind me and people would tell me things. If I knew they were guilty, I liked to roust blokes out of bed at 6 a.m. and arrest 'em — for breathing. I had a network of informants. The detectives at Glebe complained about me, said I was a bull in a china shop and interfered with their work . . . I was hauled into the CIB and given a dressing-down by old Bill Pryor, who was the chief then. He said, "You're interfering with the detectives' work." I bailed him up and said, "Compare the number of arrests I make to the number they make, look at the blokes I've put in gaol."

'After the reprimand, I walked out of the CIB headquarters thinking I didn't have a friend in the world, then Frank Mathews, one of the best detectives in Sydney, came up behind me and said, "You'll never learn, will you? Here I am trying to get you a job back in plain clothes and you go in there and blow up the boss." I said, "You know bloody well that what I said is right." He grinned at me and said, "Don't worry, you'll be all right."

Ray Blissett balls his fists and says that he is no longer the religious man he was in his younger days. 'I couldn't be anything but irreligious,' he says. 'I don't know how anyone can spend forty years among the crime in Sydney and believe in God. The bludging, graft, poverty . . . I'm no hypocrite.'

# 17

# Exile and Incarceration

Tilly Devine was one of the first to feel the sting of the new consorting laws. In January 1930, she was arrested for being in the company of disreputables: her own prostitutes. In court, she also faced two charges outstanding from late the previous year, one of riotous behaviour and another of assaulting a policeman.

She pleaded with Judge Laidlaw to let her off; her mother in London was ailing, she said, and she promised him that if he did not charge her she would leave Australia and stay in England for two years. The judge, possibly relishing some relief from the menace of Palmer Street, agreed: 'If I can be satisfied that this woman bona fide intends to leave for England within a month, and if I can be satisfied that she intends to behave herself, I don't know that that wouldn't be a very fair way out of it.'

Knowing she could leave Big Jim to run the rackets alone in her absence, Tilly went to the shipping office to buy a first-class ticket on the *Otranto*. But, mortifyingly, her reputation had preceded her and the shipping line would only sell her a third-class passage. 'My money is as good as anybody's,' squawked the vice queen. 'Nobody has the right to refuse *me* a first-class passage.' The sales clerk, it seemed, did. Tilly backed down, and made the best of it. After a month of raucous bon-voyage parties and a final all-night farewell at her Maroubra home, Tilly, wearing a snappy red beret and holding a lush bouquet, waved goodbye to Big Jim and other well-wishers from the deck of the *Otranto* as it sailed away from Woolloomooloo wharf. 'It was a swell party, believe me, boy!' she told a friend that day, referring to the Torrington Road bash. 'You ought to see the place this morning!'

With Tilly away, staying with her parents in Camberwell and perhaps being reunited with her son Frederick, Kate Leigh could not resist taking time out from her sly-grog and drug selling to lambast her enemy. 'It is my educated opinion,' she told a reporter whom she had summoned to her home, 'that Matilda Devine has ruined the lives of innocent young women by setting them to work in her brothels.' Kate ended her tirade with a snippet that she hoped would prove to the reporter's readers beyond any doubt the black character of her adversary. 'I,' she divulged, 'once loaned Tilly Devine a dog and that woman never returned it.' It was not long before Tilly learned of her rival's attack.

From London, Tilly wrote a missive of outrage to *Truth*. The tabloid, gleefully beating up the feud, published the letter on 29 June 1930 — although some of its flourishes create the suspicion that Tilly's words were embellished by an in-house hack before publication:

*Dear Sir,*

*I am writing this letter, asking a favour to keep my name out of the papers in any connection with Kate Leigh, as I don't wish to know her class. I never mixed in with her and never in my life did she give me a dog. They are my dogs! I have their pedigree, and they are a class above hers. Fancy her saying things about me now that I am out of the country. And tell her for me I don't wish to see her iron face in London as I have my parents here and they are clean. That woman! She could not*

*compare herself with my mother, who is a wonderful old-
fashioned lady and knows nothing of my doings in Sydney.
Thank God! Anyway, I must say you gave my husband a fair
go at his trial in your papers, so surely you will be fair to me.
Let dying dogs die. As I say, 'Give a dog a bad name and it
sticks.' I was not as bad as I was painted. There are lots in
Sydney who will miss me, even the police; as I hope never to
come back to Sydney. I like it but you people did not like me
because I am English. If I had been an Aussie girl there would
have been nothing said. I was too straight for half of them. I
spoke my mind as all Londoners do, right from the shoulder.
Kate Leigh! That thing of a virago! She is jealous of my youth
and prosperity. I know too much for her, that is why she hates
me, and then she has the cheek to say she doesn't mind being
called 'notorious' but she hates to be called 'the worst woman
in Sydney'. Well, I think myself a class above her. The underworld all took their hats off to me and class me a lady beside
her. Men in gaol know her class. Why is it she can do as she
likes and other women are dead frightened? No, she is handy
for the police. She is known as the biggest police top-off in
Australia. Send one of your reporters around to different pris-
ons and ask those that are doing a turn what class of woman
she is. One well-known man is doing life at Long Bay. She sent
a dinner to him last Xmas and he found out it was from her.
He packed it in a clothes bag and sent it right back to her, and
if you don't believe me, I can tell you the man's name if you
care to answer this letter. So I must thank God I was born of
good parents. My father has never taken a drink, and never
been inside a police court in his life. My dear mother is very
sick at the present time and I am nursing her back to health,
otherwise I would put my address on this letter. It would worry
them if they saw half what was in the papers about me. So,*

*trusting you will do this favour for once, as your paper is a class above the others.*

*I remain,*

*M. Devine.*

Tilly's delight can only be imagined when that same month Kate was arrested for possession of cocaine after drug squad detectives Wickham and Thompson, with sergeants Russell and McLeod, policewomen Lillian Armfield and a Mrs Mitchell, raided her Riley Street home.

In Central Court, Kate, in a black dress, fur stole and wide-brimmed hat, sat silently (for once) as Wickham and Thompson testified against her. They gave evidence that when they raided her home and were questioning her, an object fell from Kate's clothing and she had attempted to retrieve it and throw it into a fire that was burning in the room. Armfield had taken the object from Kate. On inspection, it was a small tobacco tin filled with cocaine. Another eight cocaine-filled tins had been found in Kate's bedroom — in the fireplace, in a vase and in a dressing-table drawer. 'It's a frame-up,' Kate had shrieked, and attempted to manhandle the police from the room. The sergeants had picked her up, and carried her struggling and shouting to the patrol car outside in the street. In court, Kate's lawyer, Mr Moseley, entered a not guilty plea on the grounds that the police had framed his client and, besides, she had never been involved in the drug trade in all her life.

Mid-trial, Kate's mother Charlotte died at age eighty-one, and, the day after the funeral, Kate appeared in court trembling, sobbing and wailing. Whether her histrionics were true grief or a cynical ploy to garner sympathy and buy time can only be guessed at, but Moseley called for an adjournment because, he told Judge Perry, his client was distraught and should be under sedation. 'Mrs Leigh was passionately fond of her old mother,' said Moseley, who added that at the funeral at Rookwood Cemetery, Kate had collapsed on her mother's grave. He produced a medical certificate stating that she was suffering from 'shock and neurasthenia'. The judge had little option but to adjourn the case until the defendant had recovered.

Alas for Kate, just days before the scheduled resumption of proceedings, her staunch insistence that she had never had anything to do with drugs was embarrassingly and fatally undermined when her occasional lover and latest chauffeur, Herbert 'Pal' Brown, who had succeeded Kellett Street razor victim Bruce Higgs at the wheel of Kate's limousine, was gaoled for fifteen months for cocaine possession and car theft. On 9 July, commercial traveller Leslie Tilney had parked his car in College Street, East Sydney, while he made a call. Minutes later, he saw his vehicle speeding down the street with Brown at the wheel. Tilney chased on foot for 100 metres, then commandeered an NRMA patrol cycle and overtook him in South Dowling Street. Tilney made a citizen's arrest and took Brown, who was under the influence of alcohol and cocaine, to Darlinghurst Police Station.

In court, for reasons best known to Brown and his lawyer, the long-suffering Mr Moseley, Brown feigned drunkenness on the stand. He glared at Judge Fletcher and the jury and, his eyeballs revolving and body swaying, Brown slurred, 'You call this a court of law!' Then he claimed he was not responsible for stealing Tilney's car because, on the night in question, he was inebriated, too inebriated to drive, and in fact had been drinking for six weeks. His drunk act was doused by the cold waters of cross-examination. The prosecutor proved that Brown's chauffeuring was a cover for the cocaine he distributed for Kate Leigh. Brown then confessed to cocaine addiction, and told the court that Kate often paid him with white powder. He received fifteen months in gaol.

Late in July, when she was unable to delay proceedings further, it was Kate Leigh's turn to go down. In spite of her police and political contacts, she was sentenced to twelve months' gaol and fined £250 in lieu of a second year behind bars on the cocaine possession charges.

On the stand, Tom Wickham could hardly contain his emotions at nabbing Kate at last on a drug charge: 'I have known this woman for fifteen or twenty years. She is a principal in the cocaine traffic in this city. Not only does she peddle it herself, but she is one of the biggest suppliers to other pedlars. She is titled "the uncrowned queen of the underworld" and there is no doubt that she wields a powerful influence in the underworld of Sydney. She boasts her privilege of obtaining preferential treatment of prisoners in the gaols and of her influence with high political and legal people. I regard her as a menace to the community. She is a low moral type, capable of committing any crime in the criminal calendar. Many of the recent underworld vendettas have been attributed to her and I am sorry to say that I cannot say anything for her. Many years ago, she introduced me to her daughter, Eileen. The girl was then only fifteen years old. I have seen that girl go down and down, until today she is the lowest type of woman.'

As Kate was led away in handcuffs, she rounded on Wickham and screamed across the courtroom, 'Look here, Wickham! You can't say that I've not been a mother to my daughter. I've been a better mother to my daughter than you've been a father to yours!' A few days later, a police informer walked into the CIB and claimed that, from prison, Kate had offered a hit man from Melbourne £100 to kill Wickham.

While rejoicing in Kate's incarceration, *Truth* asked why it had taken so long for her to receive a lengthy gaol term, then answered its own question: because her informing was too valuable to the police. Under the headline 'Sydney's Vicious Harridan of Underworld Should Have Been in Gaol Long Ago: Shelf, Hypocrite, Base and Vile', the piece continued:

*There are oft-repeated whispers that when she tired of her lov-
ers, the law conveniently reached out and placed them in gaol
for long periods. This might have been no more than coinciden-
tal. Kate gets hot under the collar when suggestions are made
to the contrary, but it was always Tilly Devine's most telling
verbal blow when she and Kate got into wrangling. Writing
from England some months ago, Tilly slated Leigh as the greatest top-off (informer) in Sydney, and Tilly had plenty of
fellow-believers. That there was some influence that saved
Leigh from gaol on numerous occasions goes without saying.
She was the associate of criminals and the Consorting Act
could have swept her into gaol many months ago had the
police applied it. But Kate seemed to bear a charmed life.*

The tabloid reminded its readers of how Leigh's sparkling car swept
her about the streets, driven by one chauffeur after another, how her
sly-grog shops were left alone by police, and how she was constantly
in the company of known criminals, including Wally Tomlinson.

The privileged life enjoyed by Kate on the street continued
unabated behind bars. Police, mindful of the many inmates who were
in Long Bay Gaol because of Leigh's informing, kept her isolated from
the vengeful. She was allowed a steady string of visits from Razorhurst
underlings who ran her lucrative cocaine trade and sly-grog shops
while she was indisposed. Kate, as usual, was given a cushy job in the
kitchen, where her talent for baking scones was appreciated by warders and official visitors to the prison. One such visitor was Lady
Gwendolen Game, the wife of State Governor Sir Philip Game, who
declared Kate's scones 'far better than those they serve me at Government House'.

The most-favoured treatment Kate received annoyed other inmates.
The 'Old Woman,' as she was known in gaol, 'never does any work
in the kitchen,' griped one. 'She is supposed to scrub and do other

things, but she gets the other women to do her work for her. She pays them in tobacco. She seems to be able to get unlimited supplies of tobacco although it is forbidden. She pays these silly creatures to do her work for her and then she boasts about it.'

Kate habitually took for herself the pick of the meat from the butcher's lorry, cooked it, and ate it in the officers' quarters from plates she had brought from her home. What choice meat she couldn't eat herself, she fed to Shifty, the prison dog. She recommenced her romance with Pal Brown, her driver, who was doing time for cocaine dealing. Brown worked in the prison bake-house. Her enemies carped that by being Brown's lover, she ensured herself a plentiful supply of not just sex, but sugar buns and currant loaves, which she loved. Kate had her own china teapot and wore her own shoes, stockings and underwear rather than prison-supply garb.

She was foul-mouthed and violent and often threatened to knock other inmates down, with her fists or a kitchen utensil. She threatened to throw one young fellow kitchen worker into the oven. One male prisoner who sang at a prison entertainment afternoon learned exactly what she thought of his crooning when she pelted him with vegetables and hooted, 'Give 'im the 'ook!'

Another prisoner complained, 'As soon as she arrived, the place was in an uproar. She goes where she likes in the gaol, and dobs in who she likes. I have never done time so hard in my life as I have since she came here. I have nothing to say against the officers of the female division at all. They are good and kind. But she seems to have them all on edge, too. She storms and rouses about the place all day. At any time you can hear her "clapper" going; if we spoke half so loud we would be locked up in our cells.' Other prisoners complained that Leigh would confiscate and devour any sweets or cakes sent to them by their family. As one disgruntled inmate grumbled: 'Leigh is arrogant and defies all regulations. She lives an idle and luxurious life when she is supposed to be paying for her crime.'

Apart from Pal Brown and Shifty the dog, Kate's only other real friend in Long Bay was an elderly alcoholic named Catherine Ikin. Ikin had been charged with the manslaughter of her husband Albert and was in custody awaiting trial. On 12 June 1931, Catherine and Albert, also alcoholic, had been at their home in Woy Woy, when, according to Catherine, Albert had seen her looking in the woodshed for kindling wood. He had imagined she was searching for a hidden bottle of liquor there and in a rage came at her with a razor. They had wrestled and in the melee, she told police, Albert had sustained a razor gash on his hand. The cut extended from between Albert's fourth and little fingers almost to his elbow. He bled to death. In prison, Kate was the frail and distraught Catherine Ikin's self-appointed benefactor and protector. 'She is very good to me,' Ikin said at the height of the friendship. 'She is the loveliest woman at the Bay, and she gives me half her rations and makes me a cup of tea in the mornings.'

Ikin soon had reason to retract her praise, for Kate's kindness was not motivated by altruism. In late September '31, after Ikin had been acquitted and released from prison, Kate, who herself was free after authorities, to the fury of police, paroled her after just one year of imprisonment and allowed her to pay her £250 fine in easy instalments, was waiting for Ikin at the prison gates in her chauffeur-driven limousine. The unlikely duo drove off together.

The friendship did not endure. Within a week, Ikin had reported Kate to the police for assaulting and robbing her. Kate, claimed Ikin, had wheedled from her the information that she was due a £12 pension payout because she was now the widow of an ex-serviceman. Kate had insisted on accompanying her to the Woy Woy post office, where the money was being held. Outside, Kate demanded the money. When Ikin refused, Kate produced a small knife or razor and stabbed her in the finger. Ikin fled to the nearest police station. Kate was convicted of inflicting grievous bodily harm on the elderly woman and, incredibly for one with a record as substantial as hers, merely fined a small sum.

Only months later, on 9 December, Kate was entertaining a group of customers at her Riley Street sly-grog den when an argument broke out. Rifle in hand, she ordered one protagonist, Joe McNamara (the same McNamara who was the proprietor of Mack's, outside which Norman Bruhn was gunned down in June '27), to leave the premises. He, like Snowy Prendergast (the young wannabe out to gun down Wally Tomlinson in March 1930), called the old gangster's bluff. And, like Prendergast, he paid dearly. Without further debate or ado, Kate shot him in the groin. She was arrested, but McNamara refused to identify her as the culprit and charges were dropped.

A month later, she was in trouble again when nabbed for consorting with prostitutes. An exasperated judiciary sent her back to gaol, but only for a month or two.

# 18

# Chez Devine

Tilly Devine returned from London in the first week of January 1931, after just nine months away. Jim's welcome home for her could not have been what she'd hoped for. Arriving at Torrington Road, she found her husband entertaining a strange woman. When she accused him of cheating on her, he denied it. The stranger was not his lover, he protested, but a housekeeper who had been looking after him in Tilly's absence. Tilly, in a cursing rage, threw the woman out. Jim again asserted his innocence, but Tilly was too angry to listen. In a fury himself now, Jim hit her. Then he reached for his rifle. At that, Tilly ran into the street, with Jim at her heels. From the same spot on the verandah where he'd fired at Gregory Gaffney, he now blasted away at his wife. This time his aim was less true, and she escaped unscathed.

At the sound of gunfire, the Devines' long-suffering neighbours called the police, who arrived in force and arrested Jim. He explained to them how his wife had wrongly assumed his housekeeper was his lover and had become hysterical and ran screaming into the street. To calm her down, he had fired a volley over her head. 'What else could I do?' The bloody neighbours, as usual, he said, had overreacted and involved the law. The officers, nevertheless, charged Jim with attempted murder. Before taking him in, they searched the house, and in the pocket of a coat hanging in a bedroom wardrobe, they found a razor.

At committal proceedings, Tilly, still unforgiving, glared at Jim. He met her withering looks with winks and patronising smiles. But by his trial on 16 January 1931, they'd patched things up and she refused to testify against him. The attempted-murder charge was dropped. Police then tried to have Jim Devine charged with possession of a lethal weapon, the razor. His lawyer guffawed. How on earth, he demanded of the Crown, could his client be in possession of a razor when it was not on his person but in a coat in a cupboard? That charge, too, was dismissed.

Two months later, police were back at Torrington Road. Jim Devine, face swathed in bloody bandages, told them his tale. He had been at home alone on 14 March when the doorbell rang. On opening the door, he was attacked by the visitor, a person he insisted he'd never before laid eyes on. The mystery assailant had attacked him with a razor, cutting open Jim's face. The slash extended from his ear, which was all but severed, to his mouth.

Devine said that his attacker had then fled, and he, losing blood and in terrible pain, staggered to the phone and called a friend, whose identity he simply could not remember now because he had been in such shock. The friend had driven him to St Vincent's Hospital where his horrific wounds were stitched. Nor was Tilly any help to police. 'I have never in my life topped off anybody to the coppers,' she later told reporters with what they noted was an enigmatic smile, 'and I'm not starting now.'

It has never been revealed who slashed Jim Devine that night. It could have been someone loyal to Kate Leigh, paying Jim Devine back for killing Gaffney and being part of the force that attacked Dalton and Tomlinson. Maybe it was a reprisal for Snowy Prendergast's ill-fated rampage at Kate's home. Perhaps it was just one or another of Jim's many enemies, someone he'd assaulted or cheated along the way.

And there is another possibility. At the time, the Devine marriage was floundering. Jim had been beating Tilly since they met, but recently he had escalated his violence and taken a number of lovers, possibly including the 'housekeeper'. The vicious-tempered Tilly, who never had a problem inflicting bodily harm on others, may that night have had enough of her husband's thuggery and philandering, and punished him with one of the razors that littered their home.

Because of the ugly red scar that now decorated Jim Devine's cheek, he was known for a while by the unwieldy sobriquet 'Scarface Big Jim' Devine. But whoever slashed him, the injury did not help the disposition of the ever-irascible Jim, who now kept his rifle loaded and at arm's reach in readiness for anyone else who wanted to chance their hand.

One who did was Frank Green. The friends had turned on each other after Jim was exonerated of involvement in Barney Dalton's death, leaving Green to face the rap alone, and Green had said in court he had seen the murder weapon at Jim's home. There was also, it's believed, some kind of money dispute between the pair.

On the afternoon of 16 June 1931, the bad relations between the gangsters came to a head. That day, Jim had been busy. He visited Tilly, who was locked in the Central Police Station cells after being convicted of gingering George Hudson, a customer at one her brothels, of £2. Jim had taken her a fur coat in case she was cold. He then went to the Sir Walter Raleigh Hotel in Darlinghurst for an ale. While Jim was there, Green, with Nellie Cameron in tow, confronted him. Green demanded £25. With an oath, Jim brushed Green aside, and left the hotel to meet his friend, cabbie Fred Moffitt, who would drive him home to Torrington Road.

After Jim Devine left the Sir Walter Raleigh, an affronted Green and Cameron plotted to raid the Devines' home that night and relieve Jim of either the £25 or goods of similar value. Perhaps Green was drunk, for if sober he would have remembered that Jim Devine kept a loaded rifle at Torrington Road and — as he himself had seen at powder-burn range the night Gaffney died — could use it proficiently.

Green and Cameron recruited an ally named Buller and caught a cab to Torrington Road. When they arrived, at about 7.30 p.m., it was raining heavily. Without a knock, Devine later testified, the trio barged through the Devines' front door and into the lounge room where Jim was sitting with Moffitt and a man named Les Jordan. Green rammed a nickel-plated revolver into a startled Jim's stomach and ordered him to hand over £25 — 'and if you squeal, I'll blow your guts out'. Once more, even while under the gun, Jim refused. Green's bluff had been called and, putting the gun away, he tore a £50 diamond pin from Devine's tie and, flanked by Cameron and Buller, backed out of the house.

As soon as they were outside, Jim ran to his bedroom, took his rifle and ran to the front porch. 'Stop, Frank, and give me that tie pin,' he demanded.

'Stop, nothing,' answered Green. Jim fired at Green, but missed. He fired again. The bullets lodged in a neighbour's front fence and a grassy verge.

'Come out here and don't be a dog!' cried Green from the roadside to Jim, barricaded in his favourite shooting position on the front porch.

Les Jordan watched the fracas from a window, while petrified neighbours peered from behind their curtains as their suburban street once more became a battleground. Fred Moffitt, the taxi driver, broke from the Devines' home and raced to his parked cream-and-red cab. As he was climbing in, he was confronted by Green, Cameron and Buller, who leapt in and screamed at him to drive them away. As the taxi accelerated along Malabar Road, Green fired a barrage of shots at

Jim from the open front passenger-seat window. Devine returned fire, shooting four times. Moffitt cried out and pitched forward. Then, as Jim later told police, Green, Cameron and Buller 'got out of the cab and ran towards Torrington Road and fired a shot as they were going. I had no more cartridges so I went inside and locked the house up.'

At first light, Jim peeped from the porch window and there in the street he saw Moffitt's cab, stationary at a crazy angle. All its doors hung open. After checking that Green was not lying in wait for him, he approached the vehicle. He later told police of seeing Moffitt sprawled over the wheel like a broken puppet. He added, somewhat unnecessarily, 'Poor old Fred was dead.' The soft-nosed, high-velocity bullet from Jim's rifle had torn into the taxi driver's chest, shattered his breastbone and punctured his lung. The floor of the cab was awash with blood.

At the June inquest into Moffitt's death, Jim mourned, 'I would just like to express my deepest regret at the death of Fred Moffitt, against whom I held no grudge and who was a good friend to me. When discharging the shots at Green in the direction of the taxi cab, I had no intention of striking or shooting Moffitt and I aimed at the rear of the car with a view to missing him.'

When it was her turn to be questioned by the coroner, Nellie Cameron — to open laughter from the many present who knew better — brazenly declared: 'I don't know James Devine, and have never been to his house. I don't know Buller.' Of her lover Frank Green, she allowed, 'I have heard of him . . . I think.' Despite further questioning by the incredulous coroner, Cameron refused to alter her story. The coroner, in the end, ruled that there was no evidence that Devine murdered Moffitt, but that he must stand trial for manslaughter.

At Darlinghurst Criminal Court three weeks later, before a huge crowd which spilled out of the court and onto the surrounding lawns, Jim's lawyer insisted his client had every right to shoot at Green, Cameron and Buller because, under the *Crimes Act*, any responsible citizen could apprehend a person who had committed a crime for which he had not been charged and tried. Green's gunpoint theft of his tie pin entitled Devine to take whatever steps he felt necessary to arrest his assailant. He was doing just that when the hapless Moffitt got in the way and took the bullet meant for Green. Mr Justice Stephen was not convinced, saying that Jim, in turning Malabar Road into a shooting gallery, had used unreasonable force to reclaim his tie pin. 'It is not the law that any person without qualification is entitled to shoot to kill a felon who in his opinion is trying to escape.'

Then Devine found himself with a most unlikely ally. Detective Superintendent William Mackay, head of the CIB, told the court that Jim Devine had professed his deep sorrow at the death of his old friend Moffitt and reminded the court that Frank Green was a bad man who would, without a second thought, kill anyone trying to bring him down. As every policeman in Sydney knew well, extreme measures were necessary when dealing with the vicious Green, and Jim Devine had merely taken such measures.

Next came a procession of defence witnesses who swore that Jim and Moffitt were good friends, and that Jim often gave the alcoholic Moffitt money for drinks when he needed it. Over the wails of Moffitt's widow, the jury, after only a few minutes' deliberation, acquitted Jim of manslaughter. Tilly, swathed in fur and her fingers laden with baubles, embraced her husband. And at a celebratory knees-up at Torrington Road that night, Tilly, bottle of beer in hand, cooed: 'My Jim never killed anyone . . . on purpose!'

'Guido Calletti was a ruthless, cold-blooded bastard,' Ray Blissett says. 'But like a lot of those razor-gang blokes, he wasn't particularly brave when he was unarmed, or when his victim fought back.' In 1931, Calletti was a true public enemy, mugging any likely mark who strayed into his path.

One night Calletti overreached himself for once. He struck up a conversation with a seemingly mild-mannered and well-dressed grazier in a William Street pub; probably Sharland's Strand, a favourite watering hole of his. After a few beers, Calletti suggested they strike out together in search of fun and excitement. The good-natured grazier was all for it.

In a laneway off William Street, Calletti fell behind his companion then, with a rush, struck him on the back of the head. At this point, most of Calletti's victims went down and stayed down while Calletti robbed them. Not the grazier. He absorbed Calletti's king-hit without flinching, then returned one. Calletti was very strong, and one of Razorhurst's most accomplished streetfighters, but when his 'pigeon' stood up to him the hoodlum's spirit failed him. For five minutes, the grazier, who turned out to be a skilled boxer, hammered Calletti with lefts and rights, hooks and rips and uppercuts. Each time he knocked Calletti down, he'd haul him to his feet again and start afresh. When Calletti was on the verge of unconsciousness, the man from the bush pushed and pummelled him a full kilometre through the streets to Darlinghurst Police Station.

There, he waited until Calletti was revived, bandaged, splinted and charged with assault and robbery. And when Calletti faced a committal hearing over the matter, the grazier, in spite of being warned by Calletti's friends that his health would suffer if he testified, insisted on pressing charges. 'I'm going through with this to see that that ruffian gets what's coming to him.' What was coming to Calletti was two years in Long Bay prison.

A section of Frog Hollow, Sydney's most notorious slum, in the early 1920s. The labyrinth of derelict dwellings in the Riley Street escarpment was home to many gangsters, including, in the years of World War I, Kate Leigh. From the City of Sydney Library Photo Archives

Palmer Street, Darlinghurst, dwellings in 1922 — the era when the street was Tilly Devine's heartland. From the City of Sydney Library Photo Archives

'A good sort' — Kate Leigh in 1915 aged thirty-four, in Long Bay Gaol after her perjury conviction in the wake of the Eveleigh Street Railway Workshops holdup. From the original photograph in State Records New South Wales

The slum in Hollington Street, Camberwell, London, where Tilly Devine grew up. From the Camberwell, Borough of Southwark, Library and Photographic Archive

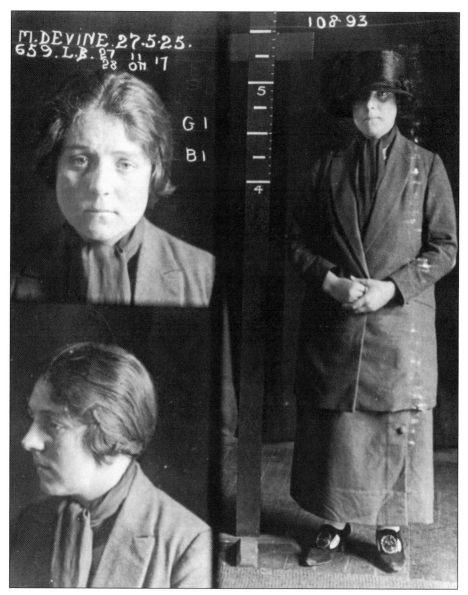

In 1925, Tilly Devine, aged twenty-five, was sentenced to two years gaol for slashing a man in a Sydney barbershop. From the Collection of the Justice and Police Museum, courtesy of the Historic Houses Trust of New South Wales

The corner of Kellett Street and Bayswater Road, Kings Cross, in 1930, at the height of razor gang activity. It was in Kellett Street that the forces of rival mob bosses Tilly Devine and Kate Leigh gathered and fought a pitched battle with razors, knives, guns, bottles and clubs on August 8 1929. Today, an inscription in the footpath commemorates the riot. From the City of Sydney Library Photo Archives

Stamping ground of the razor gangs: Liverpool Street, Sydney, circa 1930, near the corner of Riley Street, looking east. From the collection of the Justice and Police Museum, courtesy of the Historic Houses Trust of New South Wales

These razors were confiscated from The Darlinghurst Push, led by Guido Calletti. They were found in Darlinghurst Gaol by policeman Lance Hoban before being donated to Sydney's Justice and Police Museum. From the collection of the Justice and Police Museum, Sydney

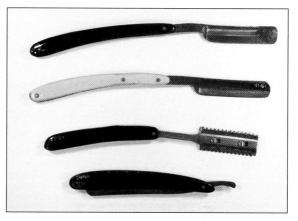

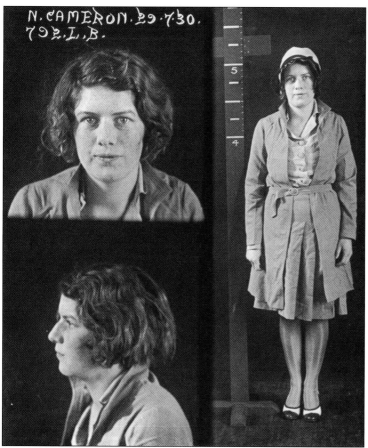

Girl of the streets — an uncharacteristically dishevelled Nellie Cameron, aged eighteen, photographed by police when arrested for soliciting in 1930. From the original photograph in State Records New South Wales

Left: Norman Bruhn, circa mid-1920s, the first leader of a razor gang. He was doomed when he challenged Devine, Leigh and Phil Jeffs. Image Library, State Library of New South Wales

Below: In October 1918, Tilly Devine was arrested as a 'common prostitute annoying by soliciting' on The Strand in London. Courtesy of London Metropolitan Archives

Continuation
IN THE METROPOLITAN POLICE DISTRICT.

Register of the Court of Summary Jurisdiction sitting at _Bow Street_ Police Court.

Thursday The 3rd day of October 1918

| Number. | Name of Informant or Complainant. | Name of Defendant. Age, if known. | Nature of Offence or of Matter of Complaint. | Date of Offence. | Time when Charged. Bailed. | Doctor's Fee (if any) | Plea. | Minute of Adjudication. | Time allowed for Payments and Instalments. |
|---|---|---|---|---|---|---|---|---|---|
| 2 | PC Bishop 280 C. | Doris Gwyn (married) (23) | Common prostitute annoying by soliciting at Coventry Street | 2/10/18 | 11.5 pm 2nd | | – | Remanded until Oct 10th | |
| 3 | PC Hebbes 116 E. | Matilda Devine (married) (19) | Common prostitute annoying by soliciting at the Strand | 2/10/18 | 10 Pm 12.00 2nd am 3rd | | – | 4/- | |
| 4 | PC Bramall 135 E | Rose Dyson (no occupation) (23) | Both Common prostitutes annoying by soliciting at the Strand | 2/10/18 | 11.30 pm 2nd | | – | 4/- or 21 days (no fixed abode) | |
| 5 | Do. | Rose Highstead (no occupation) 20 | | | | | – | 4/- or 21 days (no fixed abode) | |
| 6 | PC Hoppit 397 C | Ethel Wood (dancer) 24 | Both Common prostitutes annoying by soliciting at Coventry Street | 2/10/18 | 8.25 1.45 pm am 2nd 3rd | | p.g. | 4/- | |
| 7 | Do. | Rubina McNeilage (married) 23 | | | 1.45 am 3rd | | p.g. | 4/- | |
| 8 | SD Inspt. Collins C. | Gossie Solomon (milliner) 27 (Russian Subject) | Warrant dated 30th being the occupier of 1st floor No 13 Rupert Street, unlawfully & knowingly permit such premises to be use for habitual prostitution | 12/9 to 19/9/18 | 5 pm 2nd | | | Remanded for 7 days. Two Sureties in £25 or one in £50 | |

R Graham Campbell
Magistrate Adjudicating.

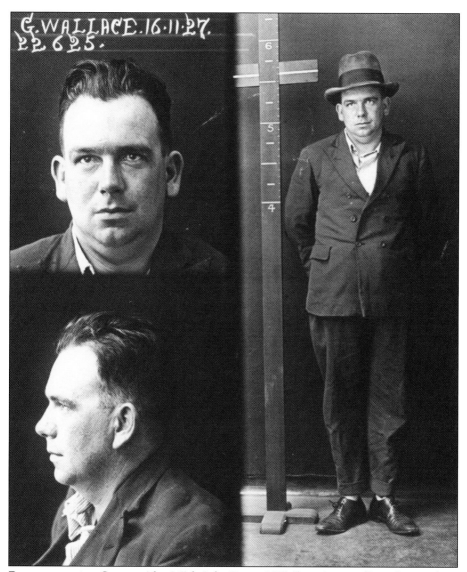

Razor gangster George 'the Midnight Raper' Wallace in a police photo taken a few months after the murder of Norman Bruhn. From the original photograph in State Records New South Wales

A 1922 police mug shot of Phil 'the Jew' Jeffs. He would realise his dream of becoming a crime tsar. From the original photograph in State Records New South Wales

Although in her later years sly-grog queen and cocaine dealer Kate Leigh enjoyed folk hero status, she was capable of violence and ruthlessness. She kept a razor in the pocket of her fur coat and a pistol in her purse. On 27 March 1930, she shot rival gangster Snowy Prendergast dead. State Library of New South Wales

Tilly Devine's house in Torrington Road, Maroubra, circa 1930, the scene of wild parties and, on two occasions, fatal shoot-outs. The Fairfax Photo Library

Tilly Devine, madam of Razorhurst, in the early 1930s. The Fairfax Photo Library

The murderous Frank 'the Little Gunman' Green, rival of Guido Calletti for the favour of Nellie Cameron.

Guido Calletti, razor-man, standover thug and terror of Darlinghurst, in the late 1920s. The Fairfax Photo Library

Future police commissioner William Mackay is decorated in 1933. Tough and innovative, he was known as a 'copper's copper'. The Fairfax Photo Library

'Pretty Dulcie' Markham, aged seventeen in 1930, 'confounded anyone who equated beauty with purity'. Image Library, State Library of New South Wales

'Big Jim' Devine during his trial for the manslaughter of taxi driver Fred Moffitt in 1931. The Fairfax Photo Library

'The Blizzard', Detective Superintendent Ray Blissett, is awarded the Queen's Police Medal for Distinguished Service in 1967. The Fairfax Photo Library

Nellie Cameron, aged twenty-six in 1938. She was beautiful, funny, smart 'and the most sought-after gangster's girl'. The Fairfax Photo Library

Frank 'Bumper' Farrell in his football days in 1950. He inspired both fear and affection among those who knew him. The Fairfax Photo Library

Above left: Lillian Armfield, Sydney's premier policewoman in the razor-gang years, attends an investiture ceremony at New South Wales Government House in the 1940s.

Above: 'A force for good' — Kate Leigh and a henchman dressed as Santa are feted at Lansdowne Street by Surry Hills locals in the late 1940s. Image Library, State Library of New South Wales

Left: 'I would give him money,' said Tilly Devine (with husband Jim in the early 1930s). 'If not, he would take it.' They divorced — bitterly — in 1944. The Fairfax Photo Library

'We'll be back when the money runs out,' said Tilly Devine, with Eric Parsons, as the Himalaya departed Sydney for London in 1953. The Fairfax Photo Library

Kate Leigh's main sly-grog shop in Devonshire Street, Surry Hills, as it is today. Note the side door to the left of the front window. Photo by the author

'I wish to God this 'ere sucking pig was Bumper Farrell!' said Tilly Devine when she cut the roast at her fiftieth birthday party. Eric Parsons is left of Tilly. The Fairfax Photo Library

Tilly Devine is seemingly unconvinced by Kate Leigh's show of affection in this 1948 photo session. The Fairfax Photo Library

'There's a bit of good old Australian history that's gone.' Kate Leigh's coffin is carried from St Peter's in Devonshire Street, Surry Hills. The Fairfax Photo Library

'By the end, she was pretty much broken.' An ailing Tilly Devine attends the funeral of her rival, Kate Leigh.

# 19

# The Girl in the Middle

Throughout Jim Devine's trial, much of the focus was on Frank Green's lover and accomplice, Nellie Cameron. Not quite twenty, her good looks, insouciance and mockery of authority struck a chord with many following proceedings. Adding to the charisma of the prostitute, thief and cocaine dealer was the much-bandied story of her fight, watched by a crowd which may have been 500-strong, in the backyard of a Darlinghurst pub with a fearsome prostitute named Black Aggie. The contretemps was sparked by a dispute over prostitution turf. Aggie 'owned' a lucrative corner and Cameron wanted it. The tale goes that both women stripped to the waist and fought it out. Aggie was bigger, but twenty years older, weaker and slower. Cameron was quick and vicious and quickly downed her opponent with blows to the stomach; then, when Aggie lay helpless on the cobblestones, Cameron raked her with her fingernails. Black Aggie left town.

Since Norman Bruhn's death four years before, Cameron had careened from Frank Green to Guido Calletti and back again. She would go on switching between the two almost until Calletti's death in 1939. The striking party girl was, on the surface, an odd companion to the mobsters. One observer noted how the manic Green's 'scowls and oaths contrasted strangely with the merry laughter of his

161

female pal and partner, sometimes known as "Sweet Nell of Tooth's Brewery".' Calletti, too, was a grim man unless committing a crime, when he brightened considerably. One newspaper reported how when both Green and Calletti fell for Cameron, 'the underworld erupted into a violent seesawing contest between them.'

Some who knew Nellie Cameron say she was worth every bruise and cut her lovers suffered. For someone whose beat was prostitution, dope-dealing, robbery and receiving, and bare-knuckle brawling, Cameron was still, somehow, a class act. Time and again, people who remember her say she was as at home in swish inner-city nightclubs such as Prince's and Romano's as she was at the Tradesman's Arms and the Fifty-Fifty Club.

Cameron had sultry good looks, blue eyes, thick glossy hair and a classy style borne of her upbringing on Sydney's prosperous north shore and her private-school education. Those who met her in her heyday recall a softly spoken, witty and fearless criminal. 'I'm no judge of beauty,' says Ray Blissett, 'but I reckon she was a great-looking dame.' To Vince Kelly, a reporter of the time, 'She had a charm that was her own, very exclusively her own in the underworld to which she descended, and a natural dignity that she never lost in the most hectic of circumstances.' And one Razorhurst scribe rhapsodised, 'Cigarette smoke curls ceaselessly from the soft lips of gangland's mystery girl, veiling the features that themselves veil with inscrutability her inmost emotions.'

Cameron's fatal flaw was her irresistible attraction to the underworld. Twice she fell pregnant to criminals who were her lovers and pimps, but lost the babies after miscarriages. By late 1931, she was a notorious femme fatale. She'd been a member of the original razor gang with Bruhn, driven a jealous Guido Calletti to cool the ardour of her suitor mobster Eric Connolly by shooting him in the stomach in February '29, vanquished Black Aggie, and been Frank Green's accomplice on the night he stole Jim Devine's tie pin and Fred Moffitt was shot. For a while, too, while Green and Calletti were behind bars or lying low, she was the lover of New Zealand standover man Edward 'Ted' Pulley.

Part of Cameron's allure was her bravery. No matter what was done to her (and in her time she was shot, slashed and beaten) she refused to squeal. Never was her adherence to the criminal code more in evidence than when, in November 1931, just five months after the death of Moffitt, Cameron was gunned down in Darlinghurst, near St Vincent's Hospital, where she had been visiting Green, himself recovering from near-fatal gunshot wounds.

Her shooting was the culmination of a bloody love-tangle that stretched back two years. In 1929, Cameron, with Bruhn in his grave, was living with Frank Green when Green fell in love with a society woman who was the girlfriend of a tearaway musician named Charles Brame. The woman was in turn smitten with Green. The gunman and the socialite became lovers. Meanwhile, Brame and Cameron repaid Green by having a fling with each other. When the society belle quickly and inevitably tired of the crude and boorish Green, the latter decided to reclaim Cameron by murdering his rival. He shot Brame in Belmore Park, near Central Railway, but Brame survived. Then, in mid 1931, just before the Devine tie-pin robbery, Green razor-slashed Brame. The musician again survived.

Green now set another trap. He persuaded Cameron to meet Brame in Liverpool Street, near St Vincent's Hospital, one night in late October. As Cameron and Brame stood talking in the lane, Green walked up. Brame later told police he saw Green reach inside his coat. He had assumed Green was drawing his pistol, so pulled out his own gun and blasted Green in the stomach. The bullet passed through Green's bowel and lodged near his spine. Green fell to the footpath, and Brame fled.

Cameron ran to the moaning Green's side and enlisted a passer-by to help her take him to St Vincent's. Doctors expected Green to die, but he slowly recovered. When questioned by police he told them he had no idea who shot him. Meanwhile, Brame, possibly guilt-wracked but more likely in mortal fear of what Green's friends would do to him, gave himself up to police, seeking safety behind bars. He was acquitted of trying to kill Green but gaoled for nine months for carrying an unlicensed firearm, for which sentence he was doubtless grateful.

At this point, in the absence of court or police records, matters grow murky. All that is known is that three weeks later, as Green's condition hovered between grave and critical in hospital, a woman in a Darlinghurst wine bar declared of him, 'It's a pity the bastard's not dead.' At that, another drinker, a friend of Green, slashed the woman on the cheek with his razor. The razor-man then left for St Vincent's Hospital to visit Green. Later that night, as the razor-slasher, Nellie Cameron and another man and woman left the hospital, they were bailed up by a gunman — like the slashed woman, there is no record of his name, but it was possibly Wally Tomlinson, who was living with the slashed woman in Cronulla and hated and feared Green. The gunman aimed his sawn-off rifle at the group, but they pounced on him and tried to grapple the weapon from his grasp. In the struggle, the gun discharged and Nellie Cameron pitched forward onto the road, shot in the side.

She was taken to St Vincent's for surgery. There, as ever, she was stoic. Though in terrible pain, she waited patiently for treatment, refused to cooperate with police when they asked who had shot her, and when a nurse wondered whether she wanted to inform her mother that she'd been shot, Cameron smiled, 'Don't worry her, nurse. I'll be all right.' Meanwhile, at about that time, the woman who was slashed in the wine bar was the victim of another razor attack, a reprisal for Cameron's shooting, in Pitt Street in the city.

When she recovered in mid 1932, Cameron was gaoled for two months for consorting with Frank Green. But a now-recovered

Green — who was due to stand trial for consorting with Cameron and other undesirables, as well as for stealing Jim Devine's tie pin — failed to keep his appointment with the magistrate and went, as they said in those days, into smoke.

The monotony of incarceration at Long Bay was broken for Cameron when she was taken from the prison to Darlinghurst Sessions Court to face a charge of gingering one of her clients, Frank Ward, of £15. Ward told the court that Cameron approached him while he was drinking in a hotel in Oxford Street. While they were chatting, the publican shouted them drinks. Cameron had then suggested he accompany her to a room nearby and he accepted. Later, he had discovered his 'roll' was missing from his vest pocket. Cameron, he was sure, had stolen it. Looking radiant and relaxed in her prison garb, she smiled sweetly when she denied the charge from the dock. How in heaven's name, she wanted to know, given that they were entangled on the bed the whole time, could she have stolen Ward's money without him seeing her?

Her ingenuousness certainly won over the normally stern Judge Herbert Curlewis, who observed to the jury: 'It's very easy [for Ward] to make these sort of charges, and sometimes it's very convenient to make an accusation against this class of woman. You know that not all married men are saints, but most of them, when a thing like this happens, have got sense enough to keep it to themselves, but Ward publishes it.' The jury quickly found Cameron not guilty, and she was bustled back to prison to tell her tale to the girls.

One person keenly following the progress of the police dragnet for the absconder Frank Green was Jim Devine. He had an excellent reason to want to see Green in custody, for before he disappeared, Green had broadcast throughout Razorhurst his intention to shoot Jim the first chance he got, then cut the ears off his damnable corpse and pin them to a wall in Stanley Street.

While Green was on the loose, Jim refused to venture from his Maroubra home without his bodyguard. So, for him, there was cause to celebrate when police finally arrested Green at a flat in Park Road, Moore Park, near the Captain Cook Hotel. As before, it was Nellie Cameron who inadvertently led the law to her lover. Police had tailed her from the moment she had been released from Long Bay, and one day an officer saw her buy two large pieces of porterhouse steak at a butcher's shop and deduced that it was unlikely that she would be eating both steaks herself. He followed her to the Park Road flat.

On 2 August, Cameron was cooking sausages for Green at the flat, where he had indeed been holed up, when police banged on the front door. High farce ensued. Green flung himself under a bed as the officers forced the door and tumbled in. 'Where's Green?' demanded Detective Sergeant Reg Kennedy of Cameron.

'Not here,' she said.

'Then whose feet are they sticking out from beneath that bed?'

'Oh,' said Cameron with unconvincing nonchalance, 'just my lover's.'

Police dragged a squirming figure out from under the bed, but, at a glance, this person looked nothing like their quarry Green. Green's hair was usually heavily oiled and elaborately quiffed, while this fellow had a bristle-cut. Green's complexion was pale, this chap's was an odd pumpkin-yellow. Green's features were mean, and somewhat battered but regular, while the man under the bed's face was contorted into a clownish grin and one of his eyes was closed tight. But the officers were not fooled for long by Green's ludicrous attempt to disguise himself. The giveaway, police said, was the trademark razor scar on the fugitive's right cheek. He had shaved his head, rubbed henna onto his face and screwed up his visage so he resembled Quasimodo. A huge wad of gum distended Green's cheek.

Kennedy chuckled, 'Well, you're certainly smart, Green. And a pretty cool customer, too. Fancy screwing up your face like that when you meet a pal. And I've been looking for you everywhere.'

An embarrassed Green spat out his gum and went quietly. 'Aw, ease it,' he told Kennedy. 'Break it down.'

'Hard luck, Frankie,' said Cameron as her man was led away.

One newspaper's headline read 'Sudden End of Gangster's Liberty', under which the article informed:

> Green is a gunman, a gangster, a night prowler, a vulture who preys on unfortunate women, a razor hand, an underworld terrorist. And the scar on his face, which an operation has failed to obliterate, makes him a marked man even when he cunningly changes his complexion with henna hair dye and screws up his face.

Green was sentenced to three months in Long Bay, and, while a prisoner, faced trial for relieving Jim Devine of his tie pin.

In the dock at Darlinghurst Court in late August, Green denied stealing the pin. Jim Devine was a liar, he snapped, and claimed that Jim had invited him and Nellie Cameron to a party at their home, then when the party was in progress Jim had become unpleasant and the two men had fought. Green knocked Jim over a lounge and Jim had picked up his gun and 'chased me and Nell out of the house'. When they were trying to flee in Moffitt's taxi, Jim had fired, killing Moffitt. Green said he had called out: 'Turn it up, Jim. You've shot the taxi driver,' and Jim had shouted back, 'Yes, and I'm going to shoot you, too.' In turn, Jim Devine angrily denied his former friend's version of events. There had been no party. Green had invaded his home. Devine reiterated how he had fired at Green in self-defence after Green stole his diamond tie pin at gunpoint.

Green's counsel, Mr McMahon, then asked the court how they could believe the testimony of a 'creature like Jim Devine, who lived on money earned by his wife on the streets'. At that, Tilly, her blonde hair coiled in hard, tight ringlets, face twisted in fury, leapt to her feet and shrieked: 'My husband never sent me out on the streets. You're a liar, Mr McMahon. He never did! He never did!' Writhing and yelling, she was ejected from the courtroom.

The jury retired, and its confused and unsettled members were unable to decide which, if either, of the men was telling the truth. So when they reconvened in the courtroom, they acquitted Green of theft. Before she left the court, grinning broadly, Nellie Cameron emitted a loud sigh of satisfaction.

# 20

# Deadline Darlinghurst

As the early 1930s continued, Australia's debt-ridden economy foundered as overseas creditors, themselves in dire financial straits, called in the money owed them. All over the land, the Great Depression took hold. Wages and pensions, like welfare spending and public works, were cut. Businesses closed their doors. Unemployment averaged 33 per cent throughout New South Wales, but in some working-class regions, such as Razorhurst, it hit 70 per cent.

The upper and middle classes of Sydney were not drastically affected. They had savings, were employed in established professions and owned their homes. But for the working stiffs who toiled in factories, shops and on the docks, the closure of these establishments meant unemployment, which meant poverty. For them, life was grim at best and desperate at worst.

Many could not afford clothing or nourishing food. Landlords turned tenants unable to pay their rent onto the street and sold their furniture. Subletting had always been rife, but suddenly there were twenty or thirty men, women and children cooped in a single terrace house. Many evicted families were clumped in appalling conditions in sheet-metal-and-paling shantytowns in Surry Hills, Redfern and Newtown. People cowered in caves in the Domain. They slept in parks in the warm months and in winter threw themselves on the mercy of church and Salvation Army charities or slept in verminous doss-houses. Some renters served with notices to quit refused to budge. They fortified their houses or flats with galvanised iron, barbed wire and sandbags, and squatted until police forcibly evicted them. There were break-ins and muggings as the destitute resorted to any means to lay their hands on money.

Unfed domestic animals roamed the alleys skinny-ribbed, plundering garbage bins and chasing rats. Abandoned litters of kittens mewed day and night. Kilometre-long queues snaked from Circular Quay where dole and sustenance coupons were handed out. Beggars fought each other for prime position on the street. Buskers wheezing Strauss waltzes on squeezeboxes and mouth organs, and singing Irish ballads and the apt new Bing Crosby hit 'Brother, Can You Spare a Dime?', provided a soundtrack for hard times.

Inevitably, the Depression bit into the profits of the racketeers. A customer to whom a big night out was drinking sly grog, having sex with a prostitute and buying a deal of cocaine now had to think twice about his evening's entertainment as he tightened his belt. Numbers at all establishments dropped. But there were still plenty among the well-heeled who could afford the goods and services they offered. Like any savvy captain of legitimate industry, Tilly and Kate reduced overheads by closing unprofitable brothels and groggeries and retrenching expendable staff.

Although Kate and Tilly's wealth can never be accurately gauged because they rarely filed tax returns, it's likely that, totting up property, cash and possessions, in the early '30s each was worth around £250 000, a fabulous sum then and the equivalent in today's money of millions of dollars.

Kate's sly-grog empire was memorably described by *People* magazine:

> *[Her kingdom is a] noisome slum which begins across the road*
> *from Central Railway Station and whose squalid, dirty, narrow*

*streets rise and fall across Surry Hills . . . The Hills are crammed with ancient hovels and terraces and life is characterised by the personalities of people, the rottenness of crime, the roughness of jungle justice, and the generous impulses of the badly-off towards the worse-off.*

Kate's was an 'empire of brothels, gambling joints, flophouses, sly-groggeries and gin mills [full of] prostitutes, pimps, thugs, blackmailers, thieves, bludgers and strong-arm toughs'. Tilly lorded it over equally seamy Darlinghurst, and pockets of Kings Cross, Woolloomooloo, Surry Hills and Paddington.

Kate and Tilly were both damned and romanticised in the press, whose relationship with the women was like that of two prisoners shackled together who hate each other but have no choice but to get along. Often the city's tabloid journalists knew more about a villain or victim than the police or politicians, since Kate and Tilly, who knew the value of public relations and were skilled spin doctors for their day, rang them to leak strategic information. Kate would telephone with news, suitably embellished, of an embarrassing incident that had befallen Tilly; Tilly would tip the paper to a crime she knew Kate had been planning for weeks. If some other gang was becoming a threat, or even getting uppity, Tilly or Kate would plant a story about their rival's operation that would bring the police down on their heads.

Knowing their readers loved it, *Truth*, *Smith's Weekly*, and later the *Sun* and the *Mirror*, chronicled every bloody street battle, every peccadillo and jape involving the women. The press splashed the story of how Tilly carried a suitcase emitting a foul smell into Central Police Court when facing trial in January 1932 for turning the Oxford Street air blue when the proprietor of the Canberra Café had sold her bad crayfish. She had then punched the police officer who arrested her. As proceedings wore on, the stomach-churning odour pervaded the courtroom. Gagging officials ordered Devine to open her suitcase. With a flourish and whoop of glee, she did so and, like a magician whipping a rabbit from a hat, revealed Exhibit A, the decaying crayfish.

Just weeks later, Tilly was back in court being convicted of consorting. She claimed she was too unwell to be gaoled since she suffered gastritis, a sore and 'probably broken' arm, and 'nervous dispairia'. All this was to no avail. When the judge sentenced her to six months' prison, she cursed out the prosecutor. On their front pages, the tabloids painted the scene. For example:

> *Devine flew into a frenzied rage. Her face turned a rich purple, her eyes became piggish, and in a berserk shriek which could be heard all over the building she poured out a stream of vile abuse upon the heads of all and sundry. 'You don't ---- give a ---- woman a chance. You're all ---- against me! You don't give a ---- woman a fair go.' It was a scene more reminiscent of a padded cell than a court of British justice.*

And also in January '32, when Kate Leigh was facing consorting charges, newspaper readers learned how she was 'smiling and smirking in the courthouse corridors, waving and wangling and bowing to acquaintances among the habitues, the press, the police and even deigning to beam upon the public'. She had brazenly faced down the prosecutor who reeled off her criminal record: perjury, consorting, possessing cocaine, found in a house in company of thieves, stealing, street fighting. 'I am a respectable woman with a lot of businesses,' she protested, 'and I have my own money.' A week later, the press made great sport of Kate's refusal to attend court to face charges of holding a gun to the face of Kings Cross woman Patsy Neill and threatening to 'blow your bloody head off, you bitch, unless you give me the two quid you owe me.'

When Kate was the following month sentenced to six months'

prison for the January charges, she complained that when Tilly Devine had been found guilty of a similar charge she was allowed to leave the country instead of doing time in Long Bay. When she learned of Kate's words, Tilly stormed into the office of *Truth*, which had fun with the encounter in its 7 February edition in an article headlined 'K-K-K-Katey . . . You're the Only "Girl" That I Abhor!':

> *Tilly made an informal — very informal — call on the editor and was in the sanctum before messenger boys, typists or secretaries could say a word . . . She had been listening to Kate Leigh's appeal against her sentence of six months for consorting. 'In the court,' declared Matilda, 'they said that a certain other underworld woman (meaning me) had been given a chance to go to England after being convicted for consorting. I was never convicted of consorting,' emphatically stated Matilda, pulling off her hat and allowing her hair to blow wildly across her face. 'I was never deported. I told the magistrate I would go to England and I went and when I wanted to come back, I came back. I'm not a bad woman. I'm not like Kate Leigh, anyway. I might drink and swear and have a run-in with the police now and then, but I don't take dope, and no one can say I have ruined young girls. Kate Leigh does all this. I'm a lady, I am. I can talk with the best people in Sydney. You might be the editor of* Truth *[and the editor blushed], but I have as much education as you.' And before Matilda left, the editor blushed some more, for, despite the fact that he sees all kinds and conditions of people, he fully realised that his 'language' education had been sadly neglected . . . when these two 'Queens of the Underworld' meet, the Marquis of Queensbury [sic] need not hang around, for his rules will not be needed.*

As well as playing up the women's rivalry and antipathy, the press did not stint when reporting on Tilly and Kate's generosity and community spirit. The two provided reams of good copy for both the crime reporters and the human-interest journalists alike. The nefarious heart of Ned Kelly beat in both women's breasts, but their kindnesses were many. Tilly and Kate did plenty to alleviate the suffering of the down-and-out in their constituencies. 'I could never knock a man back for a feed or a drink or a few bob,' Kate once said.

'Kate did a lot of bad, but a lot of good, too,' says former police-woman Maggie Baker, Lillian Armfield's right-hand woman in the Darlinghurst days. 'She made sure that no kid in Surry Hills ever went without a Christmas present. And if she saw a bloke sitting in the park in the rain she'd take him home. I was called to one of her sly-grog shops one day and there must have been at least five fellows asleep on the floor. I had to step over them. I said, "Kate what will happen if I step on one of these men?" She said, "Nothing, love, they won't feel a thing."'

Chow Hayes was another to see Kate's benevolent side, as relayed to his biographer, David Hickie, in the latter's *Chow Hayes — Gunman*. He described how every Christmas Kate erected makeshift barricades at each end of the block in Lansdowne Street in Surry Hills where she had her main beer house. She'd pay some drunks to dress up as Santa Claus, and have tables stacked with chocolates, cakes, lollies and lemonade, and toys for the local kids. Hayes pointed out that much of it was shoplifted. By turning it on for the slum children she encouraged all the customers, their fathers, to visit her place during the year '. . . because they'd say, "Kate's all right, she puts on a party every year for the kids." That went on for years. If you were sweet with Kate, she'd do anything for you and give you anything. But if you crossed her, she'd shoot you.'

Serious broadsheet newspapers railed that the tabloids' penchant for turning gangsters into folk heroes — much fun was had over Kate and Tilly's imprisonment forcing them to miss the opening of the Sydney Harbour Bridge in March 1932, for instance — was encouraging others to break the law. And while the new *Vagrancy Act*'s Consorting Clause had curbed the open gang warfare of 1927–1930, crime remained rampant.

'Small-time hoodlums are aping the dyed-in-the-wool criminals of Kings Cross and East Sydney,' claimed the *Mirror*. In the early months of 1932 alone, two policemen were beaten senseless in Market Street in the city, there was a rape and a shooting in an Elizabeth Street wine bar, and John Brady, a Chippendale thug, shot sixteen-year-old Winnie May Chown. Alexander Barrie, eighty-four, was stabbed to death by robbers who broke into his Windsor Street, Paddington, home. There were four recorded razor slashings in Darlinghurst and a score of muggings.

Tilly and Jim Devine were at a party when Jim's brother, Sid, was shot in the shoulder by a man named Guy Kingsbury. Big Jim himself was arrested in March, not for wounding or killing, but for driving without a licence. He claimed to the policeman who pulled him over that he had merely left his licence at home, but when police investigated they discovered Devine had not owned a driving licence since 1926.

# 21
# On the Town

In 1932, Phil Jeffs returned to Kings Cross from his lair on the New South Wales Central Coast. Since being shot in his own home in 1929 after the Eaton Avenue riot, Jeffs had kept a low profile while his wounds healed. To his Woy Woy neighbours, he was a legitimate businessman. Unbeknown to them, the frequent visitors who came by train to stay at his palatial home were henchmen who ran his Kings Cross brothels, gambling clubs and groggeries. Jeffs would entertain these underlings, collect his takings from them, then load them up with instructions and send them back to Sydney to take care of business.

Phil the Jew, the lowlife, cheap-flash rapist, woman-beater, gunman and razor gangster, was no more. The new Phillip Jeffs was a smoothie. He wore well-cut business suits, affected a suave, erudite manner and he dated classy women. Friends were awed by the size of his book collection, and his knowledge of philosophy and politics. The only thing that had not changed was Jeffs's burning desire to be a rich and powerful criminal.

In the '20s, Jeffs had worked as a bouncer and doorman at the Fifty-Fifty Club, a seedy dance hall and sly-grog and cocaine palace in the Chard Building (built in 1924) on the corner of William and Forbes streets. Now, in 1932, Jeffs was back at the Fifty-Fifty, having bought it cheaply from the previous proprietor, who was tired of constant police raids. When Jeffs took command, he solved that problem by heaping money on bent officers. He also forked out sums to hard men such as Frank Green as a guarantee that they would not cause trouble on the premises, and dissuade others from doing so. Jeffs considered such payouts essential overheads, much like electricity, heating, rent, liquor and drugs.

As an extra safeguard, realising his lengthy police record would attract the straight police and the press and so jeopardise the Fifty-Fifty's licence, Jeffs concealed his ownership. Until about 1935, he masqueraded as a lackey, manning the door, serving drinks and ejecting troublemakers, while his employee, a middle-aged, taciturn sly-grog veteran named Harold 'Snowy' Billington, played the role of manager. Jeffs and Billington carried on the charade for years. Giving evidence in 1933, Billington swore under oath: 'Jeffs is a general rouseabout at the place. He was very handy to me when I started. He is not employed practically as an employee. He is a pal and keeps me company. He is there for protection.' It is unrecorded whether Jeffs was on duty when a youth named Vic O'Grady fell or was pushed to his death from the top of the Chard Building onto William Street below.

A visitor to the Fifty-Fifty Club in its riotous mid-'30s heyday would enter the creaking cage elevator at ground level, and ride up past nondescript offices on floors one to three before alighting at the fourth floor. There stood a heavy door with a sign: 'Kings Bridge Club'. On the door was a side flap. A knock on the door, and the flap would be raised and a doorman, possibly Phil Jeffs, possibly Snowy Billington, would peer balefully out. The doorman would open the door, and frisk guests for firearms and ensure that they had money.

He would check whether they were a member of the club or knew someone who was.

If approved, the visitor entered a cavernous room with carpet on the floor, slightly tatty lounge suites, decorative palms and flower-filled vases, and deep chairs festooned with colourful cushions. Each window was covered by a heavy curtain so goings-on could not be seen from the street below. There were about ten bridge tables, each surrounded by four wooden chairs, at which guests sat drinking heavily or snorting cocaine from small bowls. Behind the bar were ice-chests yawning with many kinds of alcohol.

The noise from the 150 or more hooting, squealing revellers made conversation difficult. An electric fan cooled the guests and dispersed the thick, pungent fog of cigarette smoke. Patrons danced the foxtrot and the Charleston; a four-piece jazz band rattled off 'If You Knew Susie', 'Oh, You Beautiful Doll' and 'The Sheik of Araby'. When the jazzmen took a break, they would be replaced by a thin, pale youth who played sentimental favourites such as 'My Melancholy Baby' and 'Poor Butterfly' on a grand piano with a Persian silk scarf stretched exotically across its top.

One journalist partook of the Fifty-Fifty's hospitality and reported:

> [There are] Orientals, thugs, half-castes and painted women of the street mingling with well-known scions of Society, prominent actors and actresses and the leading lights of our legal and medical profession. The place has even had vice-regal connections. Unofficially, of course. Here is an Oriental, sphinx-like and furtive, dancing with an attractive young white girl. The dark-skinned foreigner opposite is an Egyptian, suspected of trafficking in that vilest of all trades, White Slavery.

White slavery or not, just about every other racket was conducted at the Fifty-Fifty Club. For all its pretensions to gentility, the Fifty-Fifty was a disreputable dive. Cocaine was freely sold by dealers, who paid a cut of their profits to Jeffs. There was gambling for those who could still afford it after paying the sky-high bar prices. Prostitutes, often supplied at a premium price to Jeffs by Tilly Devine, worked the Fifty-Fifty Club in profusion. They targeted the obviously wealthy who were slumming it for a night. Jeffs, who stood sentinel in the shadows by the bar, would exact a tithe of five shillings per client on his prostitutes, who charged around £2 for sex. Jeffs also instructed his women to insist their pick-ups buy them lots of drinks at three shillings or more. These expensive gin-and-tonics and scotch-and-sodas contained not a drop of alcohol.

On the floor above the club there were apartments where call-girls entertained. Jeffs hired 'steerers' (cabbies, hotel bellboys, barmen, waitresses) to approach prosperous-looking people and recommend that they visit the Fifty-Fifty. Some of these guests regretted their decision when Jeffs and his employees drugged them, or got them leglessly drunk and photographed them in a compromising position with a prostitute. The gulled high-roller faced the choice of paying Jeffs to destroy the photos and negatives, or seeing them sent to his family and employer.

Pickpocketing and robbery were rife at the Fifty-Fifty, but even those patrons lucky enough to escape an actual mugging were bled blind as they were hit on repeatedly by employees for tips: in the elevator as they entered, to get in the front door, to order a drink or a meal, to dance, to use the bathroom. To leave the club cost the customer a £5 'exit fee'.

Fights often broke out between soused customers and rival gangs. One night a dozen members of Woolloomooloo's Brougham Street Gang, out for blood after Jeffs sold them adulterated cocaine (the same scam that had caused the Eaton Avenue brawl), burst into the club looking for him. Jeffs, luckily for him, was elsewhere, but a bouncer suffered concussion when the mobsters smashed a bottle of gin on his head. They then tore the Fifty-Fifty apart, smashing hundreds of bottles of alcohol and glasses, destroying furniture, splattering paint and dog faeces over the walls and roughing up aghast patrons.

One unwelcome visitor to the club was Sergeant Henry Ham — the beat cop unlucky enough to be on the receiving end of one of Tilly Devine's anti-authoritarian harangues, now, four years later, a licensing policeman. He and two constables raided the Fifty-Fifty Club in March 1933, and took the names of those drinking alcohol and the waiters who'd served them. Jeffs, dropping all pretence of being hired help, stalked across the dance floor to the tables where Ham was writing in his notebook and snapped at his patrons: 'Tell them nothing. This is not a court of law.' When Ham ordered the waiters to hand over the money they had taken from the drinkers, Jeffs interrupted, 'This is money you received for sandwiches, not alcohol.' Then he barked at his employees, 'Now, don't say anything more!'

Everyone in Sydney knew that the Fifty-Fifty Club sold alcohol illegally after 6 p.m. and that gangsters gathered there. But raids by licensing police and Consorting Squad officers were rare. Jeffs paid some senior police officers to direct the honest Consortos' investigations elsewhere. After a rare bust in 1933, some detectives were called as witnesses for the defence. 'I have visited the Fifty-Fifty Club on many occasions,' said one, 'and I have never seen any liquor sold there.' Another swore, 'The club is well-conducted and I would have no objection to taking my wife there.' Nor had a third ever seen 'anything untoward take place'.

Another reason for the club's immunity was that Jeffs, like Kate Leigh, enjoyed the friendship of prominent politicians. He was, for instance, a good friend of state parliamentarian Anthony Alam, who not only had money invested in a sly-grog nightclub called Graham's, but a wife who was its proprietress. Once, in a parliamentary debate over the illegal alcohol trade in Sydney, Alam leapt to his feet to defend Jeffs's clubs: 'The Governor's wife herself could go in unattended. They are run on the most respectable lines.' One frustrated politician told the *Sydney Morning Herald*: 'We know the police have the power to put the nightclubs down, but they don't. There is a very definite reason for that, which we dare not raise.'

Late in 1933, Jeffs expanded. Again as a silent partner, he joined with Dr Reginald Stuart-Jones (an abortionist and SP bookie) and they became co-owners of the 400 Club, an upmarket sly-grog nightspot at 173–175 Phillip Street. The requisite police pay-offs were made upfront.

Still, operating the 400 Club required audacity, for it was located just a quick walk from the office of the police commissioner. Despite an outcry from the church, the press and politicians, police raids here, too, were few, and Jeffs and Stuart-Jones were always given plenty of advance warning of those that did take place. The partners co-existed cordially until 1937, when Jeffs decided he wanted the lucrative 400 Club all to himself. When Stuart-Jones refused to sell his interest in the establishment, Jeffs drugged him, then, when he was too groggy to defend himself, hurled the doctor down the stairs of the club and into Phillip Street. Stuart-Jones may have been vexed, but he was too scared to do anything about it. He walked out of his partnership with Jeffs poorer and wiser, and took up an easier life selling drugs.

The 400 was more salubrious than the Fifty-Fifty Club. Its clientele was almost exclusively what then passed for high society in Sydney. There was a main room for dining and dancing to a slick orchestra, and various bars where serious drinking took place. For guests who craved privacy, there were small, discreet dining rooms.

Exclusivity, however, did not quarantine the 400 Club from violence. One evening, two rival gangs somehow gained admittance and destroyed the classy ambience by turning on a riotous bar-room–style brawl. Well-dressed patrons fled for the exits as the gangs ripped into each other with fists and razors. At the height of the battle, a prominent advertising executive attempted to restore order by standing between the combatants and requesting in reasonable tones that they please respect their surroundings. A mobster listened politely, then sliced off the adman's ear. Phil Jeffs, appalled at the mutilation of one of his best patrons, made the best of a bad situation by picking the executive's ear up from the floor and rushing the appendage and its owner to hospital, where a surgeon reunited one with the other.

Jeffs's other establishments included Oyster Bill's nightclub at Tom Uglys Point, Blakehurst. Mobile high-flyers would make the thirty-kilometre trek there from the city to dance and drink illegally while watching the stars sparkle on the waters of the Georges River. Graham's, the up-market sly-grog shop of Jeffs's politician friend and protector Anthony Alam, was in Hunter Street. After its opening in 1936, Graham's thrived. Police headquarters was nearby, but somehow officers never seemed to notice anything untoward about Graham's, in spite of the wee-hours queues of taxis waiting to take reeling patrons home. Dick Reilly, then doing his criminal apprenticeship before becoming one of Sydney's most menacing crooks, was a cashier at Graham's. Many other villains found employment there, but so did a number of creative people attracted to the club's glamour and raciness. One of its waiters was Buster Fiddess, later a beloved television funnyman on Bobby Limb's variety shows in the '60s.

With friends in high places, such as Alam, Jeffs abandoned his sham of passing himself off as the hired help, and in the mid '30s became what he had always wanted to be: Mr Big. Dressed in tails and black tie, or in sharp dark suits, with gleaming white shirts whose high, starched collars sported elaborately patterned silk ties, he would mingle with guests at his clubs, bestowing with a smile and a wink a complimentary bottle of Johnny Walker to the showbiz high-flyers at this table, a bowl of cocaine to Miss Cameron and Mr Calletti at that. The Devines — Tilly in her expensive gowns and glittering jewellery, with her hair spectacularly coiffed; Jim, glowering, dark-suited and jittery as if he expected to be ambushed at any moment — were frequent guests at the Fifty-Fifty and the 400 Club. Jeffs always made a fuss of Tilly — a courtly kiss on the cheek, a table near the band, free champagne — and not surprisingly, because for years she had been investing parcels of her bordello profits in the astute Jeffs's enterprises.

# 22

# Pretty Dulcie

Dulcie Markham was wild at heart. She was convicted more than 100 times from 1930 until the 1960s, for prostitution, vagrancy, consorting, assaulting police and the public, keeping a brothel, drunkenness and drunk driving. 'Dulcie used to say it was easy to get a hundred pounds a night at a brothel,' recalled Lillian Armfield. 'She was completely incorrigible.' Markham's crimes were committed under an exotic assortment of aliases, including Tosca de Marquis, Tasca Damarene and Tasca de Marca, as well as the comparatively mundane Mary Eugene, Dulcie Taplin, Mary Williams and Dulcie Johnson. But to her friends, enemies and the police she was best known simply as Pretty Dulcie.

Markham, who periodically plied her trade in Melbourne at times of police clampdowns in Sydney, was a beautiful and vivacious prostitute and thief, earning herself the unfortunate nicknames 'the Angel of Death', 'the Black Widow' and 'the Hoodoo Girl', to add to the list of aliases. These nicknames seem understandable, as at least eight of her lovers were shot or stabbed to death. However, the jinx sobriquets exasperated her. 'Because men who have loved me have died, I've been called these silly names,' she sighed in the 1940s. 'I've even been sketched in one newspaper, feet apart, hair flying loose and holding a smoking gun. But I'm no gun-girl. I've never touched a gun in my life.

It's just unfortunate that those men have died. Believe me, I'm just an ordinary girl. These things have been thrust upon me.'

Like Nellie Cameron, Markham was born on Sydney's north shore, in 1913, and, after falling out with her family, she became a prostitute in Kings Cross and Darlinghurst in 1930. Until coarsened by her life and work, Markham had the ripe looks and figure of a movie star. In her most flattering photos, there is a resemblance to Ginger Rogers. As one who knew her observed, 'Dulcie confounded anyone who equated beauty with purity.' She was willowy, had piercing grey eyes, full lips, a pert nose and long blonde hair. She wore a silver slave chain on her ankle. 'She came shimmying into the underworld scene . . . and promptly created a sensation,' hubba-hubba'd the *Sun*. Markham's beauty distinguished her from most of the other women who sold themselves in Razorhurst and so she was rushed by clients who paid top money — up to £2 — for her favours when she was in her prime as a prostitute. Inevitably, she attracted the attention of Tilly Devine, who pegged her as a cash cow and installed her as a star attraction in her Palmer Street brothels.

'Dulcie had a magnificent figure and she walked better than any model,' recalls former detective Bill Harris. 'I'd rate her twelve out of ten. I'd give Nellie Cameron a seven or eight, and I'm afraid I'd only rate Kate Leigh a minus two. She was a big, fat old woman.'

Lua Niall, a Darlinghurst policeman in the '30s who knew Markham well, says the first thing you noticed about her was that she was 'absolutely beautiful'. But her good looks belied her criminality. 'She was always consorting with criminals. She made a lot of money out of prostitution. But Dulcie didn't have a brain in her head and I don't know where the money went. She certainly didn't save any, because I saw her when she was fifty and she was still working in a Darlinghurst brothel.'

In the public-enemy stakes, Markham's lovers were a league below those of Cameron, the only other prostitute as attractive. While

Cameron was fought over by gang leaders, it was Markham's fate to be romanced by foot soldiers. She married robber and extortionist Frank Bowen in 1934, but the pair parted two years later when Markham fell hard for another small-time villain, Alfred Dillon, who was just eighteen years old. Markham and Bowen would not formally divorce, but his murder in Kings Cross in 1940 would make the status of their union academic.

Ever dangerously undiscerning, Markham dumped Dillon for William 'Scotty' McCormack, the standover man who co-owned and job-shared the Darlinghurst fruit barrow with Guido Calletti. When Dillon heard he had been superseded he became mad with jealousy and told friends he would kill McCormack. Few took the young lout seriously. Then, after a day spent shadowing McCormack and Markham, Dillon cornered them in a shop doorway in William Street, just down from the Fifty-Fifty Club. Without a word, he rammed a bodkin (a large, blunt needle used to sew sugar bags) between McCormack's ribs and into his heart. Markham abandoned McCormack and fled into nearby Bourke Street. McCormack, who had not fallen when stabbed, lurched with a quizzical expression some distance along the William Street footpath. A passer-by, noticing his unsteady gait, asked him if he felt all right. 'I'm OK,' McCormack assured him — and fell dead.

Markham was hiding in a cinema when a fellow prostitute, who had been soliciting in William Street, tracked her down and told her McCormack had been killed by Dillon. Whenever she streetwalked for some weeks after, Markham wore a black wig as a sign of respect to Scotty. Dillon went to gaol and Markham was there to see him sentenced. When the judge, who had made allowance for Dillon's youth, gave him thirteen years for manslaughter, Markham, in the public gallery, waved Dillon farewell with tears in her eyes. After that, as far as is known, she forgot all about him.

# 23

# Deadly Triangle

Calletti and Green's take-no-prisoners tug of war over Nellie Cameron
was nearing its climax. Whenever the two hoodlums' paths crossed —
on the street, in gaol, in pubs — a brawl would erupt. Sergeant Colin
Delaney (whose damning character assessment of the gangster would
help scupper Calletti's *Truth* libel-suit scam in 1934) once passed a
bruised and black-eyed Calletti in the street and asked him whether
he'd been hit by a bus. 'No,' said Calletti ruefully, 'my old enemy
Frank Green and I had a disagreement.' Delaney asked if Calletti
planned to report Green for assault and Calletti laughed: 'I never go
to court. In these matters we fight it out ourselves.'

In January 1933, Cameron, then, like Markham, doing business
with Tilly Devine, was free on bail, waiting for her appeal against a
prison sentence for a drug conviction to be heard. In March, Frank
Green had just been released after serving a gaol term for consorting.
Both he and Cameron knew that her appeal would surely fail, so,
before the judge locked her up, he spirited her out of Sydney, bound
for Queensland. The pair, travelling by train with a prostitute friend
of Cameron named Maisie Allen and another man, made it only as far
as Newcastle, where Cameron fell ill with stomach pains. Green
checked her into Newcastle Hospital as 'Mrs Russell', he being the
most-concerned 'Mr Russell'.

While Green was skulking in the pubs of Newcastle waiting for Cameron's health to improve sufficiently for them to continue their journey, he was recognised by police officers who put him under surveillance. It was only a matter of time before they realised that the Mrs Russell whom Green was visiting in hospital was the bail absconder Nellie Cameron. Green soon realised that the police were onto him and would be planning to arrest Cameron as soon as she was well enough to be taken back to Sydney and gaol. So nearing midnight on 21 March, in torrential rain and lashing winds of up to 100 kilometres an hour, Green and his male friend stole into Cameron's ward, lifted the sick, weak woman out of bed, wrapped her in an overcoat and hefted her from the hospital into the gale.

As soon as a nurse saw Cameron's empty bed, the hospital reported her abduction to police, and squad cars combed Newcastle for the criminals. Green, Cameron and their friends eluded the lawmen. Drenched and freezing, they stole a car in Hamilton and drove to Sydney to hole up where they thought they'd be safe — Razorhurst.

The lovers continued to evade Sydney police, but their whereabouts was no secret to the underworld, and when Guido Calletti was released after his two-year prison sentence for his thwarted attempt to rob the grazier, he again made a beeline for Cameron, now recovered from her illness. Calletti cajoled her into agreeing to dump Green and going to live in Brisbane with him. Two weeks after the Newcastle hospital kidnap, Cameron was again heading north, but with a different lover this time. Unlike her escapade with Green, she made it all the way to Queensland. She and Calletti lived quietly in Brisbane for a month or so until local police learned they were there and gave them a choice: get out of town or be arrested. Calletti and Cameron had no option but to return to their nest and take their chances. They caught the train to Sydney. When they arrived at Central Station, an irate Frank Green was waiting.

Green and Calletti slugged it out in Woolloomooloo. Both agreed that to the victor would go the spoils, namely Nellie Cameron. That was fine by her. Their fist fight in a backstreet was watched by a cheering, wincing crowd of nearly 600. As ferocious one-on-one streetfights go, old Sydneysiders say it has been rivalled only by the legendary 1950s marathon stoush in the Domain between Jimmy Carruthers, world-champion boxer and proprietor of the local hotel the Bells, and the boxer and tough guy Ray Colman. Carruthers won that one, but when Green and Calletti fought over Nellie Cameron, there was no clear victor. For an hour, the two men punched, gouged, kicked and wrestled each other, until their bodies were bloodied and their clothes in tatters, and neither was capable of continuing. With no winner, Cameron chose to stay with Calletti, and Green could do nothing but churlishly withdraw to plan his next move to win Nellie Cameron's heart.

An opportunity arose in June when Calletti again fell foul of the law. 'I was stationed at Regent Street,' Ray Blissett says, 'and a bloke came in and said he'd been assaulted and robbed on a train. The description of the fellow who'd done it fitted Calletti. I knew where Guido hung around — Darlinghurst, Woolloomooloo — and went out looking for him. I rousted him and arrested him for vagrancy. I kept him locked up on that pretext until the man he robbed on the train arrived at the station to identify him. Calletti copped six months in Long Bay.'

Now, again, one suitor capitalised on his rival's forced inactivity. Green begged Cameron to return to his bed. He partially succeeded, but for all her charms, Cameron was a poisoned chalice. In one wild brawl with a man who'd tried to take Cameron from him, Green had his nose all but bitten off; in another, a knife fight, he nearly lost his right hand — his gun, razor and best-punch hand. After the second of these, Cameron delivered the badly injured Green to St Vincent's Hospital, where doctors did what they could to repair his hand, the muscles, arteries and tendons of which had been severed. Green told medics and police his injury had not happened when he'd been knife-fighting, but when he 'fell on a spiked fence. It seemed to rip my hand open.' Another time, he returned home to his and Cameron's flat and found a man hiding under their bed. She protested that she had no idea who the stranger was and that he must be a prowler. Green and the interloper fought, but the man was armed and shot Green in the stomach. The wound was not serious and he recovered quickly; when he was discharged from hospital, a contrite Cameron was there to nurse him back to health.

Revolving doors, swings and roundabouts. In January 1934, Green was again in gaol on a consorting charge, and Calletti, now released, reclaimed Cameron. This time, he thought, she wasn't getting away. He took her to Melbourne and married her.

Not that being Mrs Calletti earned Nellie a holiday from work. In the month they spent in Melbourne after their nuptials, Cameron was twice arrested for soliciting, once using the alias Alma Johnson and on the other occasion the poetic Nelly Kelly.

When they returned to Sydney, Calletti and Cameron declared that they were going straight and opened a fruit shop in Paddington. In *Rugged Angel*, Lillian Armfield recalled the change of image. 'I think I was one of the first to learn they were married.' They told her they were going straight, and invited her to look at their shop. 'It didn't have much stock, and I guessed it would only be a front for a sly-grog shop . . . I didn't take seriously their claim that they intended to become reformed characters. [Nellie's] record and Calletti's were too bad for me to believe that.'

In his career, Guido Calletti tried many ways to make a pound: most were illegal and required little work, unless smashing someone on the head from behind and relieving them of their wallet could be classified as such. One of his most audacious get-rich schemes was to sue *Truth* for libel in the Supreme Court, in November 1934. The spur for his action was an article in the tabloid which branded Calletti and his wife as 'disreputable'.

Hoping to be awarded a swag of defamation money, Calletti dressed up for his day in court. He wore a heavy, brown-striped suit, a colourful tie, and his short, dark hair was plastered flat with pomade. An expression of bruised innocence replacing his usual querulous one, Calletti took the stand to be gently quizzed by his counsel, Mr Williams. He was a labourer, he asserted softly, who lived in Miller Street, Hurstville, with his wife Nellie. He had been involved in crime before, but: 'Since coming out of gaol and marrying, I have turned over a new leaf. I tell his Honour and the jury that I am out to make an honest living.' To that end, he had kept away from his troublemaking friends and rented a fruit shop in Underwood Street, Paddington, around the corner from the police station, for fifteen shillings a week. He and Nellie had worked hard, and their endeavours were earning them a wage of about £4 a week. All had proceeded smoothly for a month ('I was helping her to go straight, and she was helping me to go straight') and then his noble attempt at abiding by the law was scuttled by *Truth*, whose story had defamed him.

After the article was published, claimed Calletti, 'people would not come into my shop and I had to give it up because I could not pay the rent.' Dismayed, but undeterred in his resolve to be an honest man, Calletti had borrowed money from his sister to take out a mortgage on another store in Waverley, but, again, the public shunned the shop and all because of *Truth*. He had had to close the doors of that shop, too. Since then, he had been trying to support himself and his wife by labouring. He was suing the tabloid for libel so he could clear his name and open another shop. A Sergeant James Comans appeared for Calletti. He backed the mobster's claim that while Calletti was proprietor of the Paddington store, no complaints had been made against him. Nor had any of his underworld associates been seen there. There had never been any untoward noise.

King's Counsel Watt led *Truth*'s defence. He told the court of Calletti's long and violent criminal history, and insisted that *Truth* had not libelled or defamed Calletti because it was impossible to destroy the good reputation of a man who had no good reputation to begin with. Calletti angrily responded that he had committed only a very few crimes, and most of his convictions had been a result of either mistaken identity or victimisation by police. He had certainly never heard of the razor gangs. Watt reminded the court that in the month after Calletti and Cameron had wed, she had been booked for prostitution. Again Calletti blustered, saying that she hadn't been soliciting, merely catching up with old friends on the street.

Now, Watt, who had assembled a group of policemen delighted to testify against Calletti, asked Detective Sergeant Colin Delaney of the CIB, the man whom Ray Blissett had succeeded at Glebe and who would later become police commissioner, what he knew of Calletti. Delaney didn't mince words: 'I would say that Calletti . . . a flash, handsome Australian of foreign extraction . . . is a daring and dangerous criminal. I would further say that he has been one of the worst criminals we have had in New South Wales in recent times. He is a man who I know has lived on the proceeds of bad women for a number of years. I have never known him to do any remunerative work.' Delaney then told the court how in his police career he had always tried to help criminals whom he believed were making an effort to turn over a new leaf. And, Watt asked, was the detective of the opinion that Guido Calletti was one such reformed character? 'Unfortunately,' said Delaney, 'no.'

Delaney was followed by Detective James Walker, who glared at Calletti and said: 'In my opinion, Calletti is a gunman and a man who lives on the earnings of street women. He is a man who will resort to any violence to gain his own ends.' Walker told how once he had served a summons on Calletti at the fruit shop demanding that he pay court costs that had been levied on him. Nellie Calletti had yelled at her husband, 'Aw, Guido, why don't you just go out to the "Bay" instead of paying the bloody costs?' Calletti, said Walker, had shouted back, 'I've had enough boob! I'm not going back there.'

Then, most damningly of all, a Detective Robinson took the stand and said he had arrested Calletti for consorting with criminals twice in the past eight weeks. This was a period during which Calletti claimed his behaviour had been beyond reproach.

When the time came for the jury to retire to decide whether Guido Calletti had been libelled by *Truth*, and if so, how much he should be compensated for the injury to his reputation, the judge told the jurors that before reaching a decision their task was to think hard about the evidence they'd heard and decide what kind of a man Calletti was. They had to decide whether 'a man of the worst reputation is entitled to the same measure of damages as one of unsullied and unblemished reputation'.

The jury found *Truth* had libelled Calletti, but if the criminal was hoping for a big payout, he was sorely disappointed. Financial damage to his character was assessed at one farthing, a quarter of a penny. Calletti swallowed his disappointment and eventually saw the funny side. He framed a copy of the jury's finding and hung it on his wall.

# 24

# Shady Ladies

As stated previously, Tilly Devine and Kate Leigh, for all their devotion to acquiring money and possessions, were socialists at heart. Tilly's impoverished youth in Camberwell left her with a lifelong preference for any political party whose policy was to help the poor. She was scornful of New South Wales's right-wing New Guard, and her haranguing of Francis de Groot after he disrupted the opening of the Sydney Harbour Bridge in March 1932 would not be quickly forgotten by de Groot himself nor by anyone else who heard it.

George Parsons says that in later life she became a friend of East Sydney Labor politicians and officials such as Eddie Ward. 'I don't know if Tilly ever articulated a political philosophy, but she was working class and she voted Labor. She believed in levelling up, that everyone is as good as everyone else. People need opportunities. She said, "Crime is a result of social conditions." If social conditions changed, the crime scene would change. That could have been a rationalisation for her own activities. She could never answer one question that my father would put to her: "If you steal because you're poor, why don't *all* the poor steal?"'

Kate actually politicked on behalf of the Labor candidates of Surry Hills. There is a 1931 photo of her seated at a wooden table and handing out political pamphlets. Any thirsty socialist knew they could

always get a free drink after hours at Kate's grog shops. If a similar
spirit of generosity existed at Tilly's establishments it is unrecorded.
Tilly believed that Kate supported the local politicians for other than
ideological reasons. 'Kate,' she once said, 'got away with her dope-
pushing and white slaving by means of Labor contacts in municipal
politics.'

If Tilly's charge was true, Kate's connections did her scant good in
1933 when the police, possibly embarrassed into action by her growing folk-hero status ('My sly-grogging has kept half of Sydney's poor
alive,' she'd crow, and the *Daily Telegraph* once called her 'a kindly
provider of a social service in a repressive era'), decided it was time
they made an example of her. In February, she was hauled into Newtown court on a plethora of charges from sly-grog selling to stealing,
including the theft of seven boxes of plants and five baskets of ferns
from outside a Marrickville home.

Standing in the dock, shrouded in a heavy silver-fox fur despite
high summer's heat, and wearing many rings and a huge hat, she
chuckled as the prosecution described how she was being driven by
her minions Ronald Williams and John McIntyre when she saw the
plants and decided they would be exactly what she needed to spruce
up her groggeries. She ordered her sidekicks to stop the car and steal
the plants. They did so, but were seen by neighbours and the number-
plate of her limousine was noted and reported to police. When the
three were remanded for breaking, entering and stealing, she called
to her supporters in the courtroom: 'Hurry up and get my bloody bail
fixed up! I don't want to hang around all day!'

While free on bail for those charges, in June, she faced trial on
another. The previous December she and her sometime lover and
bodyguard, hard-eyed, broken-nosed Henry 'Jack' Baker, had broken

into a store in Newtown and stolen groceries. Someone informed on them and the police came calling. In court, however, just as she and Baker were about to be gaoled, Kate's plant-stealing accomplices Williams and McIntyre stood up and confessed to the crime.

A week later, Kate, redefining the term 'incorrigible', was again in the dock, at Sydney Quarter Sessions, charged with receiving groceries and meat stolen by Baker and another underling named Walter Saari from a store in the western Sydney suburb of Liverpool in January. A Detective Tolley had entered Kate's premises in Bourke Street, Surry Hills, and found the pilfered goods. Kate conducted her own defence and made the court laugh when she accused Tolley of eating the evidence, namely a large slice of cheese. She also reduced the gallery to gales of laughter by producing a meatless hambone and challenging the Liverpool storekeeper to identify it as the one stolen from his shop. In spite of her best comic efforts, the jury in the end failed to see the funny side and found Kate, Baker and Saari guilty. Saari was sentenced to twenty-three months in prison, and Baker to three years because, said Judge Curlewis, he was an habitual criminal and 'a rotter' besides.

Knowing that she, too, would surely be sentenced to a lengthy spell in Long Bay, Kate begged leave to strike a bargain with Curlewis. After piteously explaining that her long criminal career, which dated back to 1897, was 'all a result of my never having been given a chance', she promised the judge that if he spared her from incarceration this time, she would leave Sydney for five years. Her daughter Eileen had been banished from Sydney the year before in lieu of a prison term for prostitution. The judge mused that in Kate's case, too, rustication, the legal term for banishment, would indeed save the taxpayer the cost of accommodating her in Long Bay and agreed, with the proviso: 'You are bound over in your own recognisance to refrain from dishonesty and from associating with criminals, and also that you will not come within 200 miles of Sydney for a period of five years. If you do, you will probably be sent to gaol for five years.'

Kate was visibly relieved and thanked the judge, but still could not help chirping, 'Can't I come down just once for a holiday?'

Curlewis grinned, 'Yes, but if you do, you may find yourself staying here for quite a long time.'

With much fanfare, parties, and teary farewells, Kate Leigh packed her bags, put her various sly-groggeries and other enterprises in the hands of trusted employees, and departed Surry Hills for her hometown of Dubbo.

To nobody's real surprise, her rustication did not last. In the first week of August, she was spotted in Surry Hills by a Detective Sergeant Bowie, who arrested her on the spot. This time an angry Judge Curlewis sentenced her to two years in Long Bay for breaking her recognisance. At that news, she bounded from the dock and, to Curlewis's great discomfort, embraced him and Bowie, as if to say 'better gaol than Dubbo'.

'Them mugs couldn't get me out of Sydney without they took Sydney away somewhere and buried it!' she chortled to a fellow prisoner during her first week inside. 'I'm here, and while I'm here I'll have a good time. It's better than being stuck away somewhere in the blasted bush.' In prison she was reunited with daughter Eileen, who, like her mother, had defied her rustification order, returned to Sydney and been caught.

Tilly Devine was behind bars then too, serving six months for consorting, robbery, assaulting a policeman and resisting arrest. (At Tilly's sentencing at the Appeals Court, Judge Edwards had to clear a large space on his desk to accommodate the numerous files that comprised her criminal record. 'Goodness me,' he gasped. 'Is this all hers?' When her lawyer attempted to explain that many of the charges had arisen from good-hearted rowdiness at his client's birthday parties, the judge declared, 'Well, she must be a very old woman!')

It is not known whether Tilly and Kate fraternised in prison. Most likely, each gave the other a wide berth as they fell back on their comfortable Long Bay lives of plentiful food, cushy tasks and regular visitors who briefed the celebrated prisoners on their various criminal enterprises, and never left the gaol without instructions on how to administer the rorts and rackets in their absence. There is a report of Kate lolling in the sunshine on a prison lawn conditioning her long greying tresses with a paste made of mashed onion, cream and Condy's Crystals.

In the mid 1930s, Kate was in her fifties. Her buccaneer spirit still burned, but she was slowing down. She was vastly overweight and, after a half century of bad diet, late nights and the stress only law-breakers know, beginning to suffer from the ills of old age. Conversely Tilly, nineteen years younger and in her mid thirties, was in her prime. She cut a lightning strike of colour in drab Depression days. Her hair, often dyed platinum-white à la Hollywood's Mae West — whom, with her sexy brassiness, Tilly reminded many people of — was a soufflé of lacquer-fixed kiss-curls and wavy ringlets that fell to her shoulders. Often her crowning glory was topped by a smart cloche hat. She plastered her eyes, eyes that could be limpid and laughing, or mean pit-bull slits when she was angry, with mascara in an age when few women did. Like Kate Leigh, even in summer's swel-ter she swathed herself in bulky furs. She wore diamonds and rings on every finger and even on a few toes. Her tight little mouth was painted into a bow shape. But unlike the more pragmatic Kate — who kept an expensive pianola on her premises, not to play but as a surety against bail — Tilly regarded her possessions as affirmations of how far she had come from Camberwell. She boasted endlessly of her art, furniture and jewellery.

Despite not having a telephone because she was paranoid about foes tracking her down, in her heyday in the 1930s Tilly ran a vice empire the likes of which Australia had never seen. Her operation was three-tiered. The best-looking, classiest, most experienced prostitutes administered to the well-heeled: celebrities, businessmen, politicians and senior police officers. They operated out of a handful of sumptuously furnished and decorated Darlinghurst terrace houses, complete with phonogram and bar, or in hotel rooms, or went to the customer's own home or office. They charged the premium rate, which, in the 1930s, was £2–5 a time plus a generous tip. Generally, Tilly would take one-third of this fee and allow the prostitute to keep the tip. When they were not in her employ, many of Tilly's topline sex workers were restaurant waitresses, theatre usherettes or salesgirls supplementing their wages from the major department stores.

To cater for less-wealthy factory workers and tradesmen, Devine installed in her seedy Palmer Street terrace-house brothels her 'tenement girls'. Often they were victims of the Depression: poverty-stricken young women; deserted unmarried mothers; wives from the suburbs with families to feed, who came to Darlinghurst by train or tram and returned to their homes at night; women from the bush; or young nurses and domestic staff working in St Vincent's Hospital, Sydney Hospital and Crown Street Women's Hospital. Tilly's offsiders would approach such women and tell them they knew a nice lady who might be able to help them. That nice lady, of course, was Tilly Devine. The 'tenement girls' gave their total earnings to Tilly, who banked for them four shillings out of every twenty they earned, and, from the remaining sixteen shillings, paid for their accommodation, food and medical supplies, doled out pocket money and bought them clothes, and still had a nice sum left over for herself.

Then there was the 'boat squad'. They were older, hardened prostitutes or rough-and-ready young women from the local factories, who, for a few shillings a time, gave rough-and-ready comfort to visiting merchant seamen and servicemen in squalid dockside rooms and flats, or sometimes in the sailors' tiny bunks on-board ship. These women were skilled gingerers, but, operating as they did in the more dangerous realms of prostitution, they were often beaten, abused and themselves robbed by their customers.

Tilly's prostitutes moonlighted as her shoplifting team. She would often send them out to steal from David Jones or Mark Foys, from corner shops and the Harbour wharves. Tilly would sell the stolen goods at a little less than half the retail price to friends in the trade or at the markets. Nor was she above sending her workers out to roll and rob drunks or pick the pockets of people in the crowd at cinemas, at the races, the Rugby League and cricket, and at the boxing and wrestling matches at Sydney Stadium. Stealing the clothes, wallets and personal belongings of people swimming at the Domain Baths was another popular scam.

Tilly was a benevolent despot. When one of her 'girls' was gaoled, she would arrive at Long Bay on visiting days laden with food parcels. And she would invite the more presentable of her prostitutes to add racy glamour to her many parties at Torrington Road and various Palmer Street hangouts. Inveterate party girl Tilly never needed an excuse for a celebration. She called them 'shivoos'. A birthday, the release of a friend from gaol, a bail-raising bash to help a friend in trouble with the law or fundraisers for pals down on their luck — anything would be a good reason to knock the top off a bottle or two. One of her biggest celebrations was in the mid '30s when she and Jim hosted a bail-raising party at the Maccabean Hall, Darlinghurst, for a criminal named Kelly who had been charged with attempted murder.

Tilly's parties were raucous, raunchy affairs where guests sang and danced to the piano or a gramophone playing graphite records (known as '78s' for the number of times per minute the turntable spun). People played two-up and conspired to commit crime, and snorted cocaine and made love. At some stage at every shivoo, Tilly would fling her skirt about and (warble in a voice not quite as good as she believed it to be) the music-hall hits of her London youth.

For all the fun, given the nature of those present, there were regular outbreaks of violence. Guests always ran a risk of being stabbed or shot at a Tilly Devine party. At one Palmer Street event in the early 1930s, Tilly was pestered relentlessly by an amorous drunk. At first she played along, teasing and flirting with him. But when he began to grab at her, Tilly's coquettish smile vanished. Without warning, she picked up a pair of tailor's shears lying on a sewing machine and drove the sharp end into the man's left cheek, spraying blood over his shirt and onto the wall beside him. He ran from the house with the scissors hanging, like a banderilla in a bull's flank, from his face, and Tilly kicking him and screaming abuse. When her victim had been taken to hospital for stitching, Tilly calmed down and partied on as if nothing had happened. 'There's only one way to deal with blokes who go the grope,' she declared.

In February 1934, Tilly and Jim visited Melbourne. They were in trouble almost from the moment they arrived. Big Jim got into a fight at the Palestine Club in Exhibition Road. He was hit on the head with a heavy object but not before he had knocked one man cold. Days later, Tilly was arrested for administering a brothel in Carlton with prostitute Dolly Quinn, an old friend from Palmer Street. Police had raided the bawdyhouse, which was rented by Quinn, to apprehend her and, seeing Tilly there, arrested them both. In court, Tilly claimed it was all a terrible mistake. She had no idea Dolly was running a brothel. She had decided to remain in Melbourne for a month or two and saw a newspaper ad offering a room to rent. Lo and behold, when she applied, the landlady was good old Dolly. The judge was unconvinced and sentenced Tilly to a year in gaol. Dolly Quinn received six months. Tilly sought leave to appeal. Judge Hauser agreed and asked for £100 bail.

While she was waiting for the appeal to be heard, Tilly fled home to Sydney. 'Twelve months' prison for gossiping on the street corner,' she carped on her return. 'I wasn't about to hang around for that.' In

1934 and 1935, she was arrested eleven times, for consorting, using indecent language in the street, and five times for resisting arrest.

Kate Leigh had a scare of her own in 1935. With the wowsers seemingly distracted by some other social iniquity, the State Government eyed its much-reduced revenue since closing the pubs at 6 p.m. and seriously considered extending opening hours until nine or ten. Proponents of the change argued that Queensland's hotels shut their doors at 8 p.m. and Western Australia's at nine, and neither state was Sodom or Gomorrah because of it. In England and the Continent, pubs stayed open until late and society had not collapsed there either; whereas in the United States, where total prohibition was enforced, gangsters were running riot. As well, said the trade unions, six o'clock closing discriminated against workers whose shift ended later in the evening. Moreover, early closing was encouraging drinkers to break the law by driving them into sly-grog shops, argued those who sought to liberalise the licensing laws.

But just when it seemed that the government would vote to extend licensing hours, the temperance and church groups found a second wind, complained noisily, and the situation remained as it was. Kate heaved a sigh of relief and declared that the drinks were on the house.

# PART 3
# Colourful Identities

# 25

# An Uneasy Truce

Kate and Tilly had been deadly foes for nearly seven years. Gunman Gaffney, Fred Moffitt, Barney Dalton, Snowy Prendergast and others were dead because of the women's feud. Countless lieutenants — such as Frank Green, Bruce Higgs and Wally Tomlinson — had been slashed, beaten, stabbed and shot. Then in 1936, one of William Mackay's first acts when he became police commissioner was to read the riot act to Tilly and Kate, calling the warring women into headquarters for a meeting with himself and other senior police.

Mackay told them he was not so stupid that he didn't realise what just about everybody else but the wowsers did — that selling sly grog and running brothels were victimless crimes, and that there was a demand by many, many God-fearing and respectable Sydneysiders for the services Kate and Tilly provided. He was not about to be a spoilsport and deprive the people of their fun. Heaven knew, he liked a wee drop himself.

Then came the ultimatum: if Kate could run her groggeries and Tilly her brothels quietly and cleanly and without violence, if they agreed to inform the police about the activities of other, less-favoured gangs, the present, manageable level of police harassment of Tilly and Kate (with its occasional raids, arrests and quick release from prison) would continue. But, and it is easy to imagine Mackay glowering at the pair as he spoke, the shootings and slashings and every other form of mayhem they'd been perpetrating on each other for so long had to cease immediately. Likewise the cocaine selling by Kate and Jim Devine. And the stealing, too. And no more gingering by Tilly's girls. If Tilly and Kate chose not to comply, Mackay reportedly made clear, he'd close every brothel and groggery and put both women in gaol for twenty years. He had enough on his hands coping with a spate of domestic razor-slashings and murders, and a new generation of young thugs, often in their teens, who were shooting and bashing police and the public around Central Station and Newtown.

The old enemies saw reason that day. Life, they realised, would be easier without the warfare and, of course, customers would be more likely to spend their money in places where there was not a fair chance that they'd make their exit on a stretcher. Kate and Tilly promised Mackay that they would do their best to quieten down and get along.

In the decades left to them, they mostly kept their promise. There would be many more prison terms for each — in the following months alone, Kate served four weeks for shoplifting a cardigan worth eight shillings and sixpence from McDowells, and Tilly was locked away twice for consorting. Tilly and her prostitutes did continue to ginger customers, if perhaps not as often or as brazenly, and Kate still dabbled in cocaine, though in lesser quantities. There would be public flare-ups between Tilly and Kate themselves, but from now on there was an element of gleeful street theatre in their catcalling and shoving matches. There was the odd punch-up between their gang members, for, inevitably, a lot of wounds remained open after years of eye-for-an-eye retribution. But there were no more killings or mutilations.

So, in the mid 1930s, all-out warfare between the Devine and Leigh gangs stopped. Over the next fifteen years, the two women even developed a grudging admiration (though never an actual liking) for each other. Sydneysiders knew them by sight and, repelled yet fascinated, recounted their deeds. Tilly and Kate were on their way to becoming – like Don Bradman, Bea Miles, Yabba the barracker on the hill at Sydney Cricket Ground, and Arthur Stace (who chalked 'Eternity' on Sydney's footpaths) — true Australian folk heroes.

# 26

# Blood and Roses

The Depression was easing by the mid '30s and people had more money to spend. Phil Jeffs's Fifty-Fifty and 400 clubs and Graham's nightclub prospered. They offered booze and entertainment in slicker surroundings than Kate Leigh could offer the underworld characters and what one Sydney newspaper called 'parliamentarians and men of good character, of wealth, of business standing or of good family' who queued for entry.

By 1936, the police allowed the nightclubs to sell alcohol after 6 p.m. with only the odd perfunctory raid. This may have been because of Mackay understandably designating a low priority to closing down sly-grog dealers, considering his troops better occupied catching thieves and murderers. And undoubtedly, some police still accepted the bribes of the proprietors to look the other way. Then, too, it was hard for a policeman to get too worked up over joints that always offered a cop a free meal and a beer in the kitchen when they dropped by. Night after night, the Fifty-Fifty Club, the 400 Club, Graham's, Oyster Bill's, Macleay House (a chemin-de-fer parlour in Macleay Street, Kings Cross) and Bondi's Lido Club continued to resound with the noise of popping corks and 'Here's to you!' On the rare occasions when police visited and took names, those names were not made available to the press.

Normal procedure when police raided, for example, the Fifty-Fifty Club was that officers would knock on the security door, which would customarily take some minutes to be opened. By the time the police gained entry, the alcohol would have been hidden in safes, under the floor or dangled on string from the windows, and the tipplers at the tables and the bar would be transformed into bridge players, brows furrowed in concentration over their hand of cards, and good citizens chatting over lemonade and tea. Vases of flowers would appear on each table. The orchestra which moments before had been thumping out the latest hot jazz from Harlem would perhaps be tinkling primmer fare like 'Silver Threads Among the Gold'.

One time when the police came calling on 22 January 1936, the door was opened with more alacrity than Jeffs and Snowy Billington would have wished, and patrons were caught cold drinking wine, whisky and beer. Police had no choice but to prosecute them. However, when summons were issued, all the names they had taken turned out to be false. Instead of hauling Jeffs over the coals, the police lamely grumbled that there was nothing more to be done.

In one newspaper, Graham's even *advertised* its after-hours alcoholic attractions. Perhaps genuinely outraged (but more likely out to crank up a good controversy to haul the tabloid out of a periodic circulation lull), *Truth* campaigned against Graham's and Phil Jeffs's clubs. It accused dapper, honey-tongued Upper House politician Anthony Alam of having a financial interest in Graham's and demanded that the authorities close down the nightclub.

In September 1936, the tabloid badgered Alam into granting an interview. The politician received *Truth*'s reporter at his home. Although it was late afternoon, Alam was sitting up in bed in striped pyjamas with a breakfast tray on his lap. Alam treated the reporter with withering disdain. He cavalierly denied owning a piece of Graham's but agreed that he patronised the club. He confirmed that he was an acquaintance of many staff members but said that to his knowledge they were not criminals. 'Vaughan [Graham's floor manager and a known thug] is not a basher,' said Alam, straight-faced. 'He is one of nature's own gentlemen. He cries when he sees anybody being struck, and the last time that trouble occurred down there he had to be locked in a room because his nerves were so bad. We were afraid he would scream.' Cashier Dick Reilly (a major gangster in the making who had recently knocked out three patrons, one after the other, in a dance-floor brawl then pulled a gun on another seven who wanted to avenge them) came from one of the best families in Sydney, and could have been a champion boxer 'but his mother did not like it' Alam claimed. Apparently his brother was one of the most respected members of the police force and 'Snowy' Bartlett was once the ex-boxing champion of New Zealand.

True, Alam conceded, there was a slight problem with the manager, John Sullivan. 'Sullivan has been told that if there is any more bashing, his contract will be cancelled.'

With whom, asked the *Truth* journo, does Sullivan have this contract? 'By the man who runs the place.'

Was that not Alam?

'No.'

Alam then accused the tabloid of hounding Graham's because the newspaper's managing director Ezra Norton had many thousands of pounds invested in the Trocadero, a rival Sydney variety and dance club. The reporter said he knew of no such vendetta, then returned to his desk at the paper to write his story. The article, which ran on 4 October 1936, had two repercussions. Anthony Alam served *Truth* with a £10 000 libel writ. And on 7 October, the police burst into Graham's, and arrested and fined manager Sullivan and four waiters, including the future television comic Buster Fiddess and his brother Joshua.

*Truth*'s revelations embarrassed the police into enforcing the licensing laws more strictly. A clampdown on Sydney's sly-grog nightclubs began, and it increased in intensity as the decade wore down. Graham's ceased to trade and, gradually, Phil Jeffs's political and police contacts deserted him. Between April 1933 and October 1935, police had raided the Fifty-Fifty Club just six times and levied fines totalling only £185. From 1937, the den was targeted more often, without an advance tip-off, and customers and staff were fined heavily.

Jeffs began selling his nightclubs, and by the end of the 1930s, only the 400 Club, the jewel in his sly-grog crown, remained in business. In wartime, in 1942, it too closed its doors after a national security order decreed that it be shut permanently. Jeffs, worth more than £250 000 and every bit as wealthy as the street punk of twenty years before had dreamed of becoming, retired to a life of luxury at Ettalong, north of Sydney. In his palatial apartment (part of a luxury complex he had built), he entertained often, had many lovers, and, he liked to boast, read and reread his library of philosophical works. Apart from joining Dick Reilly in a brief foray into illegal baccarat schools in Kings Cross in 1944 and a little drug dealing, Phil the Jew's criminal career was over.

# 27

# Laying Down the Law

Under William Mackay, the New South Wales Police Force was getting its act together in the 1930s. Mackay, was, however, unable to eradicate corruption — that was never likely while police pay was so low and courting informers part of policing — and he was stubborn and autocratic. His enemies in the press and in parliament called him 'Hitler' and 'a prime bully'. But thanks to the Mackay regime, police were better trained and fitter.

The force was compartmentalised into foot police, plain-clothes police, women police and mounted police, and detectives were detailed into murder, consorting, arson, drugs, betting, company crime, vice, railway theft and stock stealing squads. There were the fingerprint and photographic branches and the Modus Operandi Office, where the methods, characters and idiosyncrasies of criminals were recorded on index cards and used to identify likely perpetrators of crimes. Information on Kate, Tilly, Jeffs, Calletti and Green made the wooden boxes bulge. Sydney was divided into divisions to facilitate policing, and 100 telephone call stations (or sentry boxes), two-way car wireless and faster cars also improved the lot of the constabulary.

In the mid-1930s, numbers of murders and assaults, robberies, drunkenness and riotous behaviour rose exponentially with Sydney's growing population, but the Consorting Clause had thrown organised crime into disarray. Even allowing for the relative latitude that the police extended to Tilly Devine and Kate Leigh, the enforcing of the new law had hurt their syndicates. Police, of course, could, and did when it suited them, arrest Tilly's prostitutes, Kate's cocaine sellers and sly-grog dealers and their foot soldiers simply for meeting in a public place. Many of these minions threw up their hands and quit the underworld to seek legitimate work. Consequently, the women's crime empires shrunk. Tilly and Kate were still out-earning captains of industry and the prime minister, but by 1938–1939, their boom times were over.

Prostitution and sly-grog selling, while curbed by the consorting provisions, would never be eradicated because of entrenched public demand. To Kate's dismay, however, as her gaoling for possession served notice, the police were determined to eradicate cocaine. To that end, the Consortos and the Drug Bureau harassed and gaoled street traffickers, and shut down the rogue chemists and dentists who had been supplying the dealers. With these outlets closed by the late '30s, virtually the sole source of cocaine was Asian seamen, and after concerted raids were made on visiting vessels thought to be carrying the drug, lawmen could claim that the illicit cocaine trade was suppressed. With suddenly no peddlers, distributors, wholesalers or importers from whom to collect 'subscriptions', cocaine's eradication seriously depleted the takings of standover toughs like Frank Green and Guido Calletti, who simply preyed more on prostitutes and illegal bookies to make up the shortfall.

The end of the cocaine trade — for a time at least — put a serious dent in the infrastructure of syndicated crime. This was not only because of the money it generated, but also because drugs had long been an intrinsic part of the business of prostitution. As discussed previously, to a brothel-keeper, an addicted sex worker was an ideal employee, her need for drugs forcing her to work long hours and being under the influence of drugs making her pliable. Crime lords such as Jim Devine grew rich on their due percentage of prostitutes' earnings, then grabbed a cut of what was left in the sex worker's purse by selling her cocaine. An addicted prostitute had to remain in the game to support her expensive habit; when she grew old, she consequently retired from prostitution with no savings. With less — or no — cocaine about, many addicts left the game.

The police now turned their attention to illegal off-course SP (starting-price) bookmaking, which boomed in the 1930s. Depression times saw the poor hard-pressed to afford public transport to the track and the admission charge when they got there. It was far cheaper to stroll down to any local pub where a bookie with a telephone took their bets and they could listen to the race on the radio over a beer or two. By the time the worst of the Depression was over, off-course betting had become part of the Australian lifestyle. It remains so to this day.

Average race-day attendance at Randwick fell from 7189 in 1929 to 4064 in 1934, and on-course totalisator tax collections dropped from £14 324 to £4230. To redress the situation and get punters back spending their money at the track, racing administrators pressed the State Government to double its efforts to wipe out illegal bookmakers. The police formed an SP Squad and from 1930 to 1936, more than 20 000 arrests were made: however, in a time when pleasures were few, workers were not about to be easily deprived of their weekly flutter and this demand saw the illegal betting industry continue to flourish.

In 1938, the *Betting Act*, comprising tougher new laws, was passed. The legislation provided hefty fines for SP bookmakers. For months, police swoops on pub bookies and the fines imposed on those arrested sent the racket reeling. Three city hotels were branded 'common gaming houses' and their licences suspended. Another 200 were warned they would suffer the same fate unless the illegal bookies were run off the premises. Radio stations were forbidden to call races and allowed only to broadcast results long after the race had ended. It became a crime to telephone racing news from the track.

Betting — like sly-grogging and procuring prostitutes — was too popular to be banned by a politician's decree, however. Illegal betting operators found new ways to beat the laws. Bookmakers vacated the hotels where they could be easily targeted, and now worked from their homes and cars or in parks and halls. The latest odds were relayed to them by contacts at the racecourse who tapped out the prices with a Morse code-like contraption (known as a 'tic-tac') to men outside the track with telescopes who in turn phoned the information to bookie clients or to hives of runners who then scooted from bookie to bookie in their neighbourhood. Two specialist odds suppliers, Telesports Pty Ltd and Eatons Pty Ltd, charged illegal bookmakers a £1 fee for the starting information.

So dispersed and fragmented did the industry become that police found it extremely difficult to enforce the anti-SP laws. To please their superiors and politicians who were demanding high arrest rates, large sums of money were paid to informers to shelf SP bookies. More alarmingly, some corrupt police made arrests on trumped-up evidence to save face. There was verballing of the innocent and sometimes confessions were beaten out of framed citizens.

Another negative was that outlawing off-course betting only made the industry more vulnerable to standover toughs who leeched protection payouts from the outlaw bookies and punters. Unlike the police, the criminals had no trouble locating the bookie joints. As the *Daily Telegraph* noted:

> *The harder the police drive [to suppress SP shops], the deeper into the underworld the bookmakers will go. The government*

*will have accomplished precisely the opposite of what it set out to accomplish. SP will be so closely wedded to crime, that it will be almost impossible to clean up the mess.*

The newspaper was proved correct, as armed extortionists such as Calletti and Green now terrorised the industry.

Opposing the conservative State Government's harsh anti-SP campaign, Labor's R.J. Heffron proposed the introduction of government-run off-course betting outlets. These, he declared, would 'see the end of child runners, welshing bookmakers, standover men, and the other evils of the present vicious system. Realities must be faced. The gambling spirit of the Australian cannot be suppressed by legislation. Whether it is moral or immoral, the Australian will bet.' Government bookie joints never materialised, but when Labor eventually won office, it relaxed its predecessor's vigilance.

# 28

# Deadly Companions

The year 1937 was an inauspicious one for lovers. A botched robbery led to the death of Nellie Cameron's old flame Edward 'Ted' Pulley, a New Zealand–born standover man, housebreaker and gunman, who went nowhere without his heavy-calibre Mauser pistol and his trademark Hollywood-style sunglasses. The year before, Pulley had beaten a charge of murdering gangster Cecil 'Hoppy' Gardiner.

After spending most of 6 March 1937 drinking in the Town and Country Hotel in St Peters, in the late afternoon Pulley drove to an SP betting shop run by sisters Florence Riley and Florrie O'Halloran in Wentworth Street, Glebe. He entered the backyard, where a wireless was broadcasting the races from Randwick, and demanded £3 from the women. Riley said he was too late, she had no money to give him because 'we have been stood over enough' by other extortionists. Riley and O'Halloran went into the house and closed the back door. Pulley, drunk and in no mood to be thwarted, leapt through the window in pursuit.

In the Coroner's Court, Riley told what happened next. 'Florrie caught hold of a chocolate tin which contained our betting money. Pulley caught hold of her, trying to take the tin, and she wrestled with him.' Riley had then run upstairs, fetched a rifle from the back bedroom and returned to the kitchen, where Pulley and O'Halloran were still grappling. Riley then shot Pulley twice in the back and he fell to the floor. 'He said, "What have you done to me? I can't get up." Florrie was holding a pencil in her hand and Pulley asked, "Did you stab me with that?" He then said to call a doctor and mumbled something about his spine.' Pulley's concern about his spine was well founded for it had been severed by a bullet. He died a week later in hospital. Riley was exonerated when the court decided that killing Pulley was justifiable homicide.

No one knows if Nellie Cameron was upset by Pulley's demise, but she was certainly at her theatrical best when her husband Guido Calletti was gaoled for six months that year. He had been arrested for consorting in August, but his sentence was suspended when he promised to stay out of trouble and leave the state. He did neither. In October, Calletti was arrested for using indecent language and consorting with undesirables and now the court reinvoked his original six-month term. At his sentencing at Central Police Court: Cameron wailed: 'It's only for me that he goes out and does bad. I don't know how you can send men like my husband to gaol and then go home to sleep! Guido has been working hard for four years. You're not going to send him to gaol are you? Oh, you must give him another chance.'

Calletti moaned in his defence: 'I have been trying to keep my bond, but I am not allowed to. If a fellow known to the police talks to me, I'm booked. I don't get a chance. I might as well be dead.'

Later, as Calletti was being led through a court corridor to the cells, an hysterical Cameron appeared with a young criminal named Usher, whom she ordered to attack Detective Jack Aldridge, who was escorting her husband. When Aldridge put his hand on Cameron's shoulder to calm her down, Usher swung at the detective, who slipped the punch and swiftly overpowered the youth.

Another who had to do without her man in 1937 was Tilly Devine. For a change of scene, she and Jim had travelled to north Queensland together late the previous year; Tilly was arrested there for drunkenness and fighting in a public place, and Jim was arrested for assault. Feeling the heat, they headed south to Brisbane and Jim linked up with an old criminal friend named Wilkins and became a greyhound trainer. His sporting life ended abruptly in August when he and Wilkins were caught picking pockets at the Brisbane Show and sentenced to three months in gaol. Tilly returned to Torrington Road alone while Jim served his time.

The year brought echoes of the bad old days for Kate Leigh too, when her bodyguard and sometime lover Henry 'Jack' Baker was shot by Chow Hayes. Hayes had known Leigh since the 1920s, when she fenced the young hoodlum's shoplifting spoils. By 1937, Hayes was a gunman and standover thug. Occasionally he'd turn up at Kate's home and sly-grog shop in Lansdowne Street, Surry Hills, and demand protection money. If Kate's bodyguards were elsewhere, she'd usually pay Hayes, for whom (inexplicably to most who knew the snarling crook) she had a soft spot. Jack Baker was not long out of prison after his 1933 conviction for stealing and when he heard Hayes was demanding money from his boss, he took direct action.

Hayes told his biographer David Hickie in *Chow Hayes — Gunman* how Baker accosted him as he drank in the Lansdowne Hotel and warned him that he was looking after Mrs Leigh's interests now, and that if Hayes knew what was good for him he'd better stop bothering her for money. A few days later, said Hayes, he and a friend named Charlie Osborne stood in the shadows near Kate's house. To ensure that Baker was about, Osborne knocked on Kate's door and asked to buy a dozen bottles of beer. Baker took his money and gave him the beer. Later that night, Osborne again knocked on the door and told Baker that Chow wanted a word with him outside the Lansdowne Hotel.

According to Hayes, when Baker arrived, Hayes taunted him. 'I'm going to see Kate . . . I want to borrow a tenner from her.'

Baker said, 'You'll get fucking nothing. I told you earlier in the week.'

At that, Hayes drew his .32, said, 'Well, here you are, you can take this for your trouble,' and shot Baker in the stomach and shoulder.

Five days later, Hayes was rousted in the Railway Hotel and taken to the CIB in Central Lane by Detective Jack Parmeter (the same Parmeter who would later become superintendent). When the police-man told Hayes he was a suspect in the shooting of Jack Baker, Hayes said he'd never heard of him. Parmeter took Hayes to St Vincent's Hospital, where Baker was recovering from gunshot wounds. Baker, said Hayes, immediately insisted he had never seen him before, and told Parmeter that the man who shot him was much taller and darker than Hayes, who breathed a sigh of relief. They went back to the CIB and Parmeter said, 'I know it was you, Chow, and the only thing I can say now, is that it was a pity you didn't make a fucking good job of it.'

Jack Baker and Chow Hayes worked off and on for Kate for another fifteen years. The old sly-grogger even paid some of Hayes's legal bills and bailed him out when he was charged with consorting.

The angel of death also alighted on Dulcie Markham's shoulder. She was working in a Melbourne brothel in 1937 when she took Arthur 'the Egg' Taplin as her pimp and lover. Fellow Sydneysider Taplin was on the run from Darlinghurst police.

On 15 December he was with two friends at the Cosmopolitan Hotel in Swanston Street, Melbourne, when the trio decided to have some sport with an inoffensive-looking male hairdresser in the bar. All afternoon, Taplin and his friends pestered the hairdresser to buy them drinks and the man, suspecting there would be trouble if he declined, kept opening his wallet for them. Then Taplin left and the hairdresser, emboldened by the absence of his most menacing tormentor, refused to fund the remaining pair's party any longer. They left the pub and returned with Taplin, who smashed a beer glass on the hairdresser's head. The hairdresser climbed to his feet, drew a gun from his coat pocket and shot Taplin, wide-eyed with amazement as he fell, in the chest.

Taplin died on 22 December in Royal Melbourne Hospital. Markham was chief mourner at his funeral. The hairdresser was charged with murder but successfully pleaded self-defence.

Suddenly, however, towards that grim decade's close, the activities of Sydney's gangsters — which had appalled yet fascinated many for the past thirteen years — were overshadowed in the minds of the public by darker and more momentous events in Europe. In 1937, Hitler had rearmed Germany, annexed Austria and would soon begin his rampage through Czechoslovakia and Poland. To many, even two years before its declaration, another war seemed inevitable.

Fears of another global conflagration were briefly forgotten on Black Sunday, 6 February 1938, when five Sydneysiders drowned after three freak waves crashed on Bondi Beach. It was a typical hot and sunny Sunday, and the beach was packed with swimmers. A gentle swell caressed a sandbar about fifty metres from the shore and bodysurfers frolicked in the breakers. Eyewitnesses recall that suddenly, eerily, the sea went flat. Then, from nowhere, monster waves more than ten metres high reared up and smashed down on the sandbar. As the waves' whitewater was sucked back out to sea, it swept with it more than 200 bodysurfers. Thirty lifesavers, 'Ready Aye Ready', hit the water and swam after the stricken, screaming bathers. They saved all but five.

One week later, on 13 February, came another disaster on the water. Nineteen people drowned when the ferry launch *Rodney* capsized on Sydney Harbour. The vessel was jammed with 175 spectators farewelling the US cruiser *Louisville*, come to celebrate Sydney's 150th birthday since white settlement. As the cruiser passed the *Rodney*, the passengers on the ferry all rushed to the port side to get a better view. The *Rodney* tipped over, pitching the people into the water. Five sailors leapt from the deck of the *Louisville* into the water to rescue the drowning. They were assisted by fifteen members of the police band, who were on another boat serenading the *Louisville* out of the Heads.

Only a few years earlier, the murder of so prominent a mobster as Guido Calletti would have been front-page news, but with war looming — in August, '39, it was only a month away — public interest in his slaying was scant.

In April 1938, Calletti was released from Long Bay, where he had been gaoled the previous October for consorting. He returned to an empty nest. In spite of her teary outburst when he was sentenced, Nellie Cameron had deserted Calletti while he was inside, and left Sydney to work as a prostitute in Brisbane and Cairns. In the hope of arousing Cameron's jealousy, Calletti began squiring Dulcie Markham and grew flabby — and complacent — on the large amount of money she earned as one of Sydney's busiest prostitutes. Possibly spurred on by his money-hungry new lover, who herself had just served a month in Long Bay for robbing a tourist of £20, Calletti decided to make his play for the big time by taking control of all SP protection racketeering in Surry Hills and Darlinghurst. In a few violent months in early-to-mid 1939, Calletti and his gang beat off rival outfits and he reigned unchallenged as SP standover king of Razorhurst. Calletti at age thirty-seven had never been as powerful or feared.

Now he considered new kingdoms to plunder, and began to covet the profits that the Brougham Street Gang was making selling protection to illegal bookies in Kings Cross and Woolloomooloo. He declared war on the Brougham Street boys. Calletti's strategy was not to target the bookies themselves, but to let the Brougham Street mobsters collect, then corner individual members of the gang and relieve them of their takings. There was open brawling on Butlers Stairs, in the Domain and the wharves of the 'Loo. But soon Calletti's attacks had the Brougham Street Gang reeling. Feeling invulnerable, Calletti began skiting that he had beaten his rivals, and spoke of setting up a criminal empire the likes of which Australia had never seen.

On Sunday, 6 August, Calletti joined other mourners at his grandmother's funeral in the western suburbs, then returned to Darlinghurst to meet Dulcie Markham. Over a drink, Calletti had a rush of blood. He decided to prove his fearlessness by crashing a Brougham Street mob party being held that night to celebrate the birthday of one of the gang's girlfriends.

Conversation stopped when Calletti and Markham sauntered brazenly into the house in Brougham Street, just off William Street. The rival mobsters and their molls glared at the interlopers. One thug approached Calletti and said, 'I hope you haven't come to cause a blue.'

'No,' Calletti assured him, 'I only came to have a friendly drink.'

Warily, the Broughams called a truce with their enemy and offered him the first of many beers. For an hour or so, Calletti chatted amiably with his hosts. Then, as he became drunk, he grew obstreperous. At one point he snarled at a group of Broughams, 'I'll fucking-well fix all you fucking bastards.'

Calletti continued his tirade of abuse. A brawl ensued. The Broughams rushed Calletti, who punched and kicked out at them. Calletti was powerful, but was heavily outnumbered and getting the worst of it. He reached for his gun; one man grabbed his wrist. Women screamed. Somebody smashed the lamp with a chair, plunging the room into darkness, and there were two shots and a bellow of pain. When the light bulb was replaced, Calletti lay on the floor writhing and semi-conscious. Blood flowed from bullet wounds in his stomach. Dulcie Markham sat dazed beside him, cradling his head in her lap.

All the men fled, leaving five women in the house. One hailed a cab to take Calletti to hospital. The taxi driver arrived, looked aghast at the dying gangster and ran to a police callbox in the street. Detectives Dimmock and Jack arrived ten minutes later. Dimmock knelt beside Calletti, whose eyes were glazing over. 'Do you know me?' asked the policeman. Calletti nodded. 'Who shot you, Guido?'

Calletti gasped, 'I don't know' and passed out.

An ambulance was summoned and sped Calletti to St Vincent's Hospital. He died there two hours later. His body was taken to the Reliance Funeral Chapel in Flinders Street, Darlinghurst, where, next day, his teenage son from his first marriage wept over his body, which lay in an open coffin. Calletti was dressed in one of his gaudiest suits.

Back at Brougham Street right after the shooting, Detective Sergeant Colin Delaney combed the premises. He questioned the birthday girl, a nurse, who divulged the names of those who had been at her party. A dragnet hauled in all but two of the revellers, Robert Branch and George Allen, who police believed were the killers of Calletti.

Two days later, Guido Calletti was buried with glitzy pomp. Five thousand mourners, many weeping and almost all from the underworld, paid their final respects at the Catholic Chapel at Rookwood Cemetery where Calletti's rich oaken coffin sat engulfed by a sea of flowers. Among the wreaths were a large cross of blooms and a heartbroken message from Nellie Cameron, despatched from Queensland. Cameron couldn't make her husband's funeral, but his last lover Dulcie Markham keened melodramatically by the casket.

Acting on further information from the nurse (who had been promised immunity from prosecution as an accessory to murder), on 10 August, police arrested Branch and Allen in a house deep in bushland at Cowan Creek, north of Sydney. Both men had pistols. Knowing the accuseds' friends would try to intimidate the nurse into retracting her story, the police hid her in a Moss Vale guesthouse, where they believed the Brougham Street Gang would never find her. Then the guesthouse proprietor, who was under orders to report anything suspicious to Delaney, phoned to say that the nurse's sister had paid a visit. Delaney soon discovered that neither of the nurse's siblings were in the state and took a boxload of mugshots to the proprietor to see if he could identify the mystery visitor. The man pointed to a photograph of Nellie Cameron.

At the murder trial of Branch and Allen at Sydney Quarter Sessions, the nurse blithely denied all her previous evidence while insisting that neither Cameron nor anyone else had pressured her to change her story. She explained that now that she had had time to think about things, she realised she had made a mistake and the two men in the dock, on closer inspection, were not the men she saw fighting with Calletti at the party after all.

Cameron was subpoenaed and called to the stand by a prosecutor hoping that, in her grief over her husband's death, she would indict the suspects. He was disappointed, for she refused to cooperate. Policeman Lua Niall was in the courtroom that day: 'I was posted to observe the trial of the men charged with killing Guido Calletti. Nellie was first witness for the Crown and every question the prosecutor put to her she said, "I can't remember, I can't remember." The case fell through and the men who killed Calletti went unpunished. I remember her as quite attractive, not badly spoken, either, but she had a terrible memory.'

How to explain Nellie Cameron's behaviour? Why did she warn the nurse not to incriminate Branch and Allen, and not attempt to avenge her husband's murder on the witness stand? Cameron and Calletti were estranged at the time of his death, but they remained married after being lovers for a decade, and she had taken the trouble to send the cross of flowers to his funeral. On the evidence, the most likely conclusion is that the Brougham Street Gang offered her money to switch sides and keep silent and, knowing that Guido was past help, she took it.

Having just dried her tears after Calletti's funeral, Dulcie Markham returned to Melbourne. There she heard that her husband Frank Bowen had been shot dead in Kings Cross. She took solace in the arms of a lowlife named John Abrahams. Abrahams was out of his depth with the beautiful prostitute and was soon locked in a violent tug of war for her affections with a towering villain known as Big Doll.

On the night of 14 June 1940, Abrahams and Big Doll fought in a Collingwood gambling den. Abrahams was pummelled and, in the time-honoured way, Markham went home with the victor. At 2 a.m., Abrahams, battered, humiliated and drunk, staggered from the dive. His problems were just beginning. A man, who witnesses said was 'tall and hiding near a car', confronted Abrahams and opened fire with a revolver. The early volley missed and Abrahams ran for cover, but the tall gunman chased and shot him down. Abrahams died in the street. Markham travelled north once more, to the employ of Tilly Devine, and a Sydney about to be changed forever by World War II.

# 29

# The War at Home

War was declared on 3 September 1939, and the vice queens — Kate was nearly sixty and Tilly a flagging thirty-nine — watched helplessly as many of their customers and henchmen enlisted, and sailed away to fight. For the next six years these men would be indulging their vices not in Razorhurst, but in the roaring quarters of Cairo, London and the Pacific.

While the servicemen were away fighting, residents of inner Sydney came to terms with daylight saving and the rationing of food, clothing and petrol. People were required to carry ID cards. Cheap austerity meals, consisting of the most basic ingredients, were suddenly on restaurant and cafe menus. Then, in March 1942, came the first load of R&R-ing American servicemen. For the vice bosses, the loss of the locals was in large part compensated for by the first of many Allied invasions of Sydney. The Yanks were cashed up and keen for a good time after enduring the horrors of combat, and made a beeline for the fleshly and alcoholic delights of Razorhurst. In the interests of the war effort, the authorities were prepared to cut the visitors some slack, and left alone the criminals who catered to the servicemen.

'We found it necessary to not only turn a blind eye, but to give tacit approval to the existence of a brothel which catered exclusively to American Negro servicemen,' tut-tutted Lillian Armfield.

*It is painful to recall that such was the case, but it was, and our own Defence authorities and those of the United States forces accepted it and approved it as a necessity. On that point it is even more painful to recall that, before this establishment came into being for them, we found our own girls, sometimes very young girls, immorally associating with the Negroes. It was like a knife through the heart when we found that one Sydney girl, only twelve years old, was in the bed of a Negro serviceman, as Detective Sergeant Farrell of the Vice Squad could confirm.*

Some Americans got more than they bargained for, as they were gingered outrageously by the prostitutes and mugged by their pimps. Rat-smart locals fleeced the cocksure servicemen by selling them cigarettes made of cabbage leaves or crushed gum leaves rolled in Tally-Ho papers, and cold tea or tobacco water poured into brown bottles and passed off as beer or whisky before the sellers faded into the shadows. When they realised they'd been suckered, the Americans would set off in bands to take revenge, and brawls between them and denizens of the Cross and Darlinghurst, Tilly Devine included, erupted nightly. As former Darlinghurst detective Bill Harris recalls: 'Events began to overtake Tilly in World War II. Once a black US serviceman came to her brothel and did what he had to do with one of her prostitutes, but when he finished with her he wouldn't get off. The prostitute was screaming, and the bloke was getting ugly, then Tilly ran in with a bottle and hit him on the head and fractured his skull. She was charged with grievous bodily harm.'

As the rich, randy and thirsty Yanks stormed Sydney's hot spots, Kate Leigh, as Sydney's pre-eminent dispenser of sly grog, and Tilly

Devine, its leading brothel-keeper, had every right to expect that they would reap a financial bonanza. But the 1940s saw old warhorses like them challenged by a new generation of younger, hungrier outlaws, including Dulcie Markham's occasional lover Donald 'Duck' Day, Lennie McPherson, Abraham Saffron, Dick Reilly and old razor-man Sid Kelly, who moved in to make a profit from Sydney's vice economy.

Making his malevolent presence felt in the war years, too, was Percy 'Big' Neville, a 187-centimetre, 130-kilo standover man who deluded himself that he was Guido Calletti's successor. Neville habitually swung a gold chain and, like Calletti, preyed on the vice purveyors. Born in Moss Vale in 1916, Neville grew up in Redfern. He was a criminal minnow in the '30s, but in wartime Sydney, with Kate in decline, he wielded his size and bad attitude like a blade and established a lucrative sly-grog business. While Kate, in her own rascally way, dealt squarely with publicans and breweries, Neville stole and browbeat alcohol from the wholesalers. He was feared and hated in equal measure. 'Neville was a dingo,' said one policeman of the time. 'He was a big hulk but had no guts when it came to a showdown.' Neville was probably the murderer of his cardshark accomplice Francis Allard — together they'd travel on interstate trains fleecing travellers in rigged card games — who was found dead from head wounds in the Cooks River, possibly caused by a knuckleduster with sharpened blades. Neville moved to Melbourne after the war, and on 10 July 1948, he was shot dead in Flinders Lane. 'Percy Neville was no use to nobody,' said a policeman when he died.

In the old days, Kate and Tilly would have despatched their thugs to drive the newcomers away. There would have been gang war. But with advancing age, they were softening, growing tired of endless conflict, seeking a less stressful existence. Not only that, but even if they had been of a mind to battle for their turf, they would have had their work cut out — for Gunman Gaffney, Barney Dalton and Guido Calletti were all dead, and Frank Green, Wally Tomlinson and Big Jim

Devine were middle-aged now, and hobbled by the effects of bullet and razor wounds, drugs and booze.

Still, Tilly and Kate were too wily and determined to be put totally out of business by the interlopers, and they would rank among Sydney's wealthiest for a while yet. (Around this time, in the early war years, Lua Niall arrested Tilly, 'and she opened her purse in front of me and if there wasn't a couple of thousand pounds in it, then I'm no judge.') But in the '40s, after ruling Sydney's crime roost for more than a decade, Tilly Devine and Kate Leigh were just two more snouts in an increasingly crowded trough.

# 30

# Bumper and the Rugged Angel

Among Tilly and Kate's principal tormentors were two of the most colourful and, in their different ways, effective law enforcers Australia has seen, every bit as good at their trade as the women themselves: Frank 'Bumper' Farrell and Lillian Armfield.

It was July 1945, and with the Axis forces all but routed, Australia was abuzz with talk that World War II was at last in its dying days. Then Bumper Farrell gave Sydneysiders something else to talk about. The famous Darlinghurst cop was playing front row for Newtown first-grade Rugby League team, as usual wearing his big, baggy shorts and with his socks down around his ankles, when, fifteen minutes into the match against St George, a scrum broke up in a flurry of fists and cursing and Farrell's rival prop Bill McRitchie reeled backwards, clutching a gaping wound where his ear had been. The ear was hanging loose, attached only by a flap of skin. 'Look what he's done to my ear!' screamed McRitchie, pointing at Farrell.

Farrell's snack was front-page news. Bumper denied biting McRitchie's ear — denied it for as long as he lived — but few believed him. At a New South Wales Rugby League inquiry into the incident, McRitchie testified that 'while my head was in the scrum, Farrell bit me severely on the ear. As I was suffering, I clawed at his face with my right hand. I said to him, "For God's sake, let go!" but he continued to bite me.' Farrell, for his part, said he could not have severed McRitchie's ear because the only teeth in his head were ten on his bottom jaw. He then whipped out his upper denture to illustrate the point. McRitchie, his head swathed in a bandage, was unconvinced. 'The teeth you have were enough for you to do the job, Mr Farrell,' he snapped. Amazingly, Farrell was cleared of guilt on a vote of fifteen to twelve. McRitchie endured five months of skin grafts to remould his mutilated ear. In sporting circles, until he retired from Rugby League in 1951, Farrell would be known as 'the Cannibal'.

Born in Surry Hills in 1916, Farrell attended Redfern Patrician Brothers and Marist Brothers, Kogarah, where he got his nickname of 'Bumper' for his habit of smoking cigarette bumpers (butts) he'd find on the ground. After school, in the Depression, Farrell was an apprentice boilermaker in Marrickville and worked at Garden Island, but he quit to join the police force. Not especially tall, but stocky and strong, Farrell resembled Punch in a Punch and Judy show, with his arched beetle brows, florid complexion and hooked nose. But of all Farrell's physical characteristics, none compared with his heavily cauliflowered ears, gnarled bricks of cartilage courtesy of a thousand football whacks.

Farrell's energy, ruthlessness with criminals and the air of menace that he exuded in spite of his Luna Park grin saw him rise swiftly through the police ranks. Nor did his fame as a Rugby League star for Newtown and Australia hinder his progress. After cutting his teeth (so to speak) as a probationary constable in Darlinghurst in the mid-1930s, he became chief of the vice squad in Darlinghurst in the 1940s and dealt rough justice to local hoods. Tough as they were, Tilly Devine, Kate Leigh and their crews did not relish confrontations with Farrell.

Anecdotes about him abound. 'Bumper was a terrific cop,' laughs

Lua Niall, his sometime Darlinghurst colleague, 'but he was as rough as bags. In the late '30s and '40s, Darlinghurst Division No. 3 was the most dangerous beat in Australia. Brawls were commonplace. On Friday nights and weekends there would be drunks sprawled all over the place. Drunkenness was right out of hand. Farrell and his colleagues would stop the fights and pile all the boozers into a big paddy-wagon. We had to pick up the drunks because if we left them unconscious on the ground, the criminals would go through their pockets and steal their money.'

Farrell himself was a prodigious drinker. Niall remembers him imbibing heroically after finishing work on a Friday night. 'It was nothing for him to drink a dozen bottles or so, and then go down to Bondi for a swim at five or six in the morning. He'd be drunk when he dived in, then he'd swim straight out to sea, but by the time he swam back in he'd be stone-cold sober.'

He inspired fear in crooks. 'Once on a nice, sunny September day, a detective at Darlinghurst named Cec Holmes and I pinched Tilly Devine in Palmer Street,' Niall recounts. 'When we tried to take her in, she collapsed to the ground and was screaming so loud you could hear her at Circular Quay. She was crying and kicking her legs, yelling to the growing crowd that we were roughing her up. This went on for ten minutes. We could have made a fortune if we'd taken a hat around to the audience that gathered for her performance. Then Farrell passed in a police car. He saw us struggling with Tilly and got out. He said, "Now, Til, what the hell are you up to? Come on, get on your feet and into my car." Like a little schoolgirl, she did exactly as he said without any more fuss. Many of the prostitutes were informers for Farrell. He called them by their Christian name and they called him "Mr Farrell". He treated them properly.'

Bumper Farrell and Kate Leigh shared Irish ancestry, but in spite of being two high-profile characters of the same East Sydney patch, they were never friends. Farrell earned Kate Leigh's lasting enmity when he ordered a mid '40s blitz on her sly-grog dens. 'I was always on the attack and Kate was always on the defensive,' said Farrell years later. While on her frequent excursions to court, Kate would hail all and sundry, sharing a joke and a chat with judges, lawyers, solicitors, police and the public, but whenever she came face to face with Frank Farrell, she skewered him with a pained grimace, as if something rancid had been passed in front of her nose. 'That bloody Bumper,' she'd mutter.

Former policeman and police historian Lance Hoban first knew Farrell in 1940. He says that the wrongdoers in East Sydney knew him by sight. 'He was the eyes and ears of Darlo, and they kept out of his way. Whenever there was real trouble, a brawl at the notorious Fifty-Fifty Club, an eruption at Kate Leigh's, a misunderstanding at Matilda Devine's, or upheavals at any of the sixty-two hotels and wine bars in the patrol, it was always, "Quick, find Bumper, this looks heavy. Is Bumper on? Well, get him down there." On these occasions, Farrell was always cool and calm, rarely returning to No. 3 Station without a vanload of "guests".'

Hoban says Farrell was 'fearless, he could use his fists and he was always in good nick. He swam all year round, and he could run. He sang, too, but badly. Every Friday night we'd go to the Dolphin Hotel in Surry Hills and Frank always sang Irish songs. '"The Isle of Innisfree" was a favourite. He was always off-key. Someone said to him, "Frank, that song you sang haunted me all night." Frank said, "Well, it bloody well ought to have. I murdered it!"'

Hoban says that while prostitutes were in awe of Farrell, they had no love for him. 'Frank knew Tilly and her girls very well,' he says. 'They were his forte in vice. They considered him to be as indigestible as a Hasty Tasty hamburger. The Hasty Tasty was a restaurant in the Cross that sold terrible burgers. The joke was that if you survived a Hasty Tasty hamburger you had an iron constitution. Same with Bumper.'

Bill Harris was another detective who had the opportunity to observe Farrell at close hand. 'Bumper would bend and stretch the rules,' he says. 'Detective Ray Kelly, the famous Ray Kelly, told me when I was at the CIB that the reason Farrell was able to get away with what he did for all those years was that he knew everything that was going on in Darlinghurst and the Cross. He had incredible inside information and intelligence about all the criminals, who did what to whom, when and why. He had this information because of his network of informants whom he'd pay and bully. The prostitutes were scared of him, and with reason, because he wasn't easy on them. And, being a footballer, he wasn't gentle when he put you into the back of a police van. You went in and you went in quick! A businessman one day saw Bumper roughly manhandling villains into the back of his van and protested, "Officer, you shouldn't be so rough." Farrell said, "Oh, I shouldn't, eh? Well, come 'ere, you're in too!" and threw the bystander into the van. Bumper got away with it all. Nothing was ever done to him, he was never reprimanded, because he was so valuable.'

Bill Harris, who was a skilled acrobat when young and wrestled with Bumper in the ring at police training, also attests to Farrell's value in a street fight: 'One night he was being driven through the Cross by a young constable when they came upon a huge blue in progress outside a nightclub. There were thirty or forty blokes involved. Bumper ordered the constable to do a U-ey and pull up. The young bloke did so and Bumper piled out of the van and waded in and he was punching and kicking and knocking blokes down. He was having the time of his life. He loved to fight. He'd flatten you as soon as look at you. That was Bumper.'

Greg Brown's association with the legendary policeman, who, it's said, was never bested in a street fight, began in the mid '30s when they cruised together in a patrol car. In Wentworth Avenue one evening in the late '30s, Brown, Farrell and a colleague named Clive Tierney found themselves battling a dozen thugs in Wentworth

Avenue. Tierney was wielding his baton and inadvertently hit Farrell on the forehead, splitting his head open. Brown laughs now: 'All Bumper did, blood streaming down his face, was turn to Tierney and ask him to please be more careful when he's swinging his baton. Bumper went on with his annihilation. He wore his hair parted in the middle and that night in Wentworth Avenue it was parted good and proper!'

These days, older Sydneysiders appalled by the latest outbreak of juvenile delinquency like to cluck about how such antics wouldn't have happened in Farrell's day. No mollycoddling for Bumper, they say. He'd give us a boot up the rear and send us home to our parents. If every middle-aged or elderly man who claims to have once worn Farrell's bootprint is telling the truth, the policeman could scarcely have had time to do anything else but chase children off the street. One whose backside *did* make the acquaintance of Farrell's boot is former South Sydney and Australian Rugby League player and coach Bernie Purcell. He recalls vividly how, as a young teenager, he and a group of mates were walking from their home turf in Redfern to Luna Park. Early in their trek, a paddy-wagon cruised to a halt nearby. Farrell climbed out and advanced on the boys. 'Where are you blokes going?' he demanded to know.

Purcell told him, 'Luna Park, sir.'

'Oh no, you're bloody well not,' growled Farrell, 'you're going right back to Redfern.'

At that, says Purcell, 'Bumper planted his boot right up my bum.'

Purcell got his revenge years later when he was playing against Farrell. During the game, the big policeman was wrestling on the ground with Souths' captain Clive Churchill when Farrell lashed out with his boot and kicked Churchill in the face. Purcell raced in and socked Farrell on his prominent proboscis. The referee sent Purcell and Farrell from the field. As they trudged off to the hoots of the crowd, Farrell said in a wounded tone, 'What did you hit me for, Bern? I was only paying that little bastard Churchill back for kicking me in the balls.' Purcell explained that his punch had nothing to do with Churchill, and everything to do with that long-ago incident when Farrell discouraged him from walking to Luna Park.

As Bill McRitchie, his St George opponent would attest, there was a dark side to Farrell. In veteran Sydney journalist Geoff Allen's 1999 memoirs, *Gullible's Travails*, Allen claims that McRitchie was not the only footballer to be ripped and torn by Farrell's gnashers. Allen writes that he was covering the Newtown–Balmain Rugby League match at Sydney Cricket Ground in May 1945, two months before the McRitchie incident, when Balmain captain Tommy Bourke was escorted from the field just before half-time with a deep gash on his cheek. 'As he passed me on the way to the dressing room,' writes Allen, 'he said, "That bastard Bumper bit me."' Allen recalls Bourke returning to the field, his face bandaged. The journalist rushed back to his office at the *Sun* to write the scoop of how Bourke had been bitten.

As he was typing the story, Joe Williams, who manned the newspaper's front desk, had said to him, 'They're gunning for you, Geoff.' At that, Allen reported, 'two thuggish-looking' detectives materialised in his office and told Allen he'd be wise not to write the story. 'I contacted two executives of the paper,' says Allen, 'who called in the office legal adviser, a barrister. I pleaded with them to use the story but they were adamant and said, "Forget about the scoop, your life is at stake." A check of newspaper reports of the match confirm that Tommy Bourke suffered a facial cut that required stitching.

Investigative journalist Phillip Knightley in his autobiography *A Hack's Progress* recalls that when he was working as a copy boy at Sir Frank Packer's Australian Consolidated Press, there was a *Daily Telegraph* police reporter named Sam White who sported the first pair of suede desert boots seen in Sydney. To Knightley, White was courageous because 'the toughest cop on the Vice Squad, Bumper Farrell, had decreed that only poofters wore suede shoes, and therefore anyone wearing them could be arrested for homosexuality.'

On his retirement from the force after thirty-eight years' service in August 1976, Inspector Farrell reminisced to a reporter from the *Sydney Morning Herald*, gazing out of the window of his office at Darlinghurst Police Station.

> *Is Darlinghurst better or worse now than in the early days? You have the advent of the motor car and that sort of thing, and the crims are not concentrated like they used to be. Criminals were more physical in my day. Today you have the con-man type. The crims I knew years ago would meet you face to face. Now it's more the knife in the back. The biggest problem facing police today is the drug problem. I suppose prostitution and the like will always be around. It always has been.*

Bumper died in his sleep in April 1985, aged sixty-eight, having long outlived all his old Razorhurst adversaries. His funeral at St Joseph's Church, Narrabeen, where Farrell prayed each day at 2 p.m. after his retirement, was sumptuous. The surviving members of his Newtown and Australian Rugby League sides attended, and there was a police honour guard led by Deputy Commissioner Barney Ross. A police band played mournful airs and a selection of Irish songs. The former archbishop of Sydney, Cardinal Sir James Freeman, and Bishop Edward Kelly, Bishop of Toowoomba, a lifelong friend of the policeman, co-celebrated a requiem mass.

Farrell's old friend and fellow football champion Len Smith remembers the day as a sad one, but with lots of laughs as memories of Farrell were traded: 'Kate Leigh never liked Bumper, but she always had enormous respect for him, and that doesn't surprise me. His sincerity, his kindness. Even though he had a hard face and a hard outlook, he did many good and kind things that nobody ever knew about. Francis Michael Farrell, he was a legend.'

Lillian Armfield, Sydney's pioneer policewoman, was born in Mittagong in the Southern Highlands of New South Wales in 1885. She was a psychiatric nurse at Callan Park hospital in the Sydney suburb of Ryde in 1915 when she saw a newspaper advertisement seeking applicants for a proposed new force of women police officers. The pay would be seven shillings and sixpence a day, the work would be gruelling, and no married women need apply. (No such stipulation about marital status applied to males.) She and another woman named Maude Rhodes were the only applicants to pass muster and became Australia's first policewomen. Rhodes soon left, but Armfield had found her life's work.

Armfield's brief was to 'lend a hand in any case — from murder to shoplifting — in which a woman is concerned, whether criminally or as a witness'. Working at her always-uncluttered desk, perfectionist Armfield threw herself into her work. She recruited a dozen or so other policewomen. They were replicas of herself: no-nonsense, tough, dedicated and unmarried.

In 1916, Armfield established the so-called 'dawn patrol', rescuing homeless women from the streets. After a ritual pep talk at her desk, she would offer them food and shelter and help them find employment. Stern but fair, she came into her own when interrogating prostitutes and other women offenders who felt uncomfortable being grilled by a male. She also, curiously, took it upon herself to cut a swathe through the bogus fortune-tellers ubiquitous in Sydney in the first three decades of the twentieth century.

Another task close to her heart was taking charge of abandoned babies. She would try to trace their parents, and, if unsuccessful, supervise adoption or care. The incidence of mothers leaving their unwanted babies at hospitals, police stations and other public places where they would be found and taken on by others was common in those years of no access to contraceptives — and became even more so in the Depression when many women could not even afford to feed themselves. Armfield was renowned for bestowing exotic names on the foundlings in her care. One, left by her mother in the foyer of a theatre in a busy city street, she christened 'Royal Castlereagh'.

Armfield was tall for a woman (or a man) in those days (at 172 centimetres), had prematurely grey hair and wore a grim expression. She was tersely spoken, never using two words when one would do. In the single room in a Darlinghurst guesthouse that was home for most of her life, she was a compulsive reader of detective fiction. She was a keen swimmer and golfer until arthritis crippled her, and she trained hard to be a crack shot, being the only policewoman permitted to carry a gun. The weapon came in handy in the 1920s and '30s, when it was her responsibility to deal with the female offenders of Razorhurst.

As well as Tilly and Kate, Nellie and Dulcie, there were other notorious women criminals to deal with, such as 'Botany May' Lee. Armfield worked closely with Tom Wickham and Wharton Thompson of the Drug Bureau, and one of their targets was Lee, a cocaine dealer. Once, in 1929, it fell to Armfield to take a surveillance position in a small room overlooking Botany May's backyard, hoping to catch her in possession of cocaine. When she saw Lee take a package from beneath a loose brick in the backyard, she stormed into the woman's house. Lee was not intimidated, and attacked Armfield with a hot iron. Armfield retreated, but returned with reinforcements to make the arrest.

Armfield was also the nemesis of the lesbian thief and shoplifter Iris Webber, who vied with Tilly and Kate for the title of Sydney's most violent woman. 'Her strength was enormous,' the policewoman recalled in *Rugged Angel*, 'and she would use anything that came to hand to maim anyone she attacked.' Webber liked to steal the girl-friends of male criminals, and relished the confrontation when the men demanded the return of their lovers. 'Twice she figured in shooting affrays,' said Armfield. 'Webber was afraid of no one. The toughest gangsters in the city's underworld could arouse neither fear nor respect in her.'

The prostitute Stella Croke was another who sometimes made Armfield wonder whether she was in her right mind when she answered that recruitment ad back in 1915. Croke, a friend and employee of Tilly Devine, was a notorious gingerer. 'We had frequent complaints from men she had lured to an address for the purpose of robbing them, and she had associates handy to deal violently with those victims who resisted,' Armfield recalled.

In 1942, Croke solicited Ernest Hoffman, a cook at Royal Sydney Golf Club in Rose Bay. While he was being entertained by Croke in the bedroom of her Surry Hills home, Hoffman noticed in the gloom a woman rifling his trouser pockets. He leapt up from the bed and wrestled with the woman. Croke called for her minders — her husband Bill Surridge and a man named James Harris. The four knocked Hoffman unconscious and dumped him in a vacant lot. He was found lying there and taken to St Vincent's Hospital, but he fell into a coma and died twelve days later.

Croke, Surridge and Harris, who all had lengthy police records, were arrested after scientific squad detectives took fingerprints from Hoffman's possessions. They were convicted of Hoffman's murder and sentenced to hang, but the sentence was commuted to life behind bars. Croke was released in 1956, and Tilly Devine staged a riotous welcome-home party for her. Croke returned to prostitution, but not for long. The following year she died of a poisoned finger.

In the 1940s, Tilly was not the force of old, but Armfield still always found her a handful. When policewomen were sent out onto the streets of Darlinghurst to arrest Tilly's sex workers, they knew they were being despatched to do dangerous work. The prostitutes and their pimps were armed with razors and guns, and any interlopers who strayed onto Tilly's patch, whether law officers, freelance prostitutes or prostitutes allied to other syndicates, risked serious injury.

Tilly and her employees considered it unfair that policewomen were assigned to hound them. They prided themselves on being able to pick a plain-clothes policeman on sight, day or night, but were thrown by the undercover female police. Often policewomen were used as decoys, and would patrol the streets and lanes on the arms of men, looking like lovers out for a stroll, then pounce on the prostitutes.

But Armfield knew she was fighting a losing battle. She realised that no matter how severe the laws, nor how ingenious the methods and unremitting the efforts of the authorities, prostitution would never be stamped out. 'Centuries of experience prove that even in the most rigorously controlled social systems,' she said, 'it has always had its part, often being condoned in the highest places.'

The highest rank Lillian May Armfield attained was special sergeant first-class, but she was awarded the King's Police and Fire Services Medal for distinguished service in 1946, three years before she retired, wracked by arthritis, at age sixty-one. By then, there were thirty-six policewomen in the New South Wales Police Force, all trained in the same disciplines as the men, with the exception of firing a gun.

One of Armfield's closest, most trusted, lieutenants was Maggie Baker, who remains devoted to her boss's memory decades after Armfield's death. Like Armfield, Baker is a formidable woman and, again like Armfield, she never wed. 'We were both,' she says, 'married to our jobs.'

Now in her late seventies, Baker's stories about the almost-two decades she spent on the beat at Darlinghurst post–World War II make that long-gone era seem as immediate as yesterday.

'During World War II, I was working for Army Investigations and when the war ended, my boss, a retired police inspector, said to me, "You'll be needing a new job. Ever thought of being a policewoman?" I said, "I'm there." So we went down to see Police Commissioner Billy Mackay and I'm in this room with three fellows, commanders and superintendents, and I'm standing in the middle of the room and they're giving me the once-over and they say, "Hmmm," looking me over from every angle. I felt like a prize cow at the Easter Show. Then they huddled in a corner to talk about me, and I said, "Excuse me gentlemen, but do I get the blue ribbon?" They said, "You're in the police force."'

Within an hour, Baker was standing in the office of her new boss — the head of all women police, Special Sergeant Lillian Armfield. 'I was so nervous, I felt like a wet sponge. She was a very tall woman with arthritis. The officer with me said to her, "Here's your new recruit." Miss Armfield said to me, "Stand over there!" She was brusque to the point of rudeness, but there was something about her that I liked and admired. She said to me, "If you're no good, I'll give you hell." I thought, "This is going to be a trial." She really put me through the hoops, but I didn't worry. I was either going to be suitable for the job or not. She must have seen something promising in me. She swore like a trooper and she said, "The first time you bloody-well do something to upset me, the first time you let me down, I'll kill you." I said, "I'm not frightened of death." She snapped, "Don't be smart." But she trusted me, and once I got to know Miss Armfield, she was terrific.'

Baker worked in Darlinghurst for seventeen years, and says she went to places with Armfield 'where no other policewoman had ever been'. The women became close friends. Armfield lived in a tiny room in Darlinghurst, 'and if she needed the least little thing she'd send for me. I didn't mind. If she had a big job on, it was always her and me together.

She favoured me and would assign me before the others. She was the only policewoman with a gun. She used to take me to brothels and I met every crim she ever knew. She'd threaten them, "If you ever do anything to this policewoman, I'll shoot you." She often threatened to shoot me, too, when I displeased her, but I like to think she wasn't serious.'

Baker was often assigned to deal with Kate Leigh, and came to know her as friend and foe. After her first encounter (when Tilly had tried to stop Baker entering a Darlinghurst street and Kate came to the policewoman's assistance by sitting on the brothel queen), 'We always got on well. Kate lived her life and I lived mine and we respected each other. She was talking to Miss Armfield about me one day and she said, "I really like her." Miss Armfield always took me to see Kate whenever she paid her a visit.

'Kate Leigh respected me because she respected Miss Armfield. Kate thought the world of her, but they were on opposite sides of the law so their relationship could never be friendly, never close, and if Kate did anything wrong, Miss Armfield didn't think, "I'll go easy on her." She did what had to be done and locked her up.'

When Baker knew Kate in the 1940s, she was 'a little, fattish person. She always wore very big hats, and seemed to me to be nice and clean. She had the most gorgeous rings I have ever seen. I have never seen a woman with more rings and she wore them on every finger except her thumbs.' Baker noted that Kate's hands were gnarled with arthritis.

'I had no moral problem with sly grog, but it was my job to stamp it out. If I saw Kate doing something she shouldn't be doing, I'd go up to her and tell her to stop. She'd give me the works — would she ever! — She'd give me a mouthful of swear words and say, "Don't you ever talk to me again!" Then she'd dob me in to Miss Armfield, say, "That bloody Baker!" And Miss Armfield would say, "Oh, Kate, she's only doing her job." Then Kate would say, "Oh, I know that, Lil, but I can't be seen being nice to her."'

Armfield impressed upon Baker Kate's value as a police informer. '"Keep in Kate's good books because she's a wonderful informant, and, besides, if you know what she's doing, well, better the devil you know." Kate would tell us things no other police officers could find out. She'd say, "Come up and see Aunty Kate if you want to know something." She felt that so long as she was being helpful to us she wasn't going to get into too much trouble. I'd often drop in on Kate for a chat and some information. I've had cups of tea in Kate's place even though other officers said, "Ohhh, she'll poison you." Fact was, I didn't trust her, but we needed Kate Leigh. Police are not so brainy that leads fall out of the air.'

Baker did not enjoy such cordial relations with Tilly Devine, who took an instant dislike to the tall, young policewoman. 'Tilly sparkled with diamonds and thought she was the Queen of Sydney, but she was a vicious woman. She would see me in the street and hiss, "I hate you." I went twice to Tilly's joints alone and after that I said to the male police, "I'm not going down there again for you, never." She was unpleasant, and if she didn't want to talk to me she'd slam the door in my face. Miss Armfield and Kate Leigh could swear, but they had nothing on Tilly. I'd be walking down Oxford Street on my beat and she'd be walking up. She always gave me a couple of swearwords and I'd say, "How do you do?" One day I was in Oxford Street with a new recruit and Tilly glared at me and snarled, "You bastard." I said, "Thank you, Tilly," but my partner went red in the face. I said, "What's the matter?" She said, "I didn't like that lady." I said, "That was no lady. That was Tilly Devine."'

With cocaine trafficking largely eradicated by the time she joined the force, the most frequent problems Baker had to deal with were street prostitution, drunken brawling, pickpocketing and assault. 'I ran in drunks, but I was careful only ever to get rough with the ones I knew I could handle. I had no radio or gun, just my handbag, and I could swing that at a troublemaker's solar plexus and bring him down. I wasn't a punching bag for anyone. I wasn't especially fit, but I could swing that bag and I learned a bit of jujitsu. A bloke once was swearing at me, and I'd never heard such filthy language in all my life, so I couldn't keep my hands off him a minute longer and I whacked into him. I was never frightened to go round the streets of Darlinghurst at night. If ever I got into a scrape, I knew I had plenty of friends about to back me up. Even the prostitutes and no-hopers in Darlo would take my side if they saw me in trouble.'

And despite some notorious Armfield gruffness at times, Baker could always count on support from her senior officer. 'Miss Armfield said to me one day, "You never defy me, do you?" I said, "Why would I, you're the boss." We had a few squabbles, but if I thought she was being unfair to me, I could go to her and say, "I'm hurt," and we'd talk it out. She'd say, "Don't take any notice of me, I'm in pain."'

The arthritis in Armfield's legs worsened over the years until it crippled her and forced her resignation from the force. Maggie Baker retired in the early 1970s when she was in her fifties after she developed a debilitating thyroid problem. 'The doctor said it was a desk job or nothing. I refused to be a pen-pusher because I loved working on the street so much. I only rose to the rank of sergeant. Miss Armfield, who'd retired herself by then, called me and said, "You've done your job, health comes first. It's time to get out." Soon after, when I was in hospital having my thyroid treated, I heard that Miss Armfield had died.'

Armfield's last years had not been happy. On her retirement, she was treated shamefully by the force she had served with such dedication. She received no pension when she retired because when she joined in 1915 she was a few weeks over thirty years, the maximum eligible age to contribute to the departmental pension and insurance fund. Armfield lived in virtual poverty on about £6 a week in her Darlinghurst room. Her board cost around £4 a week, leaving her just £2 for all other expenses. Her sole pleasures were reading detective paperbacks and the Harbour cruise her old police workmates would treat her to each year on her birthday. In 1964, her arthritis painful and debilitating, she was unable to care for herself any longer and she moved from her room to a hostel for the aged in Leichhardt. The following year, the State Government came to her rescue, after a fashion, when it granted the eighty year old an extra £3/10 a week.

Just before Lillian Armfield died in Lewisham District Hospital, on 26 August 1971, aged eighty-six, Police Commissioner Norman Allan visited her. 'Now, I don't want the publicity of a police funeral,' Armfield scolded, like the crosspatch of old, 'just a quiet cremation at the Northern Suburbs Crematorium.' Allan acceded to her request, but made sure a police guard of honour was on hand to bid her goodbye.

# 31

# Hearts of Darkness

Armed with the recollections of those who lived in Surry Hills in the 1940s, it is not impossible to imagine Kate Leigh in her domain in those years. In her sixties then, she had notched up almost all of the 107 convictions she would record in her life, and had served eleven of her thirteen gaol terms. She had shot a man dead, wounded and battered others, and ordered killings and maimings.

It hadn't, however, been one-way traffic. In her years as a sly-grogger, cocaine dealer, thief and receiver of stolen property, she had been assaulted more times than she could remember, being knocked unconscious on a number of occasions, and sustaining cuts, bruises, a smashed nose and jaw. Late nights, being around smokers, and tension had turned her skin to leather, a fact which the rouge she trowelled onto her cheeks could not disguise. Her voice was a rasp. In her youth, she had been handsome enough to take her pick of any underworld blade. As she liked to say when comparing herself to Tilly Devine, '*I* never had to sell my body.' But now, although she would marry a third time, her siren days were long gone. Tilly was calling her 'the Old Bag'.

Often, in the late afternoon, Kate was seen lumbering along gritty Riley Street, a short, stout woman often in an ankle-length lavender dress and a fur stole, even in summer when the sun was hot enough to turn the dusty bitumen footpath to glue. One ring-laden mitt gripped her black handbag, in which she kept a revolver and £2000 for 'business emergencies'. On top of her tangled, greasy, patchy-black-dyed hair would be a dark wide-brimmed hat that more often than not sprouted feathers. Passers-by needed to get no closer than a metre or two to Kate to be assailed by cloying clouds of her favourite fragrance, a potion called Jicky.

At Devonshire Street she would turn left and plod into Crown, and as she passed the shopfronts and pubs, people would typically call to her, 'Hey, Kate' or 'Katie, what do you know?' If the caller was a friend, she'd laugh and respond, "Ow yer goin', love? Awright?' But if it was an enemy, or one of the neighbourhood urchins who delighted in teasing her at that stage of her life, she may have glowered and drawled, 'Sling yer hook', 'Shut yer pan' or 'Cut out the cheek, Sonny Jim, or I'll bloody-well pull yer tripe out and feed it to the cat', or perhaps, when feeling uninspired, a simple, somewhat plaintive, 'Awww, fuck off, why doncha?'

Except for a couple of trips interstate and her sojourns in Long Bay Gaol, Leigh had lived in Surry Hills since the early years of the century. So, in her old age, she may no longer have noticed the smells, sounds and sights that jolted the senses of any visitor to the suburb. The mouth-watering aroma of the bakeries and the hoppy tang of Toohey's Brewery on Broadway; or the creosote stench of outside lava-tories, gut-churning wafts of blowie-covered dog faeces, and the sickly smell of days-old household garbage that littered the streets, lanes and backyards in those days. The cacophony of cawing crows; clattering billy carts careening down hills and the shrill cries of the urchins who rode them; the distant 'choof-choof-choof' of steam trains at Central; drinkers bawling 'The Rose of Tralee' and 'If You Knew Susie' in pubs and the tinkle of 'Chopsticks' on a home piano; a paperboy spruiking *Truth*'s latest scandal; the snap of breeze-blown nappies hung on string clotheslines; or the profane din of dunny-cart men hefting the evil black buckets on their heads — 'as flat as a shit-carter's hat' went the old saying. The garbos emptying bins into large squares of hessian they'd have spread on the footpath, and the squeals of kids who leapt in and snaffled trinkets and discarded magazines before the men could tie up the hessian and heave it onto the flatbed of their truck.

On the way to her terrace home, the old criminal would shop, pushing through the fly-screen door of a butcher's, whose front window would likely be decorated, as was the custom then, with a row of severed pigs' heads, and buy a purple-skinned rabbit to stew for dinner. She may have then called into a ham and beef shop where, for a shilling or two, she could buy a bottle of milk for her tea and a pat of butter for the crisp, still-warm white loaf that the bread carter delivered to her door. She would eat dinner before her driver picked her up at nine or ten to do the rounds of her sly-groggeries. Shopping done, Kate would have continued down Crown Street, past drunks sprawled in doorways and prostitutes plying their trade. Past damp, peeling, roach-ridden terraces from whose open front windows came the chirpy wireless crackle of Roy 'Mo' Rene, George Wallace (the comedian, not the old razor gangster) and Jack Davey ("Hi-ho, everybody!"). From other windows and doors would have come the wails of babies and, if it was past 6 p.m., pub closing time, slurring voices engaged in angry domestic disputes.

If Kate was in a hurry, she would take a short cut to Lansdowne Street through any of the myriad alleyways of the area, and if it was a typical Surry Hills lane circa 1940s, it would have been wee-the-bed and ragwort speckled. The heavy trudge of her sensible shoes would have sent packs of hissing, mewing cats skittering for cover. The strays, until disturbed, may have been routing a nest of the brown, razor-toothed, puppy-sized rats that, attracted to the raw sewage and refuse strewn about, infested Surry Hills. In her 1949 novel *Poor Man's Orange*, Ruth Park would describe in horrifying detail a rat attacking a baby in a Surry Hills terrace and the baby's mother beating the squealing rodent to death. Such incidents were not uncommon in the Hills.

Home at last, Kate would have opened the front door of her large terrace with its ornate iron lacework on the upstairs balcony and a street sign reading 'Lansdowne Street' affixed to the wall, and disappeared inside as yellow street lamps fizzed on up and down the road, and a westerly carrying the tang of sea salt from Darling Harbour cooled the dying day.

Kate Leigh loomed large in Bernie Purcell's Redfern boyhood and when he knocked about later in Surry Hills. He especially recalls the Christmas street parties she turned on for the poor children of the area. To slumland kids, a Kate Leigh street party was a highlight of their year, every bit as exciting as a school or church bus excursion to Manly or the Blue Mountains. Purcell, like many others, considered Kate a force for good and a friend in need.

Lance Hoban is another with splendid recall of the time and people. His first police posting was to Bondi, in 1940. He remained there, a green and ingenuous, gentlemanly uniformed cop, until he was transferred to Darlinghurst soon after. 'My superior at Bondi was Sergeant Joe Chuck, a veteran of the razor-gang wars. He counselled me before I went to work at Darlinghurst. "Now, Lance," said Joe, "We're sorry to see you go, but when you get to Darlinghurst will you be sure to introduce yourself to a lovely lady named Matilda Devine. She's a great old friend of mine, and I want you to give her my regards. You two will get on famously, I know it."'

Impressed by Chuck's reverential tone, Hoban asked, 'Oh, is Matilda Devine a nun at St Vincent's Hospital?' Chuck just laughed. 'I was terribly naive and honestly didn't have a clue who Matilda Devine was. I didn't find out until I had to take her fingerprints.'

As the constable responsible for booking and fingerprinting at Darlinghurst, Hoban was moved by the number of prostitutes who were family women from the suburbs. 'They came from Penrith, Parramatta, Chester Hill, Burwood, anywhere. I said, "How come you travel all the way into East Sydney to be a prostitute?" They said, "Oh, we come to do a day's work at the brothel. At the end of the day we add up our takings, the owner takes her share, the protection people take theirs and we take what's left. Then we commute back to our homes." It was a low way to make a living.'

Hoban, a sweet-voiced singer good enough to perform at the Tivoli Theatre on his nights off, also became acquainted with Kate, Cameron and Markham and company. 'They were hardened women, but all very cheerful and courteous to me. Maybe because I didn't try to bully them. Kate said to me one day, "How did you come to be a policeman, young man?" I said I wanted to make my career in the force. "Awww, you're wastin' your time. You're too mild-mannered. You would have made a better bishop."' Hoban, a religious man who did, indeed, after a lifetime of charity fundraising, become a papal knight and was received by four pontiffs, replied, 'Thanks for the compliment.'

It was common practice, says Hoban, for policemen whose arrest quota was low in a particular month to go out and arrest Kate Leigh. They were on safe ground, he chuckles, because she was always up to no good. 'They'd raid her joint, confiscate the liquor and charge her. She'd pay her fine or serve her time and then go straight back into business.'

One Darlinghurst constable's arrest quota may have been lagging when on New Year's Eve 1942 he decided to don his civvies and knock on Kate Leigh's door pretending to be a thirsty punter. The sting worked. When Kate and Jack Baker loaded the liquor he had ordered into his car, he arrested them. Outraged at being set up, Kate called the constable a liar at her trial when he accused her of selling sly grog. 'I've never had a sly-grog business,' she yelled, somehow maintaining a straight face. 'But I *may* have run a private hotel where liquor was sometimes sold.'

Before Judge Wells sentenced Kate and Baker to six months' gaol and a £100 fine, there was a series of bizarre exchanges in the courtroom, not the least of which was when Kate shelfed her own man. She said if anyone had been selling sly grog it was Baker, not her, and so he should pay the penalty. 'Baker is the boss,' she said. The Crown demanded to know whether Kate was Baker's lover. She exploded, 'Don't you dare talk to me like that! Do you think I'd be sleeping with some big buck nigger?' (Baker, as far as anyone knew, was Caucasian and had been sharing Kate's bed on and off for some years.)

As the judge and prosecutor exchanged nonplussed glances, Kate stormed on: 'No one can say anything against my morals. His Worship knows me well, don't you, Mr Wells?'

The judge replied that, indeed, he had known her, in a professional sense, for 'forty-one years this month, to be exact'.

But while Kate spurned Baker, he seemed not to resent her perfidy and told the world he was smitten with her. 'There's never been a better woman lived,' he declared to reporters. 'I've lived with her as man and wife for fifteen years. You always talk about her bad points, but what about her good ones? She has a heart of gold.'

There was another uproar when a prosecutor accused Kate of hiding behind Baker. 'Have you ever heard of Tilly Devine hiding behind Jim to shield her and making him take the blame?'

At that, Kate's face turned scarlet and she leapt to her feet. 'Be careful of your words! How dare you mention my name in the same breath as that woman! I am respectable and won't be insulted. I may have sold beer but nothing else. I am a different class of person. I give to the war loan, I'd do anything for the boys fighting for us. I give £10 every week to Boys Town. I refuse to be compared to Tilly Devine. I refuse to listen to her name. The mention of it disgusts me!'

Hoban concedes Kate was an incorrigible crook, but insists she was an angel in the community who 'never knocked a bloke back for a quid or a floor to sleep on if he was down on his luck'. The more ragged they were, he said, the wider she opened her heart. 'Kate was also a patriot,' says Hoban. 'In 1941, they had a war rally in Martin Place and called for people to buy war bonds. Prime Minister Robert Menzies was there. Kate slapped down £10 000 for her bonds, and challenged Menzies. "Mr Menzies, if you match my £10 000, I'll double it."' Menzies, who, in his favour, would not have been earning a tenth of Kate's income at that time, politely declined. The crowd booed.

In Tilly and Kate's mellow years, they were content to wage a public-relations war on each other. They would telephone or call on reporters and tell them of their good deeds, then gloat when their activities were headlined in the tabloids. When *Smith's Weekly*, the *Mirror*, the *Sun* or *Truth* ran a story about her hosting a party for street urchins or the homeless, Kate would rush up and down her street, thrusting it in the face of friends and passers-by alike.

*Mirror* journalist Bill Jenkings became friends with Kate in the 1940s. In his memoirs, *As Crime Goes By*, he recalled to biographers Norm Lipson and Tony Barnao: 'We loved writing about Kate, and she encouraged it. I suppose it was free advertising for her business. I reckon Kate would have been a soft bite for any reporter down on his luck.' Jenkings often saw Kate at Central Court and the two became friendly. He said if she wasn't there to face a charge herself, she was there with money to bail out one of her myriad shady mates or to bring food to a prisoner, such as the time she arrived at Central with a large tray of succulent oysters and lobster.

Ray Blissett, however, insists Kate was no saint. 'I'm sorry, but to me Kate was a bad woman, a foul-mouthed old bitch. One night, I went to see the bludger she was living with. His name was Paddy, as I remember. She said to me, "'E ain't 'ere. 'E's in 'orrrspital" — that's how she talked. I said, "What's wrong with him?" She laughed, "I stabbed him." At Christmas she'd bung on a party for the local kids, and at Easter when Wirth's Circus came to Surry Hills, down near The Pottery pub, Kate would throw hot cross buns at the kids, and everyone thought she was an angel. But she was a *fallen* angel, as far as I was concerned. A real old villain, she honestly was.'

Before attending court, Kate would go to her bank and take a selection of rings from the thirty or more she kept in a safety deposit box, adorn her fingers with them, and don her huge hat and a fur. When people asked how she could stand wearing heavy stoles on sweltering summer days, she would show them her ravaged hands and explain, 'I have to keep warm for me arfuritis.' She knew that she was the centre of attention in the courtroom and played to the gallery. 'I know you've all been waitin' for me,' she'd boom to judge, lawyers, accused and the public as she eased her bulk into her seat in the public gallery. 'Well I'm here now, so let's get started. What's on today?' Afterwards, she would shout the reporters and cops, too, if they tagged along, to a pub lunch. She drank only Blue Bow lemonade or water, but the bill for her guests usually topped £50. Afterwards, she'd take her rings back to the bank and go home.

'Kate was a real performer in court,' recalls Maggie Baker. 'Even when she was an observer, she'd bring up whatever she was having for dinner and peel her vegies in the courtroom. The scraps flew everywhere, then she'd pick them up. I remember one judge got cross with her for disrupting proceedings. "You're not bringing your dinner into my courtroom," he said. She yelled out, "Now, wait a minute, Bill. I'll come in here with my vegetables if I want to."'

Like Maggie Baker, Lance Hoban has fond memories of Kate Leigh, but no time for Tilly Devine: 'She had a terrible tongue and was a violent woman. One night when I was a constable I had to take a message down to her place in Palmer Street. We'd locked up one of her girls or clients, and they assured us that Tilly would pay their ten shillings bail. They scribbled a note to her, and I was asked to deliver it and return with the bail money.' It was 1 a.m. when Hoban arrived at Devine's house. He knocked on the door, 'and suddenly Tilly was leaning over the balcony above my head and abusing me with a tirade of foul language. I managed to interrupt long enough to tell her so-and-so was locked up and needed ten shillings to pay the bail. Next thing, a ten bob note flutters down on my head. She didn't let her friend down, but Tilly Devine was a vile woman.'

There is a terrifying photo of Tilly that lends weight to Hoban's character reference. It is a mugshot, taken on 6 February 1943, after she had been taken to Darlinghurst Police Station for being drunk and fighting. In the picture she wears no make-up or jewellery. Her hair is not styled as usual, but hangs greasy and limp around her face. She peers, befuddled but defiant, at the police photographer. Her eyes are two-thirds closed and her mouth, not flung open in a toothy grin for once, is set in a grimace. Her cheeks sag and there are deep bags under her eyes; her nose looks thick and has been badly broken, and there are scars on her face. In this photo she looks every bit the 'worst woman in Sydney'.

No doubt she was worthy of that title but, just like Kate Leigh, her good works were many and considerable. Tilly Devine did her bit for the Allies, too, apart from tending to the carnal desires of servicemen. She gave large amounts of money to funds providing for Australian warriors overseas. She bought thousands of pounds worth of war bonds and organised parties, the proceeds of which helped Diggers and their families. She never tired of telling friends how her son Frederick was serving with the British Army in the Middle East.

Possibly born of guilt at leaving Frederick behind with her parents in Camberwell when she emigrated to Australia after World War I, she adored children. And when she was seen around Darlinghurst and Maroubra wheeling a baby boy in a pram, rumours flew that Tilly had adopted the lad. Tilly laughed off the rumours, explaining that she was looking after the 'lovely little chappie' for a friend. 'I wish the stories were true,' she said, 'but how could I look after a baby when I can't even care for myself? But it is true that I love children and I'd love to be in a position to adopt one some day.'

Tilly doled out money and gifts to local youngsters, and supported the Jesuits and the Salvation Army. At Christmas 1947, she visited Collaroy Crippled Children's Hospital. At the front desk, she refused to tell her name, just said she had something for the sick kids. In the ward, she took a wad of tightly rolled ten-shilling notes from her purse and gave one to every child. Then she had her driver bring from her car a bag of toys and handed them around to the delighted kids. Tilly was overcome by their unrestrained delight, and wept. When the nurses asked who she was, she said, eyes streaming, 'Just a woman who loves children.'

# 32

# Parades Gone By

The Devines moved from their home at the corner of Torrington and Malabar roads, Maroubra, in the late 1930s, renting it out. It is hard to imagine their neighbours being overly distressed by their leaving. In the decade or so Tilly and Jim had lived in the spacious brick bungalow, Jim had shot dead Gunman Gaffney and Fred Moffitt in gun battles at the premises and others had been wounded. Nearby cars and houses had been sprayed with stray bullets in the shootouts. The gangster couple's frequent parties were the bane of neighbours' lives. These 'shivoos' usually lasted until dawn, and drunken singing, loud swearing, fist fights and shambolic dancing and falling about on the front lawn were commonplace.

Tilly and Jim's marriage had been in trouble ever since Tilly returned from England in January 1931 and found the 'housekeeper' living with Jim. There is no record of Tilly cheating on her husband except in the line of duty in her days as a prostitute, but from early on Jim Devine had been a philanderer, drunkard and wife-basher. It was always a mystery to her friends why such a strong, proud woman as Tilly Devine tolerated for so long Jim's infidelities and violence. Friends would ask how she had received her latest black eye or facial wound and she would laugh, 'Oh, don't worry, love, it's just Jim acting up again.'

In quitting Torrington Road, perhaps Tilly was hoping that a new address would bring about a new attitude in Jim. They rented a flat in Paddington. But nothing changed. 'He never used to come home, he said that business kept him out at nights,' she later recalled. 'If I said anything about him getting home late, he would knock me down with his fist and then put the boot in.'

Around 1940, Jim Devine was gaoled for stealing £100. When he was in Long Bay, his wife's visits were few. For reasons known only to her, she still loved him, friends said, but she was glad of the respite from his brutality. Tilly left their Paddington flat and moved into a terrace house they owned at 191 Palmer Street, Darlinghurst, in her red-light empire. When Jim was released six months later, he did not return to Tilly, but took his own flat in Flinders Street, Darlinghurst, where he lived with his lovers.

Even though they were no longer domiciled together, Jim continued to harass Tilly. Every Saturday morning and often throughout the week, he would bang on her door and bellow for drinking and betting money. Usually, in self-preservation and perhaps the hope that he might return to her, she gave in to him. 'He was always demanding money,' she said. 'When he was half-drunk, I would give it to him. If not, he would take it.'

A flurry of incidents in mid 1942 finally convinced Tilly that Jim was a lost cause. In July, the Navy, Army and Air Force Ball was held at David Jones department store to raise money for Australian servicemen and women. As an ex-AIF man, Jim was given a quantity of tickets to sell. As Tilly later testified in court, she, ever the patriot, told her husband that she wanted to buy twelve tickets. He told her that if she paid now, he would get the tickets and give them to her that afternoon. She handed over the cash, but Jim didn't return with the tickets. A few days later, Tilly, in a towering rage at being gypped, tracked Jim down to a pub near his flat and demanded that he either give her the tickets or her money back. Devine did neither. 'He flattened me with his fist,' she would tell the judge at her divorce proceedings, 'and then made to hit me with a chair. My driver rescued me from further injury and carried me to my car.' As her limousine accelerated away, Jim flung himself onto the road in its path. 'Go on, drive over me!' he shouted with dubious logic. 'And then I'll have you up for murder!'

About that time, too, Jim broke into Tilly's house and, as she put it, 'ratted' her purse of £26. When she later accused him of taking the money to spend at the races, 'He KO'd me [knocked me out] clean and put the boot in everywhere. He kicked me from all angles, on the chest, thighs and stomach.'

On another occasion, Jim gatecrashed a party she was holding for her employees and friends at 191 Palmer Street, and begged her to lend him money to pay his debts. Tilly refused. He flew into a tantrum, knocked her down and dumped a table laden with beer and food on her prostrate form.

Perhaps in a last-ditch attempt to save her marriage or maybe just for old times sake, Tilly planned a spectacular twenty-fifth wedding anniversary party for herself and Jim on 12 August 1942, at Palmer Street. The catering, decorations and entertainment cost her hundreds of pounds. But Jim's drunken violence ruined the celebration. He arrived late and spoiling for a fight. Tilly didn't disappoint him. 'I put this party on for our silver anniversary,' she yelled, 'and you come in at this late hour, and you're drunk. Where have you been?'

'Been?' snorted Jim. 'You know where I've been. With the new woman I'm living with. My future wife. I intended to bring her here.'

'You bastard!' said Tilly, deeply humiliated in front of her guests. 'Don't you mention that woman's name in my house.'

At that, she later told the divorce court judge, 'Jim hauled off and hit me over the head with a bottle. He cracked my skull wide open and I had to be taken to St Vincent's Hospital. They put five stitches in my head and fourteen in my right hand. I always try to protect my face and he nearly cut my fingers off with the broken bottle. I was in bed for three weeks. My nerves have been bad ever since.'

Tilly Devine's divorce application was heard in late March 1943, and she dressed for the event. She wore an expensive designer dress, a heavy fur and a wide-brimmed black hat. Her lips were a bright-red bow and her fingers flashed with many diamond rings. Her yellow-dyed hair was an elaborate array of sausage rolls. She announced she was seeking to end her marriage to James Devine because of the 'cruel beatings' she had suffered at his hands over the previous twelve months. And when the details of the domestic hell she had endured with Jim were aired in court, even those who could not abide her sympathised.

Tilly detailed Jim's assaults that had laid her low in pubs, on the street and at her home, most spectacularly at the silver wedding anniversary party. Her lawyers called a number of her friends, who swore they had seen Jim beat Tilly. One, Olive Rodman of Kings Cross, told the court she had often seen Jim Devine knock Tilly unconscious, and had inspected the bruises and cuts Jim's fists and boots had tattooed on his wife's body. Having delivered her testimony, and overcome with emotion, Rodman collapsed in the dock. Tilly's doctor, Henry Crowe, told the court that he had treated Tilly for more than a decade, and that never had he seen her so nervous and upset as now. He surmised that her condition had been caused by 'strain and battery'.

At this point, Mr Justice Edwards demanded to see the Devines' marriage certificate, to satisfy himself that they were indeed man and wife. Neither could produce the document. Tilly explained that she had given it to Australian military officials in the early 1920s, and they had never returned it to her. The judge ordered her to procure a copy of the original from the Department of Births, Deaths and Marriages in London, and adjourned proceedings until the document could be produced.

If Tilly needed something to take her mind off the impending return bout in the divorce court, she found it when she was arrested on three separate counts in June of 1943. It was a vintage Devine performance when she fronted Mr Justice Street at Central Police Court to face a number of charges: that her home, 191 Palmer Street, and a brothel that she owned in the same street, were disorderly houses where soldiers were robbed; that her home was a haven where thieves consorted; and that she had maliciously wounded one of her prostitutes, an alcoholic cocaine addict named Ellen Grimson, at that address. The judge produced Devine's record, dating back to 1921. It covered eight closely typed foolscap sheets.

The police evidence in the Grimson matter served as a chilling reminder that while Tilly Devine may have been the victim of her husband's savagery, and may no longer have been the powerful criminal she had been in the '20s and '30s, she was still a tigress. A police officer appeared as a witness for the prosecution, and the court stenographer recorded his evidence this way: 'I heard Ellen Grimson calling out in the yard of 191 Palmer Street, "Let me go! Don't hold me while she cuts me up." Tilly Devine then said, "I'll cut her ---- guts out, the ---- . Put the ---- in there until I get my ---- gat [gun]. I'll put a hole through her."' When the police arrested Tilly, Grimson was bleeding profusely from the face. She said Tilly's friends had held her while Tilly had cut her lip with a knife. It took eleven stitches to seal the wound. Tilly explained to the officer why she turned on her employee: 'The bitch would get drunk and go out and leave the lights on. It started over that. If you hadn't come, I would have killed her.' She denied slashing Grimson with a razor or knife, but admitted hitting her in the face with her ring-studded fists.

Tilly was found guilty of the disorderly house and consorting charges. She was ordered to stand trial in August for wounding Grimson.

In late July, out on bail awaiting an appeal, Tilly was back before Mr
Justice Edwards in the divorce court. She handed him the marriage
certificate and confirmed that the details on it were correct, except her
age. The certificate gave her age as twenty-one, but she had been just
sixteen when she and Jim had married at Sacred Heart Church, Camberwell Green, almost twenty-six years before.

The judge examined the certificate but was still not ready to grant
Tilly her divorce. He said he wanted to hear further evidence cor-
roborating her claim that Jim had 'habitually and cruelly' beaten her.
Tilly's lawyer Harold Munro warned the judge that such information
might be difficult to come by, for witnesses might be too frightened of
Jim Devine to speak against him. Justice Edwards, whose jurisdiction
had obviously never extended to trying criminals, was incredulous.
'Surely you don't suggest the stage has been reached in our community when persons can be intimidated against giving evidence in the
courts?'

'There are many,' retorted Munro, 'who would rather travel to the
back of Bourke than go into the witness box and say one word against
certain notorious individuals.'

The judge was not swayed. 'I think, Mr Munro, you had better get
corroboration. Marriages are not dissolved without complete proof of
matrimonial offences having been committed when the evidence is
such that corroboration is readily available.'

Tilly now told Munro to fetch a friend named Mary Singer. It has
never been divulged what incentive Tilly offered Singer to persuade
her to risk incurring Jim Devine's wrath, but several hours later, a
tremulous Singer was in the witness box. Yes, she told Justice Edwards,
she had seen Jim hit Tilly with a bottle at the anniversary party, and
seen him blacken her eyes and try to kick down her door. She had
harboured Tilly when Jim was like a wild beast when drunk. Singer's
evidence satisfied the judge, who granted Tilly Devine her decree. In
six months' time, in January 1944, the divorce would be final.

After her divorce Tilly partied hard, but her celebrations were curtailed when she stood trial for her attack on Ellen Grimson. She was found guilty and sentenced to six concurrent months' gaol on that count and the other two June offences of which she had already been convicted.

When she was released from prison, a new man entered the recently divorced Tilly Devine's life. She became enamoured of a big, bluff seaman named Eric Parsons, who worked as a part-time barman at the Tradesman's Arms Hotel.

Parsons, born in 1905, had been a steward on board the former ferry *Kuttabul*, which was torpedoed by one of three Japanese midget submarines that sneaked into Sydney Harbour on 1 June 1942. The two-man submarines' target had been the USS *Chicago*. Their presence was discovered when they were just 500 metres from the *Chicago* and preparing to fire their torpedoes. One submarine became enmeshed in torpedo nets strung across the Harbour, and the two occupants blew it, and themselves, sky-high rather than be captured. The second sub also destroyed itself when cornered by Australian warships. The third loosed a torpedo at the *Chicago*, but it missed and exploded under the hull of the *Kuttabul*, blowing it apart. Nineteen sailors died. Eric Parsons was fond of regaling customers at the Arms with tales of how he had rescued many of the drowning seamen. The spellbound tipplers repaid him with beer.

Tilly and Eric drank and caroused together, and soon became lovers. When she invited him to live with her, he left his wife Mary and moved into 191 Palmer Street, just a stagger from the Tradesman's Arms. He loved her, and humoured her, and no doubt lent support when in October 1944 she was arrested for beating up a Fijian twice her size named Vatavata, after a misunderstanding at one of her brothels.

Eric Parsons was also a victim of Tilly's cyclonic temper. On 19 February 1945, Darlinghurst Police Station received a call from a woman who would not give her name. She told them there had been a shooting at Tilly Devine's house 'and you'd better get down there quick-smart.' Tilly opened the door when the police arrived at around 7 p.m. Her face a study in puzzled innocence, she said she knew of no shooting, and invited the officers in to look around. In a bedroom they found Eric, lying still, eyes closed, under a blanket on a bunk. Tilly, finger to her lips, whispered that Eric was snoozing. A Sergeant Gilmour shook Eric, who opened his eyes. 'What's your name, sir? Have you been shot?' Gilmour wanted to know.

'I'm Eric Parsons,' replied Eric woozily. 'And no, I haven't been shot. I'm just sleeping off the booze. Are you having a joke with me?'

'Tilly, what can you tell us?' asked Gilmour.

'*Me*? Nothing,' protested Tilly. 'I have no idea what happened. I got on the booze today. The taxation mob had me down, and they took £900 out of the £1500 I had in the bank. So I got on the booze and do not care what happens.'

Gilmour and his men returned to Darlinghurst to file a false-alarm call, but then were surprised to hear on the police wireless that a man named Parsons was being treated at St Vincent's Hospital for a gunshot wound in his left leg. When Gilmour went to the hospital, Parsons told him a different story. He *had* been shot, he conceded, but had no idea who pulled the trigger. He had been standing in Palmer Street, minding his business, when he felt a sting on his thigh and looked down and saw blood. When Gilmour was sceptical, the flustered Parsons again changed his tune and this time betrayed Tilly, stammering that she had shot him when a drinking spree turned ugly. When the police went to arrest her, Tilly denied she'd shot her lover, though she did admit they'd had 'a bit of a yike over his missus'. According to Tilly, when Eric told police he'd been shot by a mystery gunman in Palmer Street he had been telling the truth.

Though completely confused by now, police charged Tilly with attempted murder.

'My client has an answer to the charge: she is completely innocent,' said solicitor Munro in Central Court in February 1945, when seeking bail on Tilly's behalf. The prosecution asserted that Tilly and Eric got drunk, quarrelled over Eric's wife Mary and the jealous Tilly shot him. Tilly stuck to her story that Eric had been wounded by a person or persons unknown. She was remanded till 6 March on £400 bail. But at her trial the case was dismissed when Eric refused to testify against her. Three months later, on 19 May, they married.

More than seventy guests crammed into Tilly's Palmer Street terrace, now decorated with her expensive furniture and art from Torrington Road, for the reception. Aged forty-four and decidedly plump, Tilly wore a powder-blue dress and a matching ribbon in her hair. Her hard face was coated in make-up and her lips were painted blood-red. Parsons, his receding sandy hair slicked back, wore a sober suit with a white carnation in the buttonhole. Guests drank beer, wine, champagne and spirits, and ate lobster, poultry and pork. There was a two-tier wedding cake with bride and groom dolls on top and a horseshoe emblazoned with 'Good luck!' Many present mused that Eric was going to need it.

To the sentimental sobs of the newlyweds and several guests, the songs 'Sympathy' and 'Because' were trilled by a slim young man wearing, for no doubt a good reason, a black tunic and furs. The party raged all night and into the next day. Just as the newlyweds collapsed into bed about midday, Tilly wearing silk pyjamas and five rings (including her new wedding band), five fire engines and an undertaker arrived at the premises. They had been summoned by a mystery practical joker. The culprit may or may not have been Kate Leigh.

'Eric was, in Australian slang, a bit of a Flash Harry,' George Parsons laughs. 'He was my father's second eldest brother. My grandparents' eldest child was Emma, then Sid, who fought at

Gallipoli when he was sixteen, then Eric. My uncle liked the good things in life and moved in circles that were a bit dicey. Stolen property, receiving. He was married to my Aunt Mary, but he was lured away by Tilly. Most of my uncles and aunts decided Eric was persona non grata when he left Mary. Not my father, who thought Eric was wonderful. Dad was the youngest sibling and he had been looked after by his brothers. Eric was good to Dad. One time Dad did something silly at work and I remember him telling Mum he was in trouble and her getting all worried. They rang Tilly and Eric, who came over and listened to Dad's story and told him, "Don't worry, we'll take care of the problem." They sorted it, like that. Eric was a big, strong man who could look after himself with his hands.'

Eric Parsons, says George, ceased to be his own man when he married Tilly. 'It was sad. He traded his independence for a flash lifestyle. He was a classic larrikin. He liked moving in dangerous circles, and there was always danger around Til. Violence was a daily occurrence. Reciprocal paybacks, medieval honour. To be taken seriously you had to be able to show you could and would defend what you had. If you didn't defend your turf in those days you'd be eaten alive.'

Eric Parsons taught young George to box. 'He said to me once, if ever you get into a fight at school, there's only one rule: you don't let him up when he's down. That involved kicking and anything else you needed to do. Eric was hard, but not nasty. He was generous and friendly, a ladies' man *and* a man's man. He told a good story.' Of Tilly's first husband, George Parsons is less complimentary: 'Eric was a great improvement on Jim, who was a total thug. I never once heard Tilly mention Jim Devine.'

'To me,' Parsons says, 'Tilly was like a ship in full sail. She wore lots of ornate jewellery, rings on her fingers and rings on her toes. No one ever taught her to dress, she went for the overstatement. In a way it was her saying: "This is me, I'm important, I'm also wealthy. Take notice." She was like one of those big Victorian houses, so stuffed with furniture that the clutter becomes interesting. She was still a good-looking woman in her forties and fifties, but heavily overweight. She'd grab you and kiss you, and be very physical. There was a great amount of Aunty Tilly when I knew her, and she'd squash you in a big hug.'

George Parsons never saw his aunt's nasty side, never heard her mention sex, swear ('apart from "bloody" and "bugger"') nor saw her assault anyone. The Tilly she allowed him to see was loving and lovable. 'She was very kind to us. She allowed us to do things our parents wouldn't. She was always interceding on our behalf if we were playing up or making noise. She'd say, "Oh the kids are all right. Kids are kids." I remember once asking her for something that my parents refused to give me, and she slipped £5 into my pocket and said, "Go and get it, and don't tell a soul."

'When she came to our house she would give us £5 each, knowing we would pass it on to Mum. It was her way of giving my mother money, because Dad, though a lovely man, was rather feckless and spent most of his time at the pub with his union mates. She knew Mum would never accept money from her but would take it from us kids. One day when Tilly gave my sister Robyn a £5 note, Robyn held it up to the light and asked if it was counterfeit. Everyone in the room froze, wondering how Tilly would respond. To our immense relief, Til thought it was hilarious.' After initial reluctance to have anything to do with her notorious new in-law, Parsons's mother and Devine warmed to each other, 'especially as they grew older,' says Parsons. 'But I had aunts who were extremely critical that my mother would even have Tilly in our house.'

Occasionally, after Tilly moved back there with Eric, Parsons was invited to his aunt's home in Maroubra. 'It was full of furniture, some of it very good quality, some bric-a-brac. Often the girls who worked for her would be there. The first time I saw all these young women at the house I asked Tilly, "Are these your daughters?" and she thought that was terribly funny. The girls made a fuss of me, cuddled me and sat me on their laps.'

But the young Parsons did recognise, he says, 'the threat, a hint of violence that was always around Tilly'. He believes it was this frisson of danger that his uncle Eric found irresistible. 'The blokes that came to the house with her, such as Skinny the bodyguard, were like neighbours, uncles. They seemed like ordinary working-class blokes and were friendly to us. They were at Tilly's beck and call. Skinny carried a gun in a shoulder holster, and one day we said, "Can we have a play with your gun?" and he said, "No." Then Tilly said, "For heaven's sake, Skinny, take the bullets out and let the kids play with the gun." Mum was appalled. Skinny took the slugs out of his .38 revolver and we rushed around the house with it. After ten minutes, Tilly said, "You'd better give Skinny his gun back." Both of her bodyguards were armed. She must have feared an attack.'

Jim Devine seemed unconcerned by the demise of his marriage and returned to his lovers and his drinking. Not long after, he moved to Melbourne, where he had grown up, and found work as a warehouse storeman. He was only fifty-two but looked seventy. His days as a major criminal were behind him.

As far as is known, he had no contact with his ex-wife again, except on New Year's Eve, 1950, when he appeared at a party in Ramsgate Avenue, Bondi, where Tilly was a guest. Taking up where they had left off at their silver wedding anniversary bash some seven years before, they argued; he punched her on the jaw, dislocating it. An ambulance and the police were called. A Sergeant Ware arrived first to find Tilly on a bed, her damaged jaw hanging loose. This infirmity, however awkward and painful, did not prevent Tilly from foully abusing the hapless policeman. She was still in hospital when the charge of using indecent language to a police officer was heard and she was fined £3 in absentia. Tilly refused to press charges against Jim, who returned to Melbourne after the assault — 'All I want from that bastard is that he get out of my life forever.'

Big Jim Devine faded into obscurity. He is believed to have died in the 1960s.

Phil 'the Jew' Jeffs died suddenly in Ettalong on 30 November 1945, aged forty-nine. It is said that Jeffs's death was caused when the bullet wounds he'd suffered after the May 1929 riot in Eaton Avenue, Kings Cross, turned septic and poisoned him. He was buried as 'Phillip Davies', the alias he adopted when he retired from Sydney's underworld to live the life of a legitimate businessman and bon vivant on the Central Coast.

Few compadres from his Razorhurst days were at the elaborate and expensive funeral. The good burghers of Ettalong came to mourn the man they thought of as a jovial, free-spending pillar of their community. A Jewish mourning prayer was intoned as Jeffs's orchid-bedecked coffin was lowered into the ground.

At the time of his death, the one-time razor gangster, pimp, drug dealer, sly-grogger, mugger and briber of police and politicians, had realised his dream of becoming Australia's Al Capone. He left to his friends and lovers a fortune of £65 000, as well as substantial property and his valuable collections of antiques and books. Jeffs, Norman Bruhn, Tilly Devine and Kate Leigh controlled Sydney's vice between the wars, reaping literally millions from their illegal activities. But of the four racketeers, Phil the Jew was the only one cunning enough to hold on to his riches until the end.

# 33

# Old Friends

Aged sixty-six in 1947, Kate Leigh seemed an unlikely candidate to fall in love and marry. Ernest 'Shiner' Ryan was a gnome-like incorrigible thief who had spent the majority of his sixty-three years behind bars, mostly for hold-ups and break and entries. He'd known Kate since the days of World War I, when he was a friend of Leigh's lover Samuel 'Jewey' Freeman and they all shared digs in Frog Hollow. He and Freeman had, of course, pulled the Eveleigh Railway Workshop heist, and Kate had followed Shiner and Jewey into gaol for perjuring herself to protect Freeman.

When Ryan began writing to Kate out of the blue in 1946, she was elderly, her two marriages and various flings with the likes of Tomlinson and Baker in her past. But Kate enjoyed Ryan's accounts of his adventures in the country's gaols, especially his tale of how he escaped from Yatala Prison in South Australia in the 1920s after stealing the master key, and had had four keys cut from the original, arrayed them in a plush-lined case and sent it to the prison's superintendent with a note: 'To F.E. Becker, Superintendent, Yatala Labour Prison, South Australia, with the compliments of the season. December 25, 1925, from Ernest Alexander Ryan.' And she was especially intrigued when he sent her a remarkable painting he had created in her honour. *The Reclamation* was a landscape which showed two paths

— presumably his and hers — intersecting at the gates of Fremantle Gaol, where Christ held a black lamb labelled 'Shiner'. Ryan signed the work: 'To Kate "Bonnie" Leigh from Ernest A. Ryan with the compliments of the season, January 1, 1947.' Leigh was chuffed, and wrote to her admirer to tell him so. He corresponded back asking her to marry him, and she said yes.

When Ryan was released from prison in 1949 he went at once to Sydney. The press, whom Kate, naturally, had apprised of the impending nuptials, met him en masse at Sydney Airport. At an impromptu press conference, he hugged Kate and declared with a shy grin that he intended to make her 'Mrs Ryan' and take her back to Fremantle, Western Australia, with him where they would live happily together in his room above a stable. Kate turned red with embarrassment and chided him, 'Arrgghh, get out of it, you mug, before I drop you. What about all those girls I hear you've been running around with?'

'Not me, love,' her beau replied. 'I'm too shy. I don't like sheilas. You're my girl. But if you won't marry me and make your home in Fremantle, I'll up and out of your life, s'help me.'

'Aw, what's wrong with you, mate?' Kate blurted back. 'Why don't you call me Bonnie, like you used to?' Then Kate gruffly assured the reporters: 'I'm not rushin' into this. I'll see what the mug's got to say before I agree to go to Fremantle.' Ryan must have said all the right things, because, soon after, the pair hosted an engagement party at Lansdowne Street, where 300 guests made short work of hot dogs, beer and champagne.

The wedding took place in Fremantle on 18 January 1950. Kate wore a striking delphinium blue-with-silver-beading wedding gown, a black veil, white gloves and white nylon stockings. Instead of her usual cluster of rings, she sported only the simple golden band Ryan had given her. 'Ain't it ducky!' Kate called to the assembled well-wishers. 'Take a gander at me, everyone! These clothes cost *real* dough.' Afterwards, as guests hip-hip-hoorayed, the buxom Kate smothered her diminutive husband, clad in a green fedora and a fawn double-breasted suit bought by her, with hugs and kisses on the lawn outside the chapel. She laughed, 'I'll see he doesn't get down to the bloody pub again,' and Shiner replied with an unsettling glint in his beady eyes, 'If this marriage don't work out, I've got a good sharp razor.' Everyone laughed.

Each step of the way, Kate had made it clear to Ryan that she had no intention of selling up in Sydney and moving to Fremantle. Sydney was where she lived and worked, and he'd have to get used to that. Almost as soon as the newlyweds settled in Surry Hills, they began to squabble. Ryan missed Fremantle, he moaned, he would never be happy in Sydney. Within a month or two of the wedding, he was back in the west. If Kate shed a tear over Shiner's defection, she did so in private.

In December 1950, almost one year after she and Ryan wed, there was a hearing in Sydney that upheld Kate's audacious demand that as Ryan's deserted wife, he had to pay her financial support of £3 a week. In Fremantle, Ryan was incredulous. 'What a Christmas box!' spluttered the old lag. 'Apart from a few days after the wedding, me and Kate have not lived together. I went east with her for a few weeks but then returned here and haven't seen her since. What a laugh! My only income is the old-age pension and there she is with thousands of pounds and she wants *me* to support *her*. I can't pay. If Kate wants me to cut it out in the cooler, I'll do that. If I go inside she'll get nothing, but I'll get free treatment for my asthma.'

When she read in the paper of Ryan's reaction, Kate chuckled: 'Oh, he's a sly old fox. He needn't worry about me sending him to the jug. He knows me better than that.'

Shiner Ryan died in 1954. When reporters asked her for her memories of the criminal, Kate released a statement in which she praised him as best she knew: 'He was a brilliant man. He engineered the whole Eveleigh hold-up. He had brains in his fingertips. He could open any lock with a wire coathanger.' She then placed a memorial notice in the classified section of the Sydney newspapers that read: 'Shiner, we cannot clasp our hands, sweetheart/Thy face I cannot see/But let this token tell/I still remember thee/Your devoted wife, Kathleen Ryan.'

Old Edward Twiss was ailing, so in September 1948 his daughter Tilly Devine decided to pay the eighty-three year old what she thought might be a final visit to the home where she had grown up in Camberwell, London. She called a press conference at 191 Palmer Street and told the well-attended gathering her travel plans. Her itinerary would include some time with her father and then she would go to Ireland 'to have a feed,' she said, 'then tour Germany and many other European countries.'

Tilly could not help gloating to friends and reporters that she had cunningly schemed to join the *Orontes* in Adelaide so she would not be on board when the liner docked in Melbourne, where she might be arrested for skipping bail fourteen years before (when arrested with Dolly Quinn for brothel-keeping in Carlton). Tilly also took the opportunity to confide to the press that she was seriously ill. In fact, she said mournfully, her days were numbered, and this trip home was one way of 'making the most of the short time left to me'. What, if anything, was ailing her is unknown, although she suffered from chronic bronchitis from her forties onwards. Tilly booked a return first-class passage on the *Orontes* and hurled herself into a round of farewell parties.

Tilly was ever solicitous of friends serving time in prison, and these unfortunates always looked forward to the booty she would bring them. So days before she flew TAA to Adelaide to rendezvous with the liner, she had her driver motor her to Long Bay to visit her prostitute friend Stella Croke who, with her husband Surridge and an accomplice, had beaten to death the Royal Sydney Golf Club chef Ernest Hoffman when a gingering went wrong. In the boot of Tilly's limousine were vegetables, and tins of tuna and salmon. At the prison gates, she unloaded them from the car and took them inside. There, a warder made a condescending remark to Tilly, who lost her temper and abused him. Ordered from the gaol for causing a scene, she stacked all the goodies back into her car and shrieked to anyone in earshot, 'I was taking this stuff to poor Stella . . . she's serving life for murder, you know. The screws wouldn't let her have it. Fancy not allowing a woman serving life to have a paltry cauliflower. I took in a chook, too, but they said she couldn't even have that. Once a month for years I've been bringing out chooks to that poor woman and this is the first time she hasn't been allowed to have one. I was so mad I threw the chook at a screw.'

But before she sailed away to England, for who knew how long, there was something else Tilly had to do.

To those who knew the women, to those who had listened to their venomous denunciations of each other for twenty years, and seen them order the slashing and shooting of each other's gangs, the photograph that appeared in the press in 1948 of Tilly and Kate embracing was as surprising as if they'd picked up the paper and seen a picture of Robert Menzies doing the foxtrot with Joseph Stalin.

Who set up the photo shoot is a mystery. It could have been one or both of the women. Possibly it was an opportunistic tabloid editor who assigned a photographer on a slow news day, and the old crime queens heard his proposal to kiss and make up for the camera and thought, 'Oh, why the hell not?' Certainly they were no longer at each other's throats for a cut of the proceeds of Sydney vice. Kate still ran her groggeries and Tilly her brothels, and both were more than capable of, as Tilly was fond of saying, 'turning on a blue', but, older and mellower, they were now small players. Kate and Tilly were happy to leave the nasty work to the usurpers.

George Parsons says today that it was rumoured in his family that Tilly and Kate had called their truce, of which the photo was symbolic, because 'they had come to a conclusion that destroying one another was not the way forward. They were under threat from the newer gangsters, and I suppose they thought they had a better chance of surviving if they battened down the hatches and got along. Tilly wanted the street violence to end because she realised that the more violent Darlinghurst was, the more police would be there to police it and she wanted to be left alone to carry out what few activities she had left.' By the late 1940s, a good ten years after Billy Mackay's ultimatum, Tilly and Kate were content to bask in the glow of being 'colourful characters'.

For the photograph, Tilly called on Kate at her home in Lansdowne Street, on the pretext of saying goodbye before she sailed for London. Kate, on cue, welcomed her warmly and invited her in. The photographer followed. Kate gave Tilly a box of Winning Post chocolates, a plaster figure of St Therese and a charm to bring her luck on her journey. Tilly grew teary at Kate's generosity and hugged her old enemy. The women kissed each other's wrinkled cheeks. In the photo, Kate at sixty-eight looks her age but appears robust. Wearing a dark dress with floral embroidery down the front, she oozes affection as she embraces Tilly. Her leathery face is creased in a huge smile. Tilly, hair set in blonde waves, wearing a rich fur and diamond rings, looks pleased to be there, but her wry gaze at Leigh betrays wariness, almost as if she is expecting to be ambushed at any moment.

Tilly and Eric Parsons then flew to Adelaide to meet the *Orontes*. She wore a full-length mink coat, two bracelets, a huge brooch, a jewelled bracelet watch and more than a dozen diamond rings, which she had insured for £10 000. Eric waved her off, then caught a plane to London, where they planned to meet in six weeks. When the *Orontes* docked in Perth for a few days, Tilly was hectored by local pressmen, whom she managed to avoid. As the ship pulled away from the dock, she called out to the thwarted reporters and photographers, 'Ha! I'm too good for you.'

During the voyage, Tilly suffered food poisoning, which confined her to her luxury £200 single cabin on the promenade deck for a day or two. She was often observed sitting without company on a deck chair, staring at the sea listening to popular love songs on a portable wireless set and occasionally nipping into the lounge for a stiff libation. She did not mingle much with other first-class guests, but made friends with a number of people in tourist class. She invited them up for a party the day before the *Orontes* docked in England.

When the liner berthed in Southampton, Tilly (whose disembarkation regalia included a black straw hat festooned with five red roses, and huge hooped diamond earrings) entertained Fleet Street reporters with a song and a galumphing buck and wing. She then hired a Daimler sedan and driver for £12, which whisked her in high style across a London still strewn with the rubble from the Blitz and bleak with wartime deprivation. She headed to Camberwell and arrived at her decrepit family home, which was soon to be razed and made the site of the council estate there today. During their reunion, Devine attempted to persuade her widower father, Edward, to accompany her back to Australia, but he refused. (Again, no record exists of any meeting with her son Frederick.) Tilly met up with Eric as planned, and they travelled together on 'our happy honeymoon'. At the end he flew home, leaving her to say her farewells in London and reboard the *Orontes*.

On the return voyage to Sydney, a female passenger with the surname of Campbell-Bone observed the vice queen at close range and
wrote about the experience. Tilly, although she'd booked a first-class
passage, was in tourist class drinking with a group of Englishwomen
who, Campbell-Bone understood, were returning with the notorious
madam to work in her brothels. Devine had beckoned to Campbell-
Bone, who was in her early forties, to join them, and she did. After
more drinks were ordered, Tilly plied Campbell-Bone with questions
about her life. So intense was the grilling that Campbell-Bone became
convinced Tilly was assessing her suitability as a prostitute. Tilly, her
fellow-passenger thought, looked worn and old — 'No trace remained
of the attraction she may have possessed when Jim married her.' The
questioning continued as another round of drinks was ordered. 'Tilly
was most affable and seemed to be mildly amused (or thoroughly
bored) as, with her skilful questioning, my life was mercilessly
bared . . . ' Campbell-Bone must have failed the audition for, to her
vast relief, Tilly did not offer her a job.

In keeping with Kate's newfound incarnation as a gruff but open-
hearted local hero, her door was always open to reporters wanting a
colourful feature about the bad old days. Early in 1950, one journalist
from *People* magazine found her in windbag mode when he interviewed her at her Lansdowne Street terrace house, her home since
1933. When he arrived, she was standing in her usual pose at her
front door, head majestically thrown back, hands on hips. From the
outset, she made it clear to the reporter, and with no hint of irony, that
she had not sold sly grog for many years and these days she was a
'shopkeeper' selling 'oranges, biscuits and lettuce' at her establishment in Devonshire Street. The reporter left, some hours later, ears
ringing with a hoard of interesting facts.

As he wrote in his article, the local kids loved her, and crammed her Devonshire Street shop at lunchtime to buy lollies and hear her jokes. She donated large sums to the Salvation Army and church charities, and on a grassroots level hired out fruit carts for destitute friends and stocked them, free of charge, with lettuces for them to sell. But, believe it or not, the adoration of Kate Leigh was not universal, the scribe conceded: Kate told him that not long ago she had been assaulted by a guest at one of her parties. He had turned the light out, hit her on the head with a bottle and, as she lay unconscious on the floor, kicked her in the stomach.

Kate confirmed in the story that she and Tilly were on friendly terms, and, in fact, hadn't been foes for quite a while:

*Tilly Devine and me, we were enemies for years. Tilly would put the dirt in about me to friends and then I'd tear into Tilly and we'd chase each other from one street to another. But that's all done now. When poor old Til came down from the Bay last time we had a real nice couple of hours together. Til's a very good woman, mind you, no matter what the police say about her. In that, she takes after me.*

As she showed the reporter around her home, she told him: 'I've got plenty of other houses. I've got a ten-roomed house in Devonshire Street. And I won't move out of the Hills.' Her greatest thrill in life? 'To make the kids happy around here. The Hills people were pretty good to me when I had nothing and I won't leave them now. Surry Hills is the quietest place in the world now.' She added, not, it seemed, without a trace of regret, that these days 'you could fire a gun in the Hills at night and you wouldn't hit a soul.' The article continued, with Kate on a roll:

*No, I don't drink or smoke. Anyone'll tell you that's right. I don't like the taste of the stuff. I remember once a plain clothes cop was bashing a man's head on the pavement. I tore into him good and hard and he hauled me up for using indecent language. Me! And then do you know what he tried to say? That I was blind drunk! The magistrate — real nice he was — soon put a stop to that. He said, 'I know that this lady does not know the taste of liquor.' See, everyone knows that I never touch a drop.*

She then pontificated on the condition of the state's prison system, a subject on which few were better qualified to speak:

*I've been 13 [sic] times in gaol — but never once for prostitution. Are women prisoners well-treated at Long Bay? Yeah. Beautiful. Couldn't be better. If I'd got my hands on that woman that gave a story to the papers about the awful conditions out at the Bay I'd have given her the biggest damn hiding she'd ever had in her life. It's just like a palace out there for first offenders. There's no excuse for women to go in again. They give them lovely dresses when they come out and dress them up like princesses. And what happens? They come into my shop with their beautiful clothes all filthy and themselves all full of plonk! And I says to them, 'What the hell's wrong with you? Pull yourselves together.' You can't do nothing with some women.*

The *People* feature was illustrated with a photograph of Kate on her first-storey balcony. She is wearing an apron and waving her hat to an adulatory throng of neighbourhood women and children. Beside her is a man dressed as Santa Claus.

# 34

# Wrong Place, Wrong Time

By the 1950s, Dulcie Markham's beauty was gone. On 6 May 1952, when she was about to turn forty, she posed for a police mugshot. Her once-long blonde hair is dirty brown and cut short, parted on the left in masculine fashion. Her formerly clear complexion is blotchy, her expression grim and her once-sparkling eyes, now cold, glare from the frame. Markham's oft-broken nose wanders alarmingly from left to right. Her fabled features have been destroyed by too much dope and bad liquor, too much sex with strangers, too many late nights, too many beatings. Perhaps too many memories. Most of her lovers had died violently: Scotty McCormack, Arthur 'the Egg' Taplin, Guido Calletti, Frank Bowen, John Abrahams; and, after them, Donald 'Duck' Day, Leslie 'Scotland Yard' Walkerden and Gavan Walsh.

Day was an ex-jockey who had pretensions to being a big man in Sydney's underworld in the 1940s. He was one of the wave of criminals who moved in on the turf of Kate Leigh and Tilly Devine, and of Guido Calletti after he was shot dead. Day sold black-market booze to American servicemen during World War II and was a standover gunman. He and Markham were lovers on and off in 1944. Day was a bully and, like most bullies, he received his comeuppance.

On 29 January 1945, Day assaulted a man who owed him money. As the man lay on the ground, Day loudly told him (*kick*) that he would be paying him (*kick*) a call that night to collect his dosh (*kick*) or else. A few hours later, Day entered the man's flat in Surry Hills. Shots were heard by passers-by and the police were summoned. When they entered the flat, they saw the dead Day spread-eagled on a bed. He had been shot through both cheeks, his nose and chest. The officers arrested the tenant of the flat, the man whom Day had beaten earlier. In court, he said that he was terrified of Day and, knowing he was coming after him, armed himself — he had killed Day before Day could kill him. The court set him free.

In the war years, Markham, like a heat-seeking missile, zeroed in on the visiting hordes of American servicemen. She relieved them of large amounts of their leave pay in Sydney, Melbourne and Brisbane. She ran a brothel in St Kilda, Melbourne, for a while in the mid '40s. She was once arrested in that suburb for appearing in the street clad only in bra and knickers and carrying an axe. To police officers she explained patiently that she was a brothel-keeper and had been chasing a customer who dared haggle over the price.

In Melbourne, Markham met Leslie Walkerden, a criminal with a reputation for violence. When they became lovers, he was providing expensive protection for a Richmond baccarat club. The extreme measures he took on behalf of the club's proprietors made him enemies, and when, at 2.30 a.m. on 12 September 1945, Walkerden left the club, he found one of the tyres of his car flat. While he was occupied changing the wheel, three men emerged from the shadows armed, respectively, with a shotgun, a .45 revolver and a .32 revolver. All three opened fire on Walkerden. The pistoleers missed, but a load of shotgun buckshot blasted Walkerden's side. In hospital he refused to say who shot him. 'Don't waste your time,' he gasped. 'I'll fix it my way.' He never did, for Walkerden died of his wounds almost immediately.

After Walkerden's death, Markham ping-ponged between Melbourne and Sydney. She remained a prostitute, but, as her beauty faded, she could no longer earn the money she had when she was beautiful, and was reduced to servicing drunks and desperates. In Sydney, Tilly Devine was a benefactor to her old friend, and a job in one of Tilly's bawdyhouses was Pretty Dulcie's whenever she wanted it.

Back in the underworld of Melbourne in '51, Markham was drinking with a group of crims at her rented home in Fawkner Street, St Kilda, on 25 September. Among her guests was flame-haired, snappily dressed small-time wideboy Len 'Redda' Lewis, in his forties; and her boyfriend at the time, a young journeyman boxer named Gavan Walsh and his brother. Without warning, and for reasons still unknown, two armed men crashed through the front door and sprayed the drinkers with bullets. Redda was unscathed, but Gavan Walsh was hit in the stomach, his brother was shot in the hand and Markham caught a bullet in her hip. The boxer died, and it took Markham and Walsh's brother months to recover.

Two suspected shooters were arrested, but Markham refused to incriminate them. At the men's trial, a nonplussed judge mused on Markham and her cronies as if pondering the anthropology of a rare species of wildlife. 'She, in fact practically all the witnesses, moves in somewhat queer circles. As far as one can gather, the men seem to spend the greater part of their day in hotels, and a good part of their night drinking from place to place. The women seem to join them in their drinking, and to change the people with whom they sleep from month to month, without anyone worrying about it or doing anything about it.'

True to the judge's rumination, Markham quickly got over Gavan Walsh's demise and became the lover of Redda Lewis. Three months after she was shot, still in bed and with her hip encased in plaster, the two were married. Sixty guests crowded into her bedroom at Fawkner Street to hear Lewis and Markham, who wore a white plaster cast on her leg and hip, take their vows. There was a spectacular three-tiered wedding cake and other cakes, savouries and copious liquor in the form of an eighteen-gallon keg of beer (guarded by best man Les 'Butcher' Gordon) and crates of wine and spirits. A reporter asked Markham if she had any qualms about being married where Gavan Walsh had been shot dead. She looked at him as if he were mad. 'Not a fuckin' one,' she said. There is a story, possibly apocryphal, that the newlyweds sang 'You Always Hurt the One You Love'. No police were invited, but they came anyway. They took the licence numbers of cars parked outside, then entered the house and noted guests' names and addresses. When Markham realised they were harassing her friends, she was furious. 'If you have no warrant, get out!' barked the bedridden bride.

Writer Brian Matthews, whose youth, as chronicled in his memoir *A Fine and Private Place*, was spent in St Kilda, was a neighbour of Markham when she married Lewis:

> *Pretty Dulcie did not spend much time or effort on what are sometimes called the niceties. Walking out behind her one day from the ladies toilet of the Middle Park Hotel, one of my innumerable aunts, not knowing for the moment who she was dealing with, noticed that Dulcie's dress was accidentally hooked up at the back, so my aunt helpfully flicked the offending bit down for her, whereupon, before a word of explanation could be offered, Pretty Dulcie turned and intimated her gratitude by saying: 'You lay a finger on me again, and I'll have the boys break your arms.' Well, that's roughly what she said — interspersed at appropriate points with copulatory and other references; and recommendations difficult to carry out even if my aunt had the slightest idea what they meant.*

Matthews remembers watching Markham holding court outside the Prince Charles pub on the corner of Fawkner and Grey streets. It was soon after her hip was shattered by the bullet and she sat with her leg propped on a stool as lackeys brought her beer after beer. At one point she caught the spellbound Matthews and his young friend observing her too closely: 'Our elaborate and studied show of uninterested loitering was so obvious that Dulcie got wind of it and told us to — I quote — *"Fuck off!"* Unquote.'

When Markham's hip had recovered, she brought Lewis to Sydney and they set up house in Darlinghurst. The union did not survive. After a series of spats, Lewis returned to Melbourne in April 1952. He was at his mother's home in Prahran on the 23rd when the doorbell rang. It must have been an horrific case of deja vu when the caller turned out to be a gunman. He aimed at the startled Lewis, then coolly pumped three bullets into his stomach. When Lewis fell, the gunman shot him three more times, then ran off. Astonishingly, Lewis did not die. Not so astonishingly, he refused to say who shot him. 'I'll cop it sweet,' he told the police.

While Lewis was recuperating in Melbourne, his wife did not travel south to visit him. It may have been because she was busy on a crime spree, for she was arrested *twenty* times on a variety of charges in 1952. Or, more likely, she knew the marriage was doomed. Lewis and Markham never lived together again, and were later divorced.

Once, when Pretty Dulcie was sentenced to a month in Long Bay for stealing, the judge, in kindly fashion, assured her that it was not too late to go straight. 'Ha!' she scoffed. 'There are ways of making money without working for it. The trouble you get into doesn't matter, so long as you get the money.' It could have been her epitaph.

# 35

# Tilly's Grand Shivoo

Tilly Devine, to the amazement of many, had made it to fifty. She was not about to let the 8 September 1950 milestone pass without a shivoo.

A photograph exists of the grand event at her old home in Maroubra, which she had reclaimed from her tenants and used as 'my suburban address'. (The terrace at 191 Palmer Street became her chief brothel, until July 1953 when the Supreme Court declared the premises a disorderly house used for prostitution.) Front and centre in the picture is Tilly, in a white dress, her hair arranged in an improbable and towering pile that resembles a Roman centurion's helmet. Around her neck is a diamond pendant given to her as a birthday present by Eric Parsons. She is standing before a table heaving with food and drink, and is about to carve an enormous roast pig. Her hands, fingers decked with rings, daintily grasp a large carving knife and a fork which she is about to plunge into the beast. She has a prim smile on her face. What she was saying at this moment was, 'Fair dinkum, I wish to God this 'ere suckling pig was Bumper Farrell!'

She is surrounded in the photo by attractive young women and Parsons, who stares boozily at the camera. In open-neck shirt, braces and cardigan, he has not dressed up for the occasion. Parsons had provided the food and drink, which cost £500, and even prepared some dishes himself. On the menu were two pigs, forty chickens and ducklings, four turkeys, two geese, twenty lobsters, two bags of oysters and two crates of prawns. Until he misjudged his alcoholic capacity and was forced to bed early, Eric was loudly proclaiming himself 'the best bloody cook in Australia!'

More than 100 guests attended, including Jim Devine's younger brother Sid; Carbine Lottie; a man known as 'Bandages'; 'Happy Harry' Snell; and Radio William, the noted SP bookie. A reporter from *Smith's Weekly* was invited to chronicle the party. Guests bore tribute in the form of jewellery, orchids, perfume and furs. Before the festivities began, Tilly had spelled out the ground rules: 'There'll be singin' and dancin' all night. There'll be plenty to drink now and plenty to eat later. But don't any of youse put on a blue or make a rort out of my home. If anyone wants to be a galah they had better fly away now while they've got a feather to fly with!'

After the guests sang 'Happy Birthday', one Archibald St Claire, (aka Tools Carpenter) toasted the birthday girl. 'Gee, it gets my goat when I see the newspapers giving the coppers the big wrap-up. All they do for Tilly is to go her scone hot! How can anyone compare a good girl like Tilly with a mob of droobs and flat feet.' Praise indeed. Tilly responded with her customary eloquence: 'Now, you can all get stuck into the suckling pigs and other scran.' At that, St Clair quipped, 'Cripes, it's a good thing you've got your teeth in, Til!'

The *Smith's Weekly* man later pulled Tilly to one side and, notepad at the ready, asked her to reel off the names of her guests. She admonished him:

> We don't give out names at my parties. I only put them on to
> please my friends and Eric's relations. I make the parties extra
> grouse so as to nark old Kate Leigh. Her parties are always
> drack. The names of the people don't matter. Just put in the
> paper that there were jockeys and barmaids, horse owners, dog
> men, tip slingers, trainers, gay girls, my bank manager, my

*interior decorator and some of my lawyers. Say this: say every-*
*body was at Tilly's suburban menagerie except coppers,*
*top-offs, phizgigs and other mugs.*

As the night wore on, Tilly took the floor to entertain her guests with a musical selection. She sang 'I'll be Your Sweetheart (If You Will Be Mine)' and 'If I Had My Life to Live Over (I'd Do the Same Things Again)', and her *pièce de résistance* was when she crooned 'Why Don't We Do This More Often?', like a chanteuse in the music halls of her long-ago Camberwell youth.

The party ended at dawn. Many guests had faded with dancing fatigue or passed out drunk in the house or the grounds, but as the last of those sober enough to do so drove away into the spring morning, Tilly was still going strong on the front lawn, kicking her legs high and screeching her favourite song, 'Knees Up, Mother Brown'.

Tilly was honoured to accept an invitation for a drink and a chat with Arthur Helliwell, a big-name columnist for *People*, a high-circulation British Sunday newspaper. Helliwell was an acerbic fellow who wore a ratty homburg hat, a David Niven moustache and held an ever-present cigarette between his third and fourth fingers. When he arrived in Australia he was on the final leg of a 1950 world tour. He had been to the United States and Fiji, and regaled readers back in England with his impressions. Helliwell offered some novel observations of Suva, for instance. 'My first peek at a South Seas island has been bitterly disappointing,' he announced. 'The romance and glamour of the South Seas is a fake.' Detracting from his enjoyment, he noted, were the sharks, rain and 'ugly' Fijian women.

Sydney, and Tilly, fared no better. The photo accompanying his column about his visit to Sydney, headlined 'This City Gave Me Such a Shock' shows Tilly sitting in a pub with Helliwell. She is drawing deeply on a cigarette held in a hand weighed down by a heavy cluster of rings. No less than four glasses of alcohol are before them on the bar. Helliwell is grasping one tightly. He wrote:

> The typical Sydney 'sport' glosses over a marked inferiority complex with an aggressive and irritating rudeness. He laces his conversation with the army's favourite adjective to the point of monotony, insults strangers as a matter of course and generally goes around looking for trouble.

Helliwell called Sydney 'a rough, tough, money-mad good-time city.' He said it was also, in many ways, beautiful and loved by its inhabitants. 'But they love much more its Saturday afternoon at the race track, its two-up gambling schools, its rowdy night life and its schooner of beer.' He could attest to the fact that if one visited such 'smart nitespots' as Joe Taylor's Celebrity Club, or Sammy Lee's, where the food, music and floor shows compared with Mayfair's best, 'you can kiss a tenner good-bye.' He ventured into Thommo's Two-Up School 'where not so long ago one character won a small fortune by tossing seventeen heads in a row!' He was amazed by the 'cockatoos' who patrolled outside and signalled the arrival of any stranger in the vicinity with warning whistles.

And, Helliwell had decided, after at least a couple of days' intense investigation:

> [Sydney] has an underworld that puts anything I have seen in London, New York, Paris or even Marseilles in the shade. Its sordid, lawless east end [sic], terrorised by a riff-raff of thugs, hoodlums, gunmen and larrikins who would make the spivs of Soho's naughty square mile look like candidates for a charm school, is more dangerous than the jungle after dark.

One can only imagine what Tilly's ancient and ailing father Edward, reading his *People* back in London, made of the next paragraph in Helliwell's report:

*Boss of the district and certainly Sydney's most colourful char-*
*acter is the fabulous 'Diamond' Tilly Devine, a tough peroxide*
*blonde from Camberwell Green, who owns the most glittering*
*collection of jewellery in Australia. Tilly, self-confessed Queen*
*of the Underworld, was decked out in eleven diamond rings,*
*two glittering bracelets and a magnificent jewelled wrist watch*
*when I met her. 'Jest a few little trinkets, love,' she said. 'Don't*
*feel properly dressed without 'em.' Tilly, who thinks nothing of*
*donating £1000 to charity or spending £500 on a children's*
*party, is probably one of Sydney's wealthiest citizens.*

When Tilly was sent a copy of Helliwell's full-page feature, which
hit the newsstands on 5 November 1950, she was ropable, and
declared that the first thing she would do next time she visited London, was to find Arthur Helliwell and 'punch him fair on the nose'.
She was not only angry because her Sydney misdeeds were now well
known in her home town, but because the article elicited scores of
begging letters from Londoners with sob stories. 'They're biting me
for everything from thousands of pounds to six-roomed houses and
washing machines,' she complained. One man proposed marriage.

Tilly travelled south for the Melbourne Cup in November 1951. In
doing so, she realised she was risking arrest and twelve months in
prison for absconding from bail after her 1934 conviction for consorting in Melbourne. She took the chance, and came to regret it.

She was recognised by police at Flemington, not surprisingly as she
was wearing thirteen of her most ostentatious diamond rings and a
long fur coat (she also had £296 in cash in her handbag), and arrested.
'I thought you blokes would have forgotten me after all these years.
Why don't you give me a break? Please don't put me in jail,' she

begged the officers. When that tack seemed not to be working, Tilly tried another. 'I've got cancer,' she sobbed. 'I haven't much longer to live and I don't want to die in jail.' A judge sentenced her to twelve months in Pentridge (or 'Belsen', as she called the prison), but because of her age and 'cancer', she was released after five weeks.

Safely home in Sydney, Tilly, her health miraculously restored, regaled reporters with the details of her ordeal. When she was gaoled, the warders had 'stripped me down to the way I was born because they thought I might be carrying a gun or drug running. I objected to that because I've never carried a gun and I've never had anything to do with drugs. My only failure is that I like a drop to drink occasionally.' She said she was glad to be home, and thankful for the hundreds of Christmas cards, letters, telegrams and personal messages she had received from strangers wishing her well. 'My neighbours, who are on the square, came and shook hands with me when I got home. All this kindness has made me vow never to get into trouble again. As a matter of fact I haven't been in trouble since I married Eric Parsons, but no one gives me credit for that.'

She returned to Melbourne for the Cup in 1952, and this time she was left in peace.

# PART 4
# The End of an Era

# 36

# Empire in Decline

'The bloom has gone off the grog,' mourned Kate Leigh. It was 1954 and she was explaining to tax investigators why she was no longer wealthy. In her seventies, she had seen her sly-grog empire snatched from her by other dealers. Another formidable rival was the licensed club, just gaining purchase in society. Why would a drinker bother slinking up a dark lane, giving a password through a chink in a door, often imbibing gut-rotting booze in unseemly surroundings *and* risking arrest, when they could drink at their local RSL or sporting club until all hours for just a few shillings a year subscription? *And* with the blessing of the authorities.

But sly-grogging was all Kate really knew, so even though by the early 1950s she owned only a few outlets, she kept at it. Her main dispensary was a flat above her fruit-and-vegetable shop at 212 Devonshire Street. Police still raided her premises, sometimes in bursts when they needed to improve their raid quota, but usually the busts were spasmodic and gentle. She still proffered the officers information but now that she was yesterday's woman and out of the major criminal loop, the few snippets she could divulge were of little practical use to police. Yet, they humoured her. They liked her as an honourable old adversary.

'In the early 1950s,' says Ray Blissett, 'I saw a lighter side of Kate.

We had a Perth detective called Bill Neilson join us in the Consorting Squad. I thought since Bill and Kate were going to have quite a bit to do with each other, it would be a good idea to take Bill up to her house in Devonshire Street and introduce them. I knocked on the door and she opened it herself. "What do you want?" she said with a scowl. I said, "Kate, I'd like you to meet Bill Neilson, our new copper." Kate's face broke into a wide smile and she yelled, "Bill, you old bastard! What are you doing here?" I said, "So you know him?" "Blissett," she said, "I know all the shits!" They'd hooked up somehow in Perth when she went across to marry Shiner Ryan.'

The old outlaw could still spark a ruckus, however. In July 1952, after one raid, she had been charged with selling wine without a licence at the Devonshire Street shop. She beat her well-worn path to Central Criminal Court where she met her lawyer, the tall and patrician W.R. Dovey, QC (who was the father of future prime minister Gough Whitlam's wife Margaret). Outside the court, before proceedings began, Leigh and Dovey were taking in the winter sunshine when a photographer for the *Daily Mirror* snapped their picture. Leigh normally relished publicity, but, for some reason, was not in the mood for it that day. With a roar, she charged the photographer. She punched him and tried to prise his camera away, all the while abusing him, said an onlooker, 'with a stream of filthy words'. The newsman was saved only by the intervention of Dovey, who held the combatants apart and tutted: 'Now, calm down Kate. That's enough of that.'

Just one month later, in August 1952, the Vice Squad again raided 212 Devonshire Street. On bursting in, officers led by Detective Sergeant Ron Walden encountered a man with a suspicious bulge under his thick woollen jumper. When they asked him what he was concealing, he sheepishly produced two bottles of illicit wine. The fellow, who gave his name as Sloggett, confessed, 'I bought the booze from Kate.'

For perhaps the hundredth time in her life, Kate Leigh was charged with selling liquor without a licence. She attended court with Dovey. The Crown's key witness, Sloggett, failed to appear, no doubt after Kate had convinced him it was in his interests not to. Just when she was waiting for the formality of the charges against her being dismissed, Walden surprised her. He produced a signed statement from Sloggett, dated the night of his arrest, naming Kate as the liquor vendor. Judge Stewart decided the note was permissible evidence and fined Kate £200. Outsmarted, she leapt to her feet, and shouted that she had been framed and Sloggett had made his statement under duress — 'The coppers kicked Sloggett in the guts and I will produce him at the Appeals Court.' Dovey calmed Kate — 'Kate, behave yourself!' — and attempted to reason with Stewart. 'This is a case of "give a dog a bad name",' he complained, insisting over the uproar that his client ran a legitimate fruit-and-vegetable shop. But the conviction, and the fine, stood.

Through her nearly forty years as a sly-grogger, Kate had prided herself on the high quality of the liquor she sold. She would pass through her shops, complimenting customers on their good sense in coming to 'Mum's'. So Roy Fowler-Glover was shocked, and then angered, when he opened one of two bottles of wine he had bought from Kate on 22 November 1953, and discovered it contained water. Throwing caution to the wind, the Marrickville electrician (who conceded later that 'I might have had a noggin or two that day') hailed a taxi and told the driver to take him to Devonshire Street, where he would confront Kate. As the taxi idled at the kerb, Fowler-Glover knocked on the door of no. 212 and, when asked by the cockatoo, gave the password, 'Mum'.

When Mum materialised, the diminutive Fowler-Glover angrily accused her of gypping him, and demanded his money back. Kate laughed in Fowler-Glover's face. At that, he stormed outside into the street and shouted that unless he was reimbursed immediately he would hurl the two bottles of water through the front window of the shop. Kate disappeared into a back room. Fowler-Glover presumed she was going to retrieve his money. He was mistaken; she returned with her gun. Kate levelled the rifle at his head — 'Get out of here, or I will blow your brains out, you bastard!' Fowler-Glover's bravado evaporated. He leapt into the cab and ordered the driver, Ian Wheatley, to get them out of there quick-smart. Wheatley, Fowler-Glover said in court, followed his advice 'with the speed of a greyhound and the grace of a dove'.

That evening, acting on a complaint from Fowler-Glover, Darlinghurst detectives called on Kate. She was indignant. 'Wouldn't you have taken a gun to him, too? The mug was going to throw a bottle through my window.' A Detective Baldwin confiscated Kate's rifle, which was unloaded. She was charged with assaulting Fowler-Glover, selling liquor without a licence and carrying a firearm on Sunday. The judge found the sly-grog and firearm charges proved but did not register a conviction, and he dismissed the assault charge.

# 37

# Crown Witness and the End of Nellie Cameron

Like Moll Flanders's triumphant homecoming as a woman of means after she had been exiled to the colonies in disgrace, Tilly Devine's visit to London for the coronation of Queen Elizabeth II in 1953 was planned as a jab in the eye to all who had snubbed and derided her. 'She returned home to show everyone in Australia and London that she'd made it to the top,' says George Parsons. 'She was effectively saying, "I left here poor and now I've come back with money."'

Tilly, says Parsons, had no particular love for individual members of the royal family. He remembers her asking, 'How does being born on one side of the blanket make you any better than someone born on the other?' But, like most Britons, and Australians too in those days, she had an inherent respect for the institution of the monarchy. So she was keen to attend the coronation and the new queen's procession through the streets, and few of the thousands of Australians who also made the journey could have planned their odyssey with such joie de vivre. She'd been dreaming of the big day, 2 June, she breathlessly confided to friends, and unless she was 'six feet underground', she'd be there in a prime vantage point. 'My family are Londoners,' she exulted with a wink, 'and they'll grab us ringside seats!'

She filled a number of trunks with her finest clothes, including eight evening gowns, fur coats, cocktail dresses, sportswear, underwear, shoes and hats. She chose a dozen of her glitziest diamond rings, and took the diamond brooch Eric Parsons had given her on her fiftieth birthday, her diamond bracelets, a diamond watch, and pearl and diamond earrings. Her husband, too, would be a sartorial paragon. 'Eric looks a real lady-killer in his new monkey suit,' said Tilly. 'We've got the best clothes money can buy.'

Tilly hosted a series of bon-voyage parties, the swishest of which was a gala farewell dinner at the Grand Central Hotel on the evening of 4 January, the day before she and Eric sailed away first class on the *Himalaya*. 'I extend an open invitation to everybody who has a kind thought for an old sinner like me,' she announced to reporters in the days before the affair. 'I don't particularly want wallopers or screws, but if they turn up I'll do the decent thing by them.'

Tabloid pressmen mobbed the departing couple as they climbed the gangway of the *Himalaya*. 'Tilly, I love your hair!' cried one. Devine had wound her locks into a plait for the send-off.

'Thanks, love. One nob made a crack about my hair being a wig. I told the old tart what she could do. Just because a woman takes care of her coiffure, that's the kind of thing she gets.'

'How are you paying for the trip, Til?'

'We backed Dalray in the Melbourne Cup!'

'Tilly, are you glad to be travelling first class?'

'I'd rather travel tourist. Swells give me a pain in the neck. But a bit of swank is all right for a while, particularly as I'm so sick with bronchitis.'

As reporters yelled questions and well-wishers flung streamers at them, Devine and Parsons hugged each other and called down at the dock, 'Hoo-roo! We'll be back when the money runs out!'

As the liner made its majestic progress out of Circular Quay, tugs tooted and sprayed water high into the air. Once outside Sydney Heads, the excited travellers repaired to their luxury cabin. Three weeks later, after battling dyspepsia, seasickness and many a hangover, Tilly arrived in England in a vintage season for Empire. The touring Australian cricket team, with Keith Miller, Neil Harvey and the young Richie Benaud, was contesting a marvellous Ashes series with England, and New Zealander Sir Edmund Hillary and sherpa Tensing had just conquered Everest in the name of the new monarch. Tilly herself did her bit to uphold the reputation of the colonies when she disembarked at Tilbury, wearing, it appeared, most of the contents of her clothes trunks. She declared to pressmen who had received prior warning of her arrival: 'I am not a member of the underworld, and it is eighteen years since I have been in any trouble. I mix only with nice people.'

Midday 2 June 1953, and 40 000 people lined the streets of London. Tilly Devine and Eric Parsons and about nine of their friends were grouped in their allocated seats in the Mall, not 500 metres from where, nearly forty years ago, Tilly had sold herself on the Strand. They had been in position since early that morning. 'Aunty Tilly and Uncle Eric sent postcards back from London, and photos,' says George Parsons. 'They showed them sitting on chairs right on the kerb in a flag-bedecked street. They were in the front row of a crowd about twelve deep. I remember my old man saying to Mum, "Oh, Til must have paid a lot of money for those seats!"'

Tilly, wearing a hairdo created for her by a Paris hairdresser two days earlier, was ebullient and probably tipsy, for Eric had been passing a bottle around to ward off the effects of unseasonal rain and sleet. A band nearby drew smiles from the shivering masses when it struck up 'It Ain't Gonna Rain No More' and 'On the Sunny Side of the Street'. Then, half an hour past noon, as the chimes of Big Ben rang across Parliament Square, cannons in Hyde Park and the Tower of

London boomed to signify that the young Elizabeth had just been crowned queen at Westminster Abbey. At the sound of the big guns, the crowd, including Tilly and her party, and the soldiers and police who controlled it, broke into 'Land of Hope and Glory' and 'Rule Britannia'. A squadron of RAF jets screamed across the leaden sky.

Tilly's and her friends' seats in the Mall were at the end of the processional route. Before passing them, the long line of carriages rumbled from Westminster Abbey up Whitehall to Pall Mall, Piccadilly, Hyde Park Corner, East Carriage Drive, Marble Arch, Oxford and Regent streets, Piccadilly Circus, Haymarket, Trafalgar Square and Admiral's Arch before entering the Mall.

Suddenly, to thunderous cheers, the carriages were upon Tilly and Eric. Eight grey horses drew the golden state coach of Queen Elizabeth II ('her smile gay and brilliant,' the *Times* of London said the next day) and the Duke of Edinburgh, with Earl Mountbatten of Burma their personal aide-de-camp. In Elizabeth's wake were Sir Winston Churchill, who flashed his trademark 'V for Victory' sign, and Lady Churchill. Australia's prime minister, Robert Menzies, and his wife Patty were in the seventh carriage. There was the Queen Mother, whom Tilly had, in all likelihood, last seen at Circular Quay back in 1927 when she was Duchess of York; and Princess Margaret; the Sultans of Lahej, Selangor, Brunei, Jahore, Perak and Zanzibar; and the Queen of Tonga. Tilly cheered, whooped and waved as the dignitaries' horse-drawn coaches rattled and clopped along the grand red, white and blue–festooned thoroughfare — 'We want the Queen! We want the Queen!' The *Times* called the parade 'long and lovely pageantry' and lauded 'the glitter of the gold, the glow of the scarlet, the trappings and embellishments of martial pride and gallantry.'

After the procession passed by and on through the gates of Buckingham Palace, there was no sense of anticlimax as the throng, many people carrying the umbrellas and newspapers with which they'd warded off the rain, and the cardboard periscopes they'd used to see above others' heads, crushed into the West End for a huge street party. The River Thames, Big Ben, the Tower of London, the Houses of Parliament and Trafalgar Square were all illuminated by thousands of burning electric globes. Fireworks lit up the stern faces of statues in Parliament Square and the white stone of historic buildings. No one now knows for sure how Tilly and Eric spent that night, but it's a safe bet that they joined the revellers.

If the finest moment of Sir Winston Churchill, whom Tilly had so roundly cheered that day, was facing down Hitler in World War II, then 2 June 1953, Coronation Day, was probably Tilly Devine's. It was also her last real hurrah, for her life would never be such fun again. There was a portent of future tribulations when Eric developed a condition in his eye that necessitated its removal in a London hospital.

In the 1950s, Tilly Devine was a woman under siege. On her return from England, troubles piled at her door. She learned that she was being targeted by the Taxation Department, which was probing her returns over the past ten years. Tilly was worried about what the department's sleuths would turn up, and she had every right to be concerned, for each year she had routinely understated her income by tens of thousands of pounds.

Possibly to take her mind off the snooping tax investigators, Tilly planned a party at Torrington Road in honour of her old friend Stella Croke when the latter was released from Long Bay Gaol after serving fourteen years of her life sentence for murdering chef Ernest Hoffman. But the night ended in uproar when a fight broke out, guns were drawn and someone shot Croke in the upper thigh. She survived that flesh wound but died within the year when a cut on her finger turned septic and poisoned her.

Another setback followed. Tilly, who had always prided herself on her pugilistic prowess, had her eye blackened by another woman at the Tradesman's Arms. Tilly was drinking with Esther O'Hara, an Aboriginal acquaintance who lived in nearby Thompson Street. The women's friendly banter became heated and ugly as their glasses piled higher on the bar. Tilly called O'Hara a 'half-breed' and a 'black bitch'; O'Hara retorted that Tilly was a 'Pommy bastard'. They shaped up to each other, but O'Hara was quicker and struck Tilly a glancing blow that knocked her down. In times past, Tilly would have leapt straight up and torn her attacker apart, but this time, her spirit crushed and her body weakening, she slowly pulled herself to her feet and slunk from the pub.

Then, in November 1957, Eric Parsons, her rock for more than a decade, died of cancer. As she had had with Jim, Tilly and Eric had regular domestic dust-ups, but without the violence. 'Eric was a promiscuous man,' says George Parsons, 'and even when he was married to Tilly I don't think he was faithful to her all the time, and I think she suspected . . . But as he got older he calmed down. Even though he was only fifty-two when he died, when we saw him in the hospital he was a very old and broken man. They were happy together and he left her some money.'

Nellie Cameron retained her good looks for as long as she lived despite the abuses of her lifestyle. In her forties, Cameron, unlike Dulcie Markham, was able to attract wolf-whistles and admiring glances in spite of being a veteran prostitute, alcoholic and drug user who had been shot, stabbed and beaten regularly for nearly thirty years. In *Rugged Angel*, Lillian Armfield compared the beauty of Cameron and Markham:

> *Dulcie was prettier than Nellie, but Dulcie's features didn't have the rare and curious indestructibility of Nellie's. Right to the*

*finish, Nellie retained her attractive appearance and the assured poise that set her apart from all the other women of the Australian underworld. Even after being badly wounded or bashed up, she maintained her air of rather disdainful nonchalance, and she continued to queen it over men.*

Cameron had kept a low public profile since the early 1940s, with only isolated incidents thrusting her back into the newspapers. On 27 November 1944, a client she was entertaining at her flat at 253 Liverpool Street, East Sydney, was shot in the buttocks. Police believed Cameron fired on the man after he caught her gingering him, but the victim insisted that a stranger had shot him while he was sleeping with Cameron on her bed. Police had no choice but to file the shooting under 'Unsolved'.

Then, eight years later, in 1952, when they investigated moans in a passageway beside Cameron's flat in Denham Street, Darlinghurst, neighbours saw her crawling on all fours, weeping with pain and losing blood from a gunshot wound in her stomach. She was rushed to St Vincent's Hospital where the bullet, which had perforated her liver and lodged between two ribs, was removed and she was treated and released. Doctors later professed amazement at finding two other bullets from earlier shootouts in her abdomen, and numerous razor and knife scars criss-crossing her body.

Police arrested William Donohoe, a wharfie with whom Cameron had lived since the end of her second marriage, to one Charles Bourke. Witnesses had seen Cameron and Donohoe arguing in a nightclub the day before the shooting, and Cameron had ended the contretemps by hitting Donohoe on the head with a beer jug. But Cameron refused to cooperate with police and the charges against Donohoe were dropped.

The good-time girl now fell into a deep depression born of post-operation symptoms, a nervous condition and her conviction that the doctors' probing in her liver to repair the bullet's damage had given her cancer. Donohoe tried to reassure her that her cancer was all in her imagination, and doctors gave her a clean bill of health, but Cameron would not be dissuaded. She believed she was dying. She hardly ever left her decrepit apartment and spent much of each day in bed.

On 8 November 1953, she waited until Donohoe left the house, then she turned on the gas jets in the oven in her tiny kitchen. She knelt, as if in prayer, in front of the oven, opened the door and put her head deep inside. When Donohoe came home, Nellie Cameron was dead. She was forty-one.

Her funeral was held on 10 November, and it was extravagant. More than 700 friends and admirers of the darling of the razor gangs were at the church and Botany Cemetery, where her rose-covered coffin was interred. Kate Leigh and Tilly Devine, not long back from the coronation, attended. Cameron survived most of her husbands and boyfriends, but Donohoe, the last man in her life, was there. So was her one-time lover, deathly pale, balding, alcoholic Frank Green, who appeared shockingly old to those who hadn't seen him since his days as an enforcer in the 1930s. Within a year, the Little Gunman himself would be dead.

Cops mingled with mourners, taking notes and photographs. Lillian Armfield, who always had a soft spot for Cameron, paid her respects. As she recalled to Vince Kelly:

> I didn't see any tears shed for Nellie. And she didn't deserve any. And, to do her justice, I know she wouldn't have wanted any. Nellie would have been happy if there had been a brawl at the funeral, a real ding-dong affair in which a few would have been wiped out. That's the sort of funeral Nellie would have liked for herself. She was only forty-one when she died, but she had lived up every day of her life.

# 38

# The Taxman Comes Calling

By the mid 1950s, Kate Leigh's fortune was gone. This was due to the competition for the illegal alcohol pound, her compulsive clothes and jewellery buying, generous donations to the needy, the escalating cost of paying her henchmen and the police fines and bribes she paid to stay out of gaol and in business.

Tilly Devine was doing better, though she, too, was bound for financial ruin. In the late 1920s and '30s, she had owned many of the properties that housed her brothels, and at one stage she ran some thirty bordellos in East Sydney. Like Kate, she had essential overheads to pay, and her extravagant parties, parasitic loved ones and friends and trips to Europe would have bit deeply into her fortune; but from the 1920s until the mid '50s, she was never less than a wealthy woman. As George Parsons says: 'I don't know what she invested in, but she was loaded . . . There was the Maroubra house and a lot of other properties around Sydney.'

These properties included a bungalow with Harbour views in Ian Street, Rose Bay. She also owned a large house at 145 Brougham Street, Woolloomooloo, and for a time she owned or rented a beach house on Scotland Island on Pittwater, near Sydney's northern beaches. Modern-day Scotland Island resident Leicester Warburton attests to the local legend that buried somewhere on the island is a cache of Tilly's money and jewellery that she attempted to hide from the Taxation Department after they began their pursuit of her. Once Warburton was swimming 'and I dived down and saw a vague rectangular shape at the bottom, and suddenly the thought popped into my head that this may be Tilly Devine's fabled treasure trove.' To his dismay, the treasure chest proved to be no more than an old Silent Knight refrigerator someone had dumped.

While some police officers seemed reasonably content for Tilly and Kate to continue catering to the victimless vices of Sydneysiders indefinitely, so long as things didn't get too rough, the Taxation Department was not so understanding. Around the early 1950s, the department eyed the women's wealth and found it at odds with their tax statements, or lack of them. Kate, the taxman discovered, had not submitted a return since 1942, and in the returns she had filed from 1938 to 1941 her declared income was just £115. The department came down on the old woman like a Ray Blissett haymaker. It levied an assessment on her of £6191. Kate was forced to swallow her pride and protest that she could not, would not, pay, so the department sued her for the money. When various friends who had loaned Kate money to invest on their behalf learned that she was no longer flush with funds, they panicked and sued her for the return of their money.

Kate was declared bankrupt on 31 March 1954, on the petition of the deputy commissioner of taxation, and the authorities took action to claim all her assets. Her Lansdowne Street house and her remaining three Devonshire Street properties, including her sly-grog headquarters at no. 212, were sold for a total of £1830, and the tax people realised another £130 from the sale of the furniture within. Her furs, her rings, her hats were all confiscated and sold, and the proceeds turned over to the Taxation Department.

Kate was reduced to near poverty, 'Look at me,' she said at the time. 'I'm almost as poor as the lowest derelict I ever helped. The only lesson I've learned is the old one, that crime — if you can call sly-grogging a crime — doesn't pay.' In June, Kate suffered a stress-induced blackout when climbing stairs and fell heavily.

She recovered, and was in Bankruptcy Court in August as tax officials continued to try to untangle her finances. The press flocked to report on her humiliation. When W.D.T. Ward, the lawyer representing the official receiver, placed Kate in the witness stand, she, possibly to win sympathy, began her evidence by telling Ward that she had not been well, and was quite deaf. The lawyer was unmoved and proceeded to dismantle his quarry. He made her agree that she had paid out thousands upon thousands of pounds in police fines over the previous ten years and demanded to know where she got the money. 'Selling liquor, but I have given away more liquor than I have sold. I have given it away for nothing.'

Ward then asked her to explain how she had been able to pay her solicitor, Mr Roach, who had been so busy on her behalf. 'Mr Roach has been very good to me. I have not paid him several times because I haven't had any money. One day I might be able to give him £1000 or £2000 because I might win the lottery, or something.' And with what did she pay her barristers, including the expensive Dovey? 'Mr Roach has paid the barristers,' she said quietly. She also claimed that 'samaritans' had given her money over the years. 'I've helped a lot of people when they were down and out and now they've come good while I'm down and out,' she said. Ward looked at his notes and saw that a Mrs Parsons was one of Kate's creditors. Was she the notorious Tilly Devine? 'Oh cripes, no,' Leigh chuckled. '*This* Mrs Parsons is respectable.'

Ward quizzed Kate on the sly-grog business. 'Well,' she replied, 'I buy wine for four shillings a bottle and sell it for seven, eight or ten shillings a bottle. But business has fallen off. There are many others in the game these days. And the cops get most of the takings when they fine me. The good old days are gone. And even when times *were* good, Jack Baker was the principal and got most of the money. I haven't got one penny piece. You could turn the place from Sydney to England and you would not find a penny piece belonging to me. I'm stony broke. I live on less than £2 a week, eating neither meat nor potatoes and making a loaf of bread last a fortnight. I haven't bought clothes for three years.' Ward asked what had become of her fabulous diamond rings. 'Lost two down the drain, lost one in flour, gave my nephew one. I sold one and bought clothes with it.'

Another to take the stand was William Beahan, son of one of Kate's siblings and recipient of a ring, who managed the fruit-and-vegetable shop at 212 Devonshire Street. Beahan was asked to shed light on Kate's financial situation. He said she was 'a proud woman' but she was poor. She had not been wealthy for years. In earlier times, Beahan said, when Kate was told a woman was wearing a £50 hat, she would boast 'Well, *my* hat costs £200.' She didn't say things like that anymore. Beahan said he paid his aunt, who now lived upstairs in a squalid room at 212 Devonshire Street, £2 a week rent to sell produce in the shop, but would often supplement that with gifts of fruit and vegetables. Beahan added that Kate 'puts on parties for kids, but she has never smoked or drunk in her life'. Yes, she did sell sly grog, but he had never had anything to do with that.

Broke and embattled, Kate did her best to earn a little money selling illegal alcohol from friends' homes and rented rooms. Then, in 1955, the New South Wales Government put her out of business for good when it ended the six o'clock swill, extending hotel trading hours to 10 p.m. Suddenly there was absolutely no reason for a drinker to imbibe illicitly, and the era of sly grog, and with it Kate Leigh's criminal career, was over. Kate's only income was what she could scrounge occasionally hiring out hand-carts to vegetable and fruit hawkers for two shillings and sixpence a day.

The following year, it was Tilly Devine's turn to be mugged by the Taxation Department. In October 1955, it ordered her to pay more than £20 000 in unpaid income tax and fines. It sequestered £3862 from her bank account towards the bill and warned her that if the balance wasn't forthcoming, more fines would be levied upon her. For once, there was no party going on when a reporter telephoned Devine at her Maroubra home. 'Tell me, where am I going to get twenty grand?' the distraught Tilly asked. 'I'm a sick woman and won't be able to pay the dough before I die. The whole thing has got me beat. The Taxation Department gave clearances to me and my husband before we went to England in 1948 and 1953. I am a trifle deaf in the left ear and did not understand the taxation people recently when they asked me to call and see them. Had I understood the message and turned up, all might have been straightened out. I've battled all my life to get where I am today, and now I get this slug. I'm in a ton of trouble. I'll certainly have to ask the taxation blokes for time to pay.'

Tilly, like Kate, had to sell her assets to pay the Taxation Department, although somehow she managed to hang on to the Maroubra home. 'I'm broke,' she wailed. 'I've had to sell everything I own.' At one point, she claimed to police that she could not sell her diamonds and give the proceeds to the taxman because a former friend had stolen them. She had been drinking heavily at Torrington Road with the friend and had passed out. When she awoke, the rings on her fingers were gone. The authorities refused to believe her.

By 1959, Devine, 'the Queen of the Night' who had once presided over so many thriving brothels, had just one establishment, and a shabby affair at that, in Palmer Street, to her name. 'The taxman finished her,' says George Parsons. 'It was the classic Al Capone scenario. They couldn't get him for the murders he committed, but they got him for not paying his tax. That's how they got my aunt.'

# 39

# Last Rites for Razorhurst

In 1955, a man threw Dulcie Markham from the balcony of a first-floor flat in Bondi. In hospital, she insisted the fellow was a stranger, but the police believed he was a client. Markham never really recovered from the serious internal injuries and broken ribs she suffered in the fall. She became known in the neighbourhood as 'the Limping Blonde'. *Mirror* man Bill Jenkings saw her soon after her accident, in Central Court where she faced a soliciting charge. He remembered it as resembling a celebrity's return when she entered the court building. '... Down at the court she was smiling, waving at friends, including me, and [was] stylishly dressed in a mauve frock. She sported a becoming blonde coiffure ... tough old Dulcie.'

Virtually crippled by the fall, she could no longer work as a prostitute. She met an Irish sailor who, a novelty for her, had no criminal connections, and she lived with him in East Sydney until 1964. She was happy and they lived quietly, staying out of trouble (if a few vagrancy and soliciting charges are discounted) until one day the sailor was savagely beaten by a man in their flat. Soon after, the Irishman was gone.

There was a minor brouhaha in the late 1950s when a fire broke out in a house where Markham was living in Botany and she complained to the police that it was a case of arson. She attempted to cut a deal with Detective Sergeant Bill Harris. 'She walked into my office,' he recalls, 'and she had some mongrel of a bloke with her and I said to him, "You're not welcome here. Get out and wait in the street." He did so, and that left Dulcie and me alone. She said, "Sergeant, I know the fire was deliberately lit and I want you to find who did it and deliver him to me because I want to deal with him." I said, "Why is it so important that you get him?" She said, "I had many thousands of pounds sewn up in a settee that was destroyed in the fire and I believe some bastard stole the money first then burned the house down. If you deliver the bloke to me, there'll be a score of quids in it for you." I said, "Dulcie, forget it. When I find out who set the fire I'll arrest him first and tell you second." It turned out it was Dulcie's niece who started the blaze.'

Bumper Farrell once told a judge that, in his opinion, Dulcie Markham was 'past redemption', but he was wrong, for in the early 1960s she went straight. A short while after her Irish lover departed, she married another solid citizen, named Martin Rooney. For twelve years they lived together, peacefully and within the law, in a neat two-storey semi-detached house in Moore Street, Bondi. They had a dog.

Then, on 20 April 1976, when Markham was sixty-three, she said goodnight to Rooney and retired to bed just after 9 p.m. As she always did before closing her grey eyes and drifting to sleep, she lit a cigarette. This night, she dozed off while the cigarette was still burning. It set fire to her bed and Dulcie Markham was asphyxiated by the smoke before her husband could rescue her.

'I loved the woman,' Martin Rooney sobbed after his wife's body had been taken away by ambulancemen. 'She was a wonderful housewife and we both wanted to forget the past. She was Mrs Rooney, not Pretty Dulcie.' Her funeral service was held at St Patrick's Church in Bondi and she was cremated at the Eastern Suburbs Crematorium.

Frank Green once boasted to his lover Nellie Cameron, 'No bullet will ever get me.' He was right. It was a knife, a 30-centimetre carving knife, which, in 1956, ended the life of the last of the razor-men.

In his fifties, Green was wizened and frail, a shadow of the murderous street fighter and gunman that he was in his younger days. He now disguised his baldness with a greasy comb-over. A neighbour once told police, 'I have never seen Green any other way than the worse for liquor, either morning, noon or night.' It wasn't just the alcohol that had destroyed Green's constitution. He liked to joke that he had so many bullets in his body — indeed, at his autopsy, eight were discovered — that he rattled when he walked. These days, about all that would give a passer-by pause on coming face to face with Green in a desperate part of town was the large razor scar on his right cheek and his intense dark eyes.

Green had lived in obscurity since his career as a major criminal finished at the end of the 1930s. Like Kate Leigh and Tilly Devine, he found himself marginalised by the new breed of bad-man. In the Second World War he was employed by various new Mr Bigs to collect standover payments from gambling dens near army bases. At war's end, he opened his own illegal betting shop in Paddington. When that quickly foundered, he was reduced to painting houses Monday to Friday and working as a cockatoo at a Woolloomooloo SP betting shop on Saturdays.

In the mid 1950s, Green rented a shabby flat in Cooper Street, Paddington. His live-in lover was a woman named Beatrice 'Bobbie' Haggett, a saleswoman in a city department store. They fought often in the two years they lived as man and wife, usually after they had been drinking heavily. A frequent source of arguments was Green's penchant for pawning everything that was not nailed down, including an electric razor and wireless of Haggett's, to fund his booze sprees. One October night in 1955 after a particularly nasty argument, Haggett walked out on Green to live with someone new. When Green learned her whereabouts, he stalked her. 'Frank and another man came looking for us with iron bars,' she later told a court. 'He kept sending me rude messages about different men I was supposed to have been with, or telling me to pay off goods he'd bought on time payment.'

But even while he was, in his inimitable way, trying to entice Haggett back to his fold, he had replaced her in his bed with a prostitute from Kings Cross known as Larry. She, to Green's jealous fury, had a tattoo on her arm reading 'Phil', the name of her husband. What Larry thought about the woman's breast tattooed on Green's arm is not recorded. For six months, Green and Larry lived together. As well as frequent drunken arguments, there were tender moments. 'He had an old bullet lodged at the base of his spine,' Larry would tell reporters. 'It used to break out into an abscess, and every four hours I'd bathe it for him. Another old bullet had caused a cyst in his stomach and from time to time it would swell. He would not go near a doctor and would deflate the swelling by sticking a needle in it.' But such quality times were not enough, and Larry left Green in early April 1956.

The old crook didn't grieve for long. Within days of Larry's exit, Beatrice Haggett succumbed to Green's pleas and returned to live with him at Cooper Street. She knew what she was returning to. 'In drink, he would become very violent,' she later told reporters of her first stint under Green's roof. 'His eyes would bulge and he would bare his teeth and everyone would become terrified. [Once] I came home and Frank had been drinking all day. He kept nagging me all the time, and for no reason at all he got this knife off the cupboard and stabbed me in the left shoulder. Five stitches were inserted in the wound. He used to sleep with the knife under his pillow or mattress.' Green stabbed Haggett on two occasions and, she said, hit her on the head with an iron bar.

Frank Green spent most of 26 April drinking with a friend named

Hunkus in Kings Cross pubs. In the early evening, they bought a crate of beer and continued their carousing at Green's flat. Beatrice Haggett was there. When Hunkus left at 10 p.m., he later told police, Green was reeling drunk, careening off the walls of his living room.

Sometime in the next hour, Green and Haggett were sitting at the kitchen table drinking beer when he accused her of having an affair with his brother Bill. 'I'll do for you!' he growled, and reached for the carving knife that lay on the tabletop. Haggett, not as drunk as him, was quicker: she grabbed the knife first and plunged it into her tormentor's heart. Green lurched back in his chair.

Haggett ran from the flat and banged on a neighbour's door. 'I think I've killed Frank,' she screamed. 'Will you go in and try to help him while I go to the hospital for a doctor?' The neighbour found Green dead at the kitchen table. Still sprawled in his chair, his head was tilted straight back and his mouth gaped wide. His arms hung at his sides. His shirt and trousers were drenched in blood. The knife lay on the table, beside a glass of flat beer.

Later, when Green's body was removed, Haggett sobbed to Detective Sergeant Workman of Rose Bay Police Station: 'I'll plead guilty. I stabbed him. What more is there to say? Frank was nagging me. It's been going on ever since I came back to him. Nag, nag, nag.' At her murder trial, Haggett had no trouble convincing the jury that she slew Green because she was in mortal fear that he was about to kill her. She was acquitted in fifteen minutes.

In the days after Frank Green's death, Sydney's newspapers were full of epitaphs for the fallen hoodlum. Larry offered a heartrending eulogy to assembled reporters that had those who knew him wondering whether she wasn't talking about some other Frank Green:

> *Frankie liked to act tough, but he wasn't so tough when you got to know him. Do you know, he used to say his prayers . . . kneel down and pray every night. He taught me the Lord's*

*Prayer. I never knew it before. He was cuddlesome, too, and loving. He'd get up and go out late at night to the Cross to get me something for my asthma. Faults? He had one. He couldn't cook tripe proper. Oh yes, and he went real crook if he found bobby pins on the bathroom floor . . . He loved music and he loved kids. There was a little girl who used to come up his place and say, 'Mr Dween, can I have my favourite record on?' I was married to Phil. He was a singer and I like singers. Met him on Wednesday, got married on Saturday, pawned his ring on Monday, left him on Tuesday. But the only man I ever loved was Frank.*

More realistically, *Truth*'s obituary read: 'Frank Green, scar-faced gangster extraordinary, died on Thursday night and underworld associates, police, newsmen who knew him in his criminal heyday, the many victims of his vicious forays for easy money, knew no regrets.'

Kate Leigh certainly had none. When asked by a reporter whether she'd be attending the funeral of the man who had waged such ferocious war against her in the razor-gang years, Kate barked: 'Go to his funeral? Hell, no. But if I do find out where they bury him, I'll go and dance on the bludger's grave.'

# 40

# The Bitter End

It was the early 1960s, and gradually Sydney had become a different place. Men didn't wear grey felt hats anymore, or dangle an Ardath cigarette from their lower lip like a fashion accessory. Chinese and Italian restaurants were springing up, families were smaller. The dunny man had gone the way of the ice carter and the rabbit-oh — into nostalgic recollection. Sentimental ballads about June and the moon had been drummed off the radio by British beat music and the surfin' sounds of southern California. People were no longer gathering in lounge rooms in a semi-circle to stare at the family wireless set while listening to John Dease, Jack Davey, *Yes, What!* and *The Search for the Golden Boomerang*. These days they were grooving with Brian Henderson on television's *Bandstand*, and following the phlegmatic cop heroes of *Homicide* and the fortunes of garrulous Barry Jones and brave, doomed Frank Partridge on Bob and Dolly Dyer's Monday night quiz show *Pick-A-Box*.

And suddenly, Kate Leigh was no longer out and about in Surry Hills. Ubiquitous for fifty years, nowadays she rarely ventured into the streets of her heartland. An octogenarian, she preferred to rest her aching bones in the small, dark room upstairs at 212 Devonshire Street where she lived alone with her memories, the bottles and bouncers of her lost sly-grogging days having long since vanished. Few people nowadays bothered to visit her, but she always kept her pantry stocked with biscuits and tea in case someone dropped in for a chat.

Kate no longer bothered to go to Central Criminal Court to support her friends. No point, for most of them were dead. She'd stopped staging parties for the local children or to help the hopeless and homeless. She was the one who needed assistance now. She lived in the past and reminisced a lot. 'I could never knock back a bloke for a feed, a drink or a few bob,' she told *People* magazine, and anyone else who'd listen. 'They used to come to me in droves and the more destitute they were, the derelicts, the impoverished, and the ragged, the wider I opened my heart.'

For the first time she expressed regret at killing Snowy Prendergast that morning in March 1930 when he invaded her home looking for her lover and henchman Wally Tomlinson. And where was Wally now? In fact, in his white-haired but wiry sixties, Wally was still in a gang, but now it was a Sydney County Council tree-lopping gang at Carlingford in the city's north-west. Kate, however, would never be drawn on the demise of Norman Bruhn, even though she undoubtedly knew well who pulled the trigger in Charlotte Lane that winter's night in 1927.

For a moment, in July 1960, she was back in the headlines. When Sydney eight-year-old Graeme Thorne was kidnapped, she piped up, saying that yes, she'd done some bad things in her long life, but she had never stooped to kidnapping. Kidnappers, she growled, were beneath contempt. 'Why, I've got one of the biggest butcher's knives in Sydney and it would give me the greatest pleasure to use it on the mongrels. I hope I will hear something that will put me on their trail. By the time I finish with them, they'll make a good meal for the dogs' home.' Fortunately for Graeme Thorne's abductor and murderer, Stephen Leslie Bradley, it was the police, and not Kate, who ran him down.

From time to time, Kate would visit the shops or a friend's house, where she would bitterly complain about the bad hand life had dealt her in her final years. When she walked, she moved slowly and gingerly. Her arthritis had spread and she was often in pain. Those who saw her commented on how much weight old Kate had lost, how shaky she looked and what a shame it was that she no longer went to the trouble of dyeing her white hair black or chestnut. Kate's neighbours often remarked that it seemed like only yesterday that she was the queen of Surry Hills, the feared sly-grog and drug dealer, owner of property, fine clothes and a strongroom of cash. Where had it all gone? They pondered that, and felt old themselves.

On Friday, 31 January 1964, Kate Leigh, aged eighty-two, suffered a stroke in her Devonshire Street room. She was rushed to St Vincent's Hospital. She slipped into a coma. Though her brain was dead, her piratical heart beat on over the weekend and then, on the night of Tuesday, 4 February, it stopped.

Her funeral was held on 7 February at St Peter's Church in Devonshire Street and the Catholic Cemetery at Botany. Her daughter Eileen, a couple of Kate's surviving siblings, nephew William Beahan, Tilly Devine, a few old lags from the underworld, police and masses of people from Surry Hills attended. There was also a scattering of minor celebrities hoping for a picture in the next day's *Daily Mirror* which, just as the young turks of crime had superseded Kate, had taken over from *Truth* as Sydney's raciest tabloid.

'When Kate died,' Maggie Baker told this author, 'I felt, well, there's a bit of good old Australian history that's gone. I didn't go to her funeral. Not into the church, at least. I heard on the radio that she had died and that there was a huge funeral planned. I knew I wouldn't have been able to get into the church, so I stood outside in the street. I've never seen so many cars, so many people from all walks of life. Even the metho drinkers. Poor old Kate, for someone who was supposed to be such an old villain, she sure got a good send-off.'

In the church and at the grave side, praise rang for the deceased. There was no trace in the eulogies of the crime tsar who helped create Razorhurst, the venal gangster who rode roughshod over East Sydney's hardest men, the profiteer who sold cocaine, the biting, clawing, king-hitting street fighter, the harridan who thought nothing of ordering a rival's murder or of shooting a man dead herself. Invoked instead on that hot, cloudless day was the other Kate Leigh — the gruff but good-hearted, more-sinned-against-than-sinning Samaritan.

Veteran detective Jack Aldridge praised Kate to the heavens in his eulogy. And, said another mourner, former deputy commissioner of police W.R. Lawrence: 'Kate used to go to the courts nearly every day and she would do all she could to help first offenders. On many occasions I saw her actually paying the fine of people who were not in a position to pay. I spent nineteen years at the CIB and Kate was one who gave me lots of information and help. There was another side to her life. Certainly she had a criminal record, but she did all she could to help the needy and young offenders. She warned many of the youngsters about the futility of crime.'

At the back of the congregation, Tilly Devine, aged sixty-three and frail as a sparrow now, may have smiled wryly.

Tilly survived Kate by six years. In 1970, as old as the century, she was a croaky-voiced wraith. The once-buxom madam with the boundless energy was bone-thin and walked with a stoop. She wore big, round, thick-lensed glasses that made her wizened face look tiny, like a discarded Victorian doll. Sydney had largely forgotten her. The newspapers that once gasped disapprovingly at the sensational incidents of her life were now preoccupied carping on about the 'shocking and outrageous' demands of Women's Liberation. Another media obsession was the decline of society, as evinced, the moral guardians claimed, by the tens of thousands who marched in the streets protesting the Vietnam War — in which in March that year in the battle of Nui Dat nine Australian troops were killed and twenty-nine injured.

Almost everyone Tilly knew from the days of knees-ups and rorts was dead. Her husband Eric was gone. Her parents and some of her siblings were, too. And so was Kate Leigh — 'God rest the old bitch's soul,' she'd say with a smile warmer than any she expended on Kate when her great rival was alive. Nellie Cameron, Guido Calletti and 'that bastard' Frankie Green, Norman Bruhn of course, Phil the Jew, Stella Croke — all in their graves. Certainly Gunman Gaffney and Fred Moffitt were no longer among the living, and she should know, for her own Big Jim had shot those poor blighters dead. There were many others who had passed away, but lately she was having the devil's own trouble remembering their names. Dulcie Markham, who in 1970 still had six years left to her, was pretty much the only member of the old crowd she knew of who was still living.

Everything was changing, and the changes bewildered and irritated Tilly, made her cracked lips curl. The music that came out of her kitchen transistor or the radio in the hospital where she was spending too much time lately, or over the speakers at the Tradesman's Arms, where she still drank occasionally — the songs of the Beatles, the Rolling Stones, Bob Dylan and Billy Thorpe and the Aztecs — must have sounded as unintelligible and discordant to her as the frantic babble of the Chinese merchants at the Municipal Markets in the 1920s. Give her 'Ain't We Got Fun!' any day. In the old times, if they'd been behaving themselves, she used to shout her girls to the flicks, to see Joan Crawford and Clark Gable, Laurel and Hardy, Shirley Temple and Charlie Chaplin, or, to show them what life was like back in London, Noel Coward's *Cavalcade*. These days, she complained, without a trace of irony, all you got was sex and violence: *Easy Rider*, *Midnight Cowboy*, *Women in Love*.

In lucid moments, Tilly could remember the sights and sounds of London during World War I, when she was one of the prettiest girls working on the Strand. She'd never go home again, she knew. She could recall craning with the other English war brides for a view of her adopted city as the *Waimana* steamed into Sydney Harbour in 1920, twelve years before the Bridge was completed. Billy Hughes was prime minister, and since 'the Little Digger' she had seen prime ministers Stanley Bruce, James Scullin, Joe Lyons, Earle Page, Bob Menzies, Arthur Fadden, John Curtin, Francis Forde, Ben Chifley, Menzies again, Harold Holt and John McEwen come and go.

Back when she blew in, East Sydney — Razorhurst, they used to call it — was wide open, a frontier town by the sea. Darlinghurst was virgin territory, so to speak, ripe for exploitation. Acquire the premises, install the girls, hire the razor-men to protect your interests or protect them yourself if you had to. Be feared. Get rich. The money, and the good times, had lasted, more or less, a long time, through the Roaring Twenties, the Depression, another world war and well into the '50s. The luxury jaunts back home were worth every penny.

Much younger criminals, more vicious than she ever was, or so she liked to say, ruled the roost nowadays — weak and weary, she gladly left them to it. There was Abe Saffron. And there had been Joe Borg, a stocky young Maltese immigrant with a mean streak as wide as William Street, who bashed and extorted his way to establishing a string of twenty-six brothels in East Sydney. Borg made many enemies and was dealt with in a way Tilly would have understood. In 1968, he was blown apart when rival gangsters planted a 2.5 kilogram gelignite bomb under the seat of his car.

Tilly had been law-abiding since '68, when she switched off the red light at her last remaining brothel in Palmer Street. She quit the game for good after she was terrorised by local heavies, possibly the same ones who killed Borg, who wanted to reign over an East Sydney prostitution monopoly. For a while, she resisted their threats, more out of instinct than any real desire to remain a force in vice, but she threw up her hands and stalked off when the hoodlums hurled a firebomb at her brothel and broke into her home, smashed it up, and stole her collection of cut glass. That year as well, the crazy old law that allowed women, though not men, to live off the immoral earnings of prostitutes, was repealed.

As a widow on an old-age pension, Tilly struggled to make ends
meet. She spent her time in lonely anonymity, testily turning away the
occasional reporter who sought her out to talk about her life and times
for 'Where Are They Now?' features in the Sunday papers or *Pix*,
*People* or *Australasian Post*. One of her few remaining joys was writing
to her favourite niece, Maureen Cocks, in England, and quietly entertaining friends in her Maroubra home, now bereft of the fine
furnishings and art the taxman had taken. At these low-key gatherings, Tilly talked endlessly of the old days. Just as Kate Leigh had done
in her final years, Tilly griped about how the Taxation Department
had destroyed her. She complained about her health, and with good
reason, for as well as the bronchitis she had suffered for years, she
now really did have cancer, and rheumatism in her hands and feet and
cirrhosis of the liver, too. There would be no more blues or shoot-outs
for her, no more high-kicks and sozzled singalongs on her front lawn.
'By the end she was an anachronism,' says George Parsons. 'She was
pretty much broken.'

Stories never end. After the first edition of *Razor* was published in
2001, a number of people contacted this author to share their memories of Tilly Devine and Kate Leigh, and the gangsters and police of
the era covered in the book. There was a priest who administered last
rites to a number of the protagonists and a nurse from Sydney Hospital who tended the wounds of the warring villains. Peg Donnelly,
daughter of Monte Gildea, a proprietor of the gangsters' pub of choice
in the late 1920s, the Tradesman's Arms, recounted how her father
'kept a waddy at the back of the till in the bar' and her brother, who
worked in the pub, vaulting the bar to quell the disturbances that

erupted regularly among the drinkers. 'I saw many street brawls while looking through the lace curtains of the music room on the first floor.'

Most interestingly, there were messages seeking a meeting from Richard Twiss, a friendly and garrulous Sydney man who is Tilly Devine's grandson, son of her son Frederick. This came as a shock, because Freddy, many interviewees had assured me, had been killed in World War II. In fact, he emigrated to Australia in 1955 with his wife, Maude, and their young sons, Richard and David. Fred had been a singer of popular songs at a club in Coogee, a vocation also adopted by Richard. Freddy and his mother had a rocky relationship. He died around 1980.

I learned, too, that as well as Frederick, Tilly and Jim Devine had another child. Alice Teresa, born premature, who lived just one day and died on 9 March 1918, at the Twiss family home at 57 Hollington Street, Camberwell.

Then there was an unsettling voice message from a gentleman gruffly identifying himself as 'John Parsons . . . I'm the bloke who doesn't exist. The bloke you didn't write about in your book.' When I called him back, the number he had left had been disconnected. I persevered and after a time I traced John to Adelaide. He turned out to be a sweet-natured, sincere man of fifty-four. 'My birth mother was a friend of Tilly's,' he explained to me.

*She fell pregnant and, being a Catholic and unable to have an abortion, had a girl. Tilly tried to adopt her but the authorities would not allow her to. The following year my mother had me. This time Tilly hired a solicitor and paid £500, and at just a few weeks old I became her adopted son. I grew up with Tilly and Eric Parsons in the big house at Torrington Road. Yes, there were wild parties and brawls and I recall gun shots, but they cared for me well. Eric I remember as an elderly man who wore a cardigan and was always producing threepenny*

*Cadbury chocolates from its pockets for me. Tilly was very tough, but I think mostly she was fair. She was affectionate and hugged me and I knew better than to get on her bad side. Because I was Tilly's kid I was shunned in the neighbourhood and was never invited to parties. I was a bit of a ratbag. I think these days I'd have been diagnosed ADD, they tell me I'm quite intelligent . . . I did well when I left school and went to work, as a projectionist at the Barclay theatre in George Street in Sydney's Haymarket, and later in the record business.*

*Tilly loved Eric, but Jim Devine was the real love of her life. Each year she and I would travel to Melbourne for the Melbourne Cup and we'd stay with Jim in Fitzroy where, at age 71, he was still working — as a bouncer at the local pub. To me, Big Jim was a gentle giant. He had a little wooden figure of a black boy which dispensed cigarettes, popping them right into his hand. He and Tilly were always glad to see each other, but before long they'd be yelling. They couldn't help themselves.*

I was contacted by Maureen Cocks, Tilly's niece, the daughter of her brother William. On the phone and later when I visited her and her sister Margaret in London, this dedicated keeper of her family's flame shared memories of her aunt and gave me family photos and scores of wonderful letters — letters resounding with loneliness, regret and recrimination that Tilly had mailed to her revealing her preoccupations as her life wound down.

On 7 June 1965, Tilly wrote to Maureen:

*Sorry I never answered your last letter before as I have not been too good. My feet and hands have been playing up with me and it is taking me all my time to write this. I received a letter from Peter [Twiss, her nephew in England] . . . telling me the [British] newspapers said I was dead. So I am going to*

*take a writ out against them. Peter sent me the cutting out of*
*the* People. *He seems to be the only one who seems to take*
*notice. How I wish [Eric] was alive he would be the one to take*
*things up for me but as you know I am one out in this country.*
*Freddy don't seem to care.*

She had sent Freddy's family a handmade dresser but had not been
thanked for her trouble.

*Well, girl, if you must know I am only seven stone in weight — I*
*take an SS [sized] women's dress. All my good clothes I have*
*given away. So now you know how worried I get . . . In Peter's*
*letter he told me to forgive my sister and brother and Caty for*
*writing that letter to John about me dead. It came as such a*
*shock to both of us. John said he would not ever write to Caty*
*again for sending him such a letter but, Maureen, if you knew*
*how they treated us you would not . want to know any of them*
*again. As you know, you are the only [family member] I write to*
*so I won't forget you later on. Lots of love from John and myself.*

Tilly wrote to Maureen on October 24 the following year, again
apologising for her tardy reply, and revealing that she had stayed in
touch with her ex-husband, Jim.

*I could not answer [your letter] as the night of my birthday they*
*put on a birthday party for me at the club so you bet your life*
*I got well drunk and I [burned] my two fingers so I have had*
*a very bad time with them . . . Well, my dear, you never met*
*Jim [Devine], but your Dad did. Well, he passed away two*
*months ago, not a bad age, seventy-four, but he was a very sick*
*man at the last. I was going over to Melbourne for the Cup this*
*year as I always went to see him and we used to talk about old*
*times, so I don't think I will be going over this year . . . I am*
*home nearly all day so I look at TV to pass the time away . . .*

Some time later, in an undated letter, Tilly told Maureen that she was in hospital with a broken hip. '. . . seven years ago they put a pin in my leg so now they have taken it out as it was causing a lot of pain. Well, my dear little girl. I don't think I will ever be coming home to England any more as to tell you the truth nobody cares [about] me there. My sister [Alice is] nothing to me now.' She railed about the inhospitable ways of her family when she last she visited England and no one offered her a place to stay, 'but if anyone from London came to my place I always had a room.' She pined for Eric Parsons. 'I have been lonely ever since I lost Eric. All I have now is my little John. He is my only little mate.'

At Christmas, 1968, Tilly applied for a Housing Commission flat in which she and John could live. The rent in the flat where they were living was $18 a week, and Tilly's pension provided just $18. There was virtually nothing left in the bank.

On 14 April 1969, writing from Sydney's Concord Repatriation Hospital, she told Maureen that she had been ill with cancer. 'I have been in hospital twice . . . I have asked to go home for Easter as you know I have little John to look after and [school holidays] start tomorrow. I want to be home with him. As you know, we have a big Show here at Easter and all the kids love to go. I suppose you will read about it in the papers [and see it] on TV.' Always a devoted royals watcher, Tilly told Maureen that 'We have the Duke and Duchess of Gloucester visiting here. They are having the time of their life each day at the Show.' The news reports of a few years back that she had died still rankled and she asked that if Maureen saw her relatives to reassure them yet again 'that I am alive and kicking.' Then she rancorously added:

> I don't want anything [to do] with their likes. They are a lousy mob, even my sister Alice. [And after] all I did for them while the war was on. She said I was a wicked woman — to tell such lies . . . Alice got the lot, but she may need a friend again, let her two sons look after her . . . I never want to see them again.

*They are all too greedy. So Maureen, don't get messed up with them. My brother Billy was the best of them all and my Eric liked him very much when they used to go to the dog racing.*

For a time in mid-1969, Tilly considered returning to England. She wrote to Maureen Cocks, 'I wonder if you would go to Australia House for me and see if they have a small flat or cottage as I am a war widow and also incapacitated.' She could be home for Christmas if a suitable abode became available, but of course there was no offer of accommodation.

While Tilly was being treated for her stomach cancer at Darling-hurst's Sacred Heart Hospice in August 1969, Sister Mary St Joseph gave Maureen a progress report on her aunt's health and state of mind.

*I'm calling you 'Maureen', as it seemed so distant to write 'Mrs' when you are the niece of one for whom I have a real admiration; and one who has been so very kind to others during her lifetime. If only you saw the joy on your aunt's face when your letter arrived, and then the flowers — lovely pink gladiolas, pink carnations and pink sweet peas. It was a delightful array. They are still looking fresh. Perhaps it's Aunt's joy and pride at their presence and above all that they were sent from England. John sends his love and will write soon. He calls frequently to see Aunt. You asked re her condition. Well, she remains about the same and is rather weak. I look forward to my visit to her daily. I think I previously mentioned that she is only seven stone in weight . . . I'm sure you all enjoyed hearing of the brave Astronauts. Aunt had a TV on which she saw all to be seen.*

*Much love from Aunt, John and myself. May God bless you and yours always.*
*Yours sincerely in Christ, S.M. St Joseph RSC.*

Sister Mary, who organised for friends to take Tilly on drives around Sydney to break the monotony of her hospitalisation, reflected how, 'Aunt is very brave and bears things well. It is such a change to see this once-active person now in bed.'

Another woman, a nurse at the hospice, has an abiding memory of Tilly. In her last months, while being cared for at the hospice, Tilly took the nurse aside. 'I want my medication, nurse,' she pleaded.

'But Matilda, you've had it. It says here on the ward sheet you were medicated at four o'clock.'

'Not *that* medication,' chided Tilly. 'Now go back to the fridge, and you'll find my medication in a bottle. It's got "Sheaf Stout" on the label.'

By April 1970, the now teenaged John Parsons was at work and, Tilly told Maureen on 18 April, doing well. 'He is earning a fortune, $40 per week, and is putting it into the bank. Soon he will be richer than any of us. Last week I bought him a portable record and radio player. He is thrilled to pieces with it. It cost $40.' Tilly informed Maureen that once more she was at war with her biological son. This time it was over some bail money she gave Freddy that had been incurred by a relative who had transgressed, and Freddy had not returned it. 'He even had the hide to blatantly lie to me — stating that the court case was in April when it had been in August.'

In November 1970, Tilly suffered a stroke and lost her speech. Incapacitated, in terrible pain and shockingly emaciated by her cancer and cirrhosis, Tilly was again admitted to Concord Repatriation Hospital. As the widow of two servicemen, she was entitled to treatment there. She never left the old building with the big red cross on its side on the banks of the Parramatta River. On the night of Tuesday, 24 November, Tilly Devine groaned, closed her eyes, and died.

Recalls John Parsons, 'I had trouble believing it when Tilly died. There had been a few false alarms. In 1968 I was in a boys' home because Tilly was in and out of hospital, and I got a call from the hospice saying she was really crook and going to die. When I went to her bedside she was sitting up having a smoke. Then, two years later at five-thirty in the morning I was eating breakfast in the canteen of the boys' home and I heard a phone ring. I knew, *I just knew*, that it was for me and it was to tell me Tilly had died. And it was, and she had.'

On 11 December, Sister Mary St Joseph sent her condolences to Maureen Cocks. '

> *. . . Your Aunt Matilda's death was announced over the radio, and it was a big shock to me. Needless to say, I'd like to have been with Aunt at the end. My one consolation is that she had made her peace with God, and even whilst here [at the Sacred Heart hospice], she was twice anointed. Aunt's wishes were carried out re her funeral, which was from our Sacred Heart Church . . . she had a beautiful coffin. While the coffin was being carried out I played 'Nearer My God to Thee'. Requiem Mass was celebrated on November 26. I had my pupils singing for the occasion, 'The Lord's My Shepherd' and other hymns. John was very grieved, as you'd imagine. He must tread the highways of life alone now Aunt has gone. Aunt is in my prayers daily at Holy Mass. I send you greetings for the holy season of Christmas, so near us now. I feel inclined to add those of your dear Aunt also. She won't be unmindful of you in eternity.*

The public tributes, so fulsome for Kate Leigh, were sparse and grudging for Tilly. Police Commissioner Norman Allan declared: 'She was a villain. I used to prosecute her and she gave me hell, but who am I to judge her?' The tabloids predictably despatched reporters to the Tradesman's Arms Hotel to interview drinkers, but if they were seeking warm-hearted reminiscences, according to them, they got none. 'Tilly never had many friends and no-one here is collecting for a wreath,' one woman reportedly sneered. 'She was a hard bitch and I don't want to talk about her any more.' One newspaper painted a scene of a customer proposing a toast to their pub's departed patron: '"Here's to dear old Til!" he chimed. But nobody drank.'

*Daily Telegraph* columnist Ron Saw penned an obituary headlined 'They'll Shed Only Crocodile Tears for Tilly Devine'. Calling her 'a vicious, grasping, high-priestess of savagery, venery, obscenity and whoredom', Saw said Tilly made Kate Leigh ('a scapegrace [but] a kindly and generous old trot with many friends') look like 'a Christmas fairy'. Tilly, Saw wrote, 'lived high off the whore's back, she gave nothing away that could not be prised from her with a knife, and if she had friends they were cowed and unwholesome low-lifers.' She was 'one of the most frightening creatures spewed up by the razor gangs. She was charged with everything from consorting to malicious wounding, from indecent language to attempted murder. But above all, she was a brothel keeper.' He blasted her for flaunting her furs and glittering rings in a Sydney grey with Depression and then wartime austerity, and scoffed at her repeated explanation that she could only afford such luxurious trappings because she'd backed last year's Melbourne Cup winner. 'To make that much money,' Saw said, 'she'd have had to back every Melbourne Cup winner back to Carbine. She was making her money from brothels and everyone knew it, but there was nothing anyone could do about it because she couldn't be charged . . . She was a wretched woman.'

Nearly forty years later, Saw's words still infuriate John Parsons. 'His obituary was both cruel and wrong,' says Parsons. 'The patrons at the Tradesman's Arms spoke only good of Tilly to me in the days after she died, and bought me many beers in my mother's memory. She did good things, as well as bad.'

Tilly Devine was cremated at Botany Cemetery with Catholic rites. There was only a handful of mourners. Indeed, most Sydneysiders were surprised to read of her death. Hadn't she died years ago? 'I think Tilly died too late,' says George Parsons. 'If she had passed away at the height of her infamy, her funeral would have been one of those gangland extravaganzas like in the movies. But when she died, her time had gone.'

Tilly left a will. 'I give, devise and bequeath to my adopted son John Eric Parsons and my niece Maureen Cocks and my nephew Peter John Twiss the whole of my real estate.' This comprised $6,190.41 in this once-wealthy woman's account at the Bank of NSW on the corner of Oxford and Crown Streets ($13.69 of which was in her purse when she died at Concord Hospital), jewellery to the value of $360 and a $20 social services funeral benefit. But before the bequest was dispersed, there were liabilities to be subtracted. The NSW Government took $1,088.61 in death duty and the Federal Government put its hand out for $13.05. Thomas Dixon Pty Ltd, the company that staged her funeral, charged $396.60, and the carpenters at Timmins Builders took $16.67 for building the coffin. G.F. Osborne, solicitor, levied a charge of $142.20. Another sum was kept aside to cover the Estate Solicitor's costs.

Not a day goes by when John Parsons, who arranged the funeral, does not remember Tilly. 'Of course I think of her. She was my mum.'

Maureen Cocks is fairly sure 'Tilly was accepted into heaven . . . for the nice things she did . . . I have two abiding memories of her, as clear to me as if they happened yesterday. She was staying at our home on one of her visits to London and I ventured into her bedroom, and she was under the covers and when I called her name to wake her, two hands covered in rings reached out and pulled the blanket down to show her face and her mass of bright yellow hair. And there was the time when the whole family went to the Sultan pub in Camberwell, in Sultan Street which was near Hollington Street where Tilly grew up and her dad used to sell cat meat door to door. Tilly put on a song and dance that stopped the pub. The number she performed was "Pistol Packin' Mama"!'

Like John Parsons, who christened his daughter Brooke Matilda, and Maureen Cocks, Tilly's nephew George Parsons remembers her fondly:

*Tilly gave freely to good causes. She loved children. She was a pillar of the Catholic faith and was revered by the Salvation Army and the down-and-outers she helped. Aunt Til wasn't too bad, given the way she was treated as a girl. She had a hard, working-class life in her youth. She was a good-looking, poor woman with no real hope of achieving anything unless she sold her body. She always struck me as being bright. She had a naïve intelligence about her and was mad-keen on education. 'If you are educated, there are hard, dirty, demeaning jobs you never have to do,' she'd say. She could sense a business opportunity. She was an entrepreneur who knew how to hold on to her money. To be as successful as she was for so long she needed to be a good administrator. She was organising a lot of girls and I've no doubt if they didn't come up to scratch, she'd get rid of them. She had to control a string of pimps to patrol her territory. And for years she successfully fought off invaders who tried to take over her business. Tilly had to be special. How else could she and Kate Leigh have run the Sydney crime scene for so long? It could not have been easy for them. They were up against some hard boys. But they thrived.*

In East Sydney in the wild years of the twentieth century, there was cruelty and crime, squalor and meanness, but there was stoicism, bravery and charity to be found in those twisting, tumbledown streets, too. Let's say of Kate Leigh and Tilly Devine, and those others who lived and loved and broke the law in Razorhurst, that they were people of their place, people of their time.

# References
## General works

Allen, G., *Gullible's Travails*, self-published, Sydney, 1998.

Anderson, H., *Larrikin Crook: The Rise and Fall of Squizzy Taylor*, Jacaranda, Milton, 1971.

Blaikie, G., *Wild Women of Sydney*, Rigby, Adelaide, 1980.

Boast, M., *The Story of Camberwell*, Southwark Council, London, 1972.

Booth, C., *Life and Labour of the People in London*, Macmillan, London, 1889–1897.

Carroll, B., *Growing Up in the '30s*, Kangaroo Press, Sydney, 1982.

Crombie, I., and Ennis, H., *Australian Photographs: A Souvenir Book of Australian Photography in the Australian National Gallery*, Australian National Gallery, Canberra, 1988.

Department of Corrective Services, *Long Bay Correctional Complex: Conservation Plan*, Government of New South Wales, Sydney, 1997.

Evans, H., *The Oldest Profession: An Illustrated History of Prostitution*, David & Charles, Newton Abbot, London, 1979.

Fabian, S., and Loh, M., *Australian Children Through 200 Years*, Kangaroo Press, Sydney, 1985.

Farwell, G., *Requiem for Woolloomooloo*, Hodder & Stoughton, Sydney, 1971.

Francis, R., *The History of Female Prostitution in Australia*, Women's

Issues and Social Empowerment (WISE), University of New South Wales Press, 1994.

Heads, I., *Backpage: Australia's Greatest Sporting Moments*, Lester Townsend Publishing, Sydney, 1989.

Helliwell, A., 'This City Gave Me Such A Shock', *Sunday People*, 5 November 1950, p. 6.

Hickie, D., *Chow Hayes — Gunman*, Angus & Robertson, Sydney, 1990.

Holledge, J., *Inside Kings Cross*, Horwitz, Sydney, 1963.

Keating, C., *Surry Hills: The City's Backyard*, Hale & Iremonger, Sydney, 1991.

Kelly, M., *Faces of the Street: William Street, Sydney, 1916*, Doak Press, Sydney, 1982.

Kelly, V., *Rugged Angel: The Amazing Career of Policewoman Lillian Armfield*, Angus & Robertson, Sydney, 1961.

—, *The Racket Buster*, Horwitz, London, 1963.

Kent, Jacqueline, *Out of the Bakelite Box: The Heyday of Australian Radio*, ABC Enterprises, Sydney, 1990.

Knightley, P., *A Hack's Progress*, Jonathon Cape, London, 1997.

Lipson, N., and Barnao, T., *As Crime Goes By: The Life and Times of 'Bondi' Bill Jenkings*, Ironbark Press, Sydney, 1992.

Lowenstein, W., *Weevils in the Flour: An Oral Record of the 1930s Depression in Australia*, Highland House, Melbourne, 1978.

McCoy, A., *Drug Traffic: Narcotics and Organised Crime in Australia*, Harper & Row, Sydney, 1980.

—, 'Two Cities and their Syndicates — A Comparative Urban History of Organised Crime' in Davidson, J. (ed.), *The Sydney–Melbourne Book*, Allen & Unwin, Sydney, 1986.

Matthews, B., *A Fine and Private Place*, Pan Macmillan, Sydney, 2000.

Morton, J., *Gangland International: The Mafia and Other Mobs*, Little, Brown and Company, London, 1998.

Murray, J., *Larrikins: 19th Century Outrage*, Lansdowne Press, Melbourne, 1973.

Park, R., *The Harp in the South*, Angus & Robertson, Sydney 1948.

—, *Poor Man's Orange*, Angus & Robertson, Sydney, 1949.

Ramsland, J., *With Just But Relentless Discipline: A Social History of Corrective Services in New South Wales*, Kangaroo Press, Sydney, 1996.

Saw, R., 'They'll Shed Only Crocodile Tears for Tilly Devine', the *Daily Telegraph*, 25 November 1970, p. 6.

Whitburn, D., *Penthouse History of Crime in Australia*, Part V: 'The Law of the Razor', Horwitz, Sydney, 1988, pp. 120-127.

# Anonymous newspaper articles

'Crime and the Police', the *Sydney Morning Herald*, 11 June 1914, p. 8.

'Eveleigh Robbery Sequel', the *Sydney Morning Herald*, 14 October 1914, p. 11.

'Sydney's Welcome — A Glorious Scene', the *Sydney Morning Herald*, 28 March 1927, p. 3.

'The Razor Gang', *Truth*, 12 June 1927, p. 15.

'Razor Attacks', the *Sydney Morning Herald*, 13 July 1927, p. 12.

'The Great Mistake', *Truth*, 17 July 1927, p. 1.

'Razor Terror', *Truth*, 1 January 1928, p. 3.

'Flogging for Razor Slashers', *Truth*, 15 January 1928, p. 1.

'Sweep the Gangsters from Sydney's Streets', *Truth*, 16 September 1928, p. 24.

'Clean Up Razorhurst!', *Truth*, 23 September 1928, p. 5.

'Stop This Dilly-Dallying!', *Truth*, 30 September 1928, p. 21.

'Gangland Silence', the *Sun*, 16 May 1929, p. 2.

'Scenes at Gang War Inquest', the *Sydney Morning Herald*, 3 August 1929, p. 9.

'Mysterious Disappearance of Maisie Wilson', *Truth*, 12 January 1930, p. 17.

'Is He Marked for Death?', *Truth*, 6 April 1930, p. 3.

'Apples on a Stick', *Truth*, 15 June 1930, p. 13.

'Says Tilly to Kate — Underworld Hymn of Hate', *Truth*, 29 June 1930, p. 15.

'Sydney's Vicious Harridan of Underworld Should Have Been in Gaol Long Ago: Shelf, Hypocrite, Base and Vile', *Truth*, 19 October 1930, p. 17.

'Razor Attacks', the *Daily Mirror*, 6 January 1932, p. 14.

'Foul Blot on City's Night Life', *Truth*, 31 January 1932, p. 14.

'K-K-K-Katey . . . You're the Only "Girl" That I Abhor!', *Truth*, 7 February 1932, p. 21.

'Tilly Lets Off Steam', *Truth*, 6 March 1932, p. 12.

'Bridge Arrest', the *Sydney Morning Herald*, 20 March 1932, p. 1.

'Sudden End of Gangster's Liberty', *Truth*, 7 August 1932, p. 14.

'Night Clubs Stay Open', the *Sydney Morning Herald*, 16 September 1933, p. 4.

'Calletti Associate of Criminals of Worst Type', *Truth*, 25 November 1934, p. 17.

'Rid Sydney of Night Club Vice', *Truth*, 4 October 1936, p. 1.

'Betting Raid', the *Daily Telegraph*, 22 November 1936, p. 9.

'Study in Scarlet: An Uncrowned Queen of Slumland Drips With Diamonds and Charity', *People*, 15 March 1950, pp. 11–15.

'No "Blues", No "Cops" at Lobster Spread', *Smith's Weekly*, 23 September 1950, p. 3.

'London Stops for Coronation', the *Times*, 3 June 1953, p. 1.

'Gangster Dies', *Truth*, 29 April 1956, p. 24.

'Farrell of the Force to Leave the Cross', the *Sydney Morning Herald*, 25 August 1976, p. 7.

# Index

339